Writers of Italy Series

General Editor
C. P. Brand
Professor of Italian
University of
Edinburgh

I

ARIOSTO

© C. P. Brand 1974
Edinburgh University Press
22 George Square, Edinburgh
ISBN 0 85224 246 8
Printed in Great Britain by
R. & R. Clark Ltd.
Edinburgh

190061

Ariosto

Edinburgh University Press

Ludovico

ARIOSTO

A preface to the 'Orlando Furioso'

C. P. BRAND

*

Contents

Preface   vii

Part One
Background

1. Life   1

2. Minor works   15

Part Two
Orlando Furioso

3. The Literary Tradition   46

4. The Theme of Love   57

5. The Theme of Arms   84

6. Dynastic, Political and Other Themes   107

7. The Arts of Narrative   126

8. The Arts of Poetry   142

9. Problems of Language and Composition   165

10. Fortune; Conclusion   184

Select Bibliography   197

Index   202

Preface

Ariosto's *Orlando Furioso* is acknowledged as the poetic masterpiece of the Italian Renaissance and has long exerted an appeal in this country, from the time of Spenser, who aimed to 'overgo' Ariosto in the *Faerie Queene*, and of Harington, who made the first English translation in 1591, to the English Romantic writers who were, almost all of them, familiar with Ariosto's poem. Sir Walter Scott, for example, used to take it to read on Salisbury Crags overlooking Edinburgh, and has described how his first attempts at narrative were made in imitation of it; and Keats learned Italian by studying it 'six to eight stanzas at a time'. We are not so well-read in the Italian poets as our great-grandfathers, but interest is reviving, and it is encouraging to know that a new translation is soon to be published by Penguin Books.

The present study is intended, like others in the *Writers of Italy* series, to explain and interpret the work of a major Italian writer. It is addressed primarily to those able to read Ariosto's poetry in the original language, but is designed also to be intelligible and of interest to those whose knowledge of Italian is slight. For this reason translations are given of quotations in Italian and only minimal assumptions are made of background knowledge.

The *Orlando Furioso* exerts a ready attraction even to those who know little of Italian romance or the Renaissance, but like so much great literature it can appeal at several levels, and some patient study is necessary in order to savour fully its richness. It is intimately associated with the Italian romance tradition and is closely bound up with the political and cultural situation of its day; and its very length and the complexity of its material and style are not easily mastered. The form of this book is intended to help the reader in these respects. The first three chapters concern the poet's life and the court of Ferrara where he worked (1), his minor works (2) and the literary tradition which he inherited (3). The next three (4–6) attempt to convey the breadth of the poet's canvas in the main thematic divisions of the work; and the three following chapters examine in some detail the poet's method, assessing his achievement in terms of narrative (7) and poetic skill (8), and analysing the linguistic and structural problems he faced (9). The final chapter surveys the European fortune of Ariosto and draws some conclusions.

A literary classic accumulates a formidable accretion of critical commentary and analysis, and original insights into the *Furioso* have been rare. Nevertheless each generation and each reader bring their own reaction to the poem. I have tried in this book to explain my personal appreciation of the *Furioso*, and at the same time to give a picture that takes account of most shades of modern critical opinion. For some chapters I have found a wealth of secondary material; for a few I have had little help. I have not thought it necessary to equip the text with footnotes, but I have indicated in the bibliographical notes at the end the editions of Ariosto's works quoted and the other principal sources which the reader may wish to pursue. The reader is also referred to the indexes, at the back of the book, of names mentioned in the text and of references to characters in the *Furioso*.

I am grateful to many pupils, friends and colleagues in Britain, America and Italy for their help – particularly for the facilities provided by Italian and British libraries, and by the University of Cornell during a term's leave of absence from Edinburgh University. I should like especially to thank Dr D. E. Rhodes, Mr R. M. Pinkerton, Dr Alan Freedman and Dr Patrick Boyde for help and criticism; and I owe a special debt to Professor Peter Brown for much valuable advice. I thank Mrs Peter Harvey for her patience in typing the various drafts of this book, and my wife for her criticism and sympathetic support. None of the above bear any responsibility for the book's deficiencies.

C. P. B. *Edinburgh, March 1973*

NOTE. References in the text are to canto and stanza numbers (for the *Furioso*), to poem and line numbers (for the lyrics), and to act and scene numbers, preceded by (i) or (ii) where necessary to indicate whether the earlier or later version is cited (for the comedies). Details of the editions used are given in the Bibliography at the end of the book.

1. Life

Ariosto's life and his poetry were closely bound up with the court of Ferrara, where his father had been an official. Ludovico himself, as a young man, entered the service of the Estense family, and strayed only briefly and reluctantly from Ferrara during the rest of his life. His *Orlando Furioso* was addressed to the Estensi, the same family to which his predecessor, Count Matteo Maria Boiardo, had dedicated the *Orlando Innamorato*, and to which later in the century Torquato Tasso was to dedicate the *Gerusalemme Liberata*. It is no accident that these three outstanding poems were all composed at the Ferrarese court or in close connection with it. The significance of the court in the Renaissance as a centre of social and cultural life is clear – nearly all the Italian writers were associated with one or more of the courts where they found in varying degrees patronage, companionship, facilities for graceful living and leisure for their art. Much as they complained of the envy, tyranny, malice and exploitation of princes and fellow courtiers they were attracted to the court as by a magnet, drawn by the patronage of its rulers and the stimulus of its culture.

Ferrara's special appeal at the turn of the fifteenth century was not confined to writers, although there were special reasons why it attracted the romance-poets. Ferrara had long been a stopping-place for travellers making their way from France along the valley of the Po, the principal route by which French culture entered Italy. Pilgrims and minstrels brought the Carolingian and Arthurian tales to Ferrara and Venice, where the first Italian versions appeared and the Estense dukes were to build up in their library the best collection of romances in Italy. Ferrara had grown precisely because of its key geographical position in Northern Italy, at the intesection of the Po and the highways from Romagna, Tuscany, Mantua and Verona. The course of the river has changed considerably since the Renaissance, but the two main branches, the Po di Volano and the Po di Primaro, at that time met close to the walls of Ferrara. Travellers by boat between Milan and Venice could stop off at the major cities along the river, and Ferrara was important strategically as commanding the last practicable passage of the Po before it spread into its delta – and it stood in a particularly vital position for communications between Venice and Bologna. Hence the covetous eyes of both Venice and the Papacy were constantly on the Ferrarese.

Ferrara's place in the political situation of Italy in the fifteenth century requires some explanation, for it has a direct bearing on the poet's career and occasions numerous allusions in his poetry. A number of independent states had emerged during the two previous centuries, of which the most prominent were Milan, a powerful tyranny established by the Visconti and carried on by the Sforza; the Republic of Venice, with its wide commercial empire in the Mediterranean and considerable territory on the Italian mainland; Medici Florence, with its extensive commercial and banking interests, on uneasy if not hostile terms with her neighbours and rivals; the Papacy, which had recovered from the Great Schism and was eager to assert its authority in temporal as well as spiritual matters; and Naples, where Alfonso of Aragon had established a despotic rule over Southern Italy and Sicily. The smaller states, Genoa, Mantua, Ferrara, Lucca and others were able to retain their independence only by alliances with the larger ones; so a balance of power was established whereby no single state was allowed to extend its territory and authority beyond a point considered tolerable by the others. Italy thus remained divided at a time when other European peoples had acquired central governments and national armies. Throughout most of the fifteenth century this balance of power was maintained without any large-scale or prolonged foreign invasions. There were incursions by the Turks, and disputes between the Angevins and Aragonese over Genoa and Naples; and there were several internal wars of short duration between different groupings of the Italian states. But the country at this time had not yet experienced the bitter military conflict it was to suffer in the late fifteenth and early sixteenth centuries.

Ferrara's position in this political structure was somewhat delicate. The Este family had dominated the city from the early thirteenth century. Obizzo II, who also gained control of Reggio and Modena, was allocated by Dante to the river of boiling blood where tyrants and murderers were punished. Following the struggle between the Papacy and Venice for possession of Ferrara in the early fourteenth century the Estensi were recognised in 1332 as Vicars of the Church in Ferrara; and members of the Estense line were to retain control of the city until the end of the sixteenth century. In Borso d'Este's time (1450–71) Ferrarese territory included Rovigo, Modena and Reggio, the two latter being held as fiefs of the Emperor who raised them to a Duchy in 1452. In 1471 Sixtus IV eventually acknowledged the Estensi as Dukes of Ferrara. In addition the Garfagnana, a mountainous region north of Lucca, asked for Ferrarese protection in the fifteenth century and was for some time under Estense control. Ferrara was therefore in the mid-fifteenth century a state of considerable size, stretching across Italy from the Adriatic to within a few miles of the Ligurian sea, and this strategic position inevitably involved her in the wider political life of the country.

During this time the city and its dependent territories were organised by successive rulers into a strongly centralised state which, small as it was, succeeded in maintaining its independence in a world of much larger aggressive powers. The economy was based on the agricultural produce of its extensive fertile plains and the fish and game to be had from the rivers and canals which ran through its low-lying land and which a laborious system of dykes kept from flooding the fields and orchards. These resources and its key situation for trading and travel provided the wealth for the Estense rulers to build up a magnificent court and city. Their rule was despotic, and often harsh. Borso d'Este had to be alert to maintain his authority and repressed insubordination and insurrection severely. Taxes and fines were frequent to provide money for his splendid court; and money and men were needed for defence of his power and the economy – there were both compulsory military service and compulsory drafts for labour on the dykes in case of flooding. Yet in spite of his severity, Borso was a popular ruler, a patron of artists and writers and the leader of a brilliant court. In the only significant conflict of his time, the war between Milan, Florence and Naples against Venice and the Papacy (1467–8), the Estensi supported the Pope, and Ercole I, Borso's successor, gained a considerable reputation for bravery. But the war barely touched Ferrara and these were the times to which the Ferrarese were to look back as a period of happiness and prosperity: 'Non son più i tempi del duca Borso' became a proverbial saying when Ercole was struggling to pilot Ferrara through the wars and political storms of the late fifteenth century.

Ercole succeeded his brother Borso in 1471 and Ariosto's father Nicolò was in Ercole's service as captain of the *cittadella* of Reggio when Ludovico was born there in September 1474. Members of the Ariosto family had been prominent in Bologna in the twelfth and thirteenth centuries and Nicolò is recorded in the *Diario ferrarese* as

having the title of 'Conte'; he had associated himself closely with
Ercole's cause when the old Duke Borso died in 1471, and he was
suspected of being involved in the plot to poison Ercole's rival. At
any event Ercole appointed him to Reggio to command the garrison
staff, and it was probably there that he met Daria Malaguzzi, whom
he married in the summer of 1473. Daria was then a girl of 20, a
member of one of the principal families in Reggio, and she brought
Nicolò a substantial dowry. Ludovico was the eldest of the ten
children she bore him, five boys and five girls. These children were
to prove a considerable responsibility for the poet.

In 1481 Nicolò Ariosto moved to another Ferrarese dependency,
Rovigo, as captain of the garrison, and found himself quickly in
trouble when hostilities broke out the following year between
Venice and Ferrara. Disputes between the Pope and Naples, and the
old rivalry between Venice and Ferrara, had led to a new grouping
of powers and to a war in which Venice and the Pope opposed the
Neapolitan League, including Ferrara. The Venetians were eager to
extend their southern border and the Pope resented Ercole's reluctance to fulfil his obligations to the Church. The Venetians invaded
the Polesine north of the Po, and when they approached Rovigo the
townspeople, left by Ercole without support, capitulated and forced
Nicolò to surrender. He came back to Ferrara with his family
in January 1484: it was not a very cheering sight for the young
Ludovico – the war had cast its shadow over the normally gay city;
trade was at a standstill; poverty and disease were widespread; there
was a good deal of lawlessness. However, the war came to an end
later that year, when the Pope turned against Venice, but Ercole
was obliged to accept a humiliating treaty whereby he lost Rovigo
and all the Polesine and had to restore Venice's trading privileges
in Ferrara. Nicolò Ariosto set about recovering his fortunes. He
managed to buy himself an important post in the communal administration of Ferrara and seems to have used it quite shamelessly
to acquire a substantial income. He was very unpopular but so were
most of the Ducal officials, who harassed the people severely.

Nicolò was sent to Modena as Captain in 1489, leaving Ludovico
behind in Ferrara, probably in the care of his uncles. The young poet
enrolled in the University, in the Law Faculty, in the autumn of
1489, and spent the next five years in his studies there. Student life
at Ferrara was rowdy and undisciplined, but probably not so rowdy
as at Bologna or Pavia where the students dominated their teachers
with threats of strikes and emigration. We know that the poet wrote

'baje', verses, now lost, in celebration of student life, and we have a Latin poem in honour of Ercole's son which shows a good knowledge of Virgil, Catullus and Ovid. Most of Ariosto's early writings were in Latin, as were Boiardo's, and it was not until 1503-5 under the influence of Bembo that he began to use the vulgar tongue for serious composition. He had a good Latin teacher, Gregorio da Spoleto, who, however, left Ferrara in 1497 to go to Milan to teach Francesco Sforza; and Ludovico may have learnt a little Greek shortly after this. He started a Latin poem, he tells us, concerning 'gesta di duci e fatti guerreschi', which he abandoned; and he composed various lyrics, pastoral eclogues etc., dedicated to women or poets and philologists among his friends, Ercole Strozzi, Alberto Pio, Pietro Bembo and others.

While the young poet was busy with his studies and his Latin verse the invasion of Charles VIII (1494) came as a bombshell to end nearly half a century of comparative peace and stability in Italy. Ariosto's thoughts flew at once to a classical parallel and he composed some well-turned Latin hexameters assuring his readers that however the war clouds threatened he himself would continue to recline comfortably beneath his tree and sing the praises of his fair Philirrhoe. Duke Ercole was striving his utmost to keep Ferrara out of the war. For many Italians Ludovico Sforza's invitation to Charles to cross the Alps in pursuit of his claim to Naples was the critical incident that opened the floodgates to the foreigner and precipitated the series of disastrous foreign invasions that were to culminate in 1527 in the sack of Rome. Ercole had established close relations with Milan (his daughter Beatrice was married to Ludovico Sforza in 1491), and with France (he sent his son Ferrante to serve in Charles' army). When the Italian League was formed to repel Charles, Ercole's sympathy for the French roused the suspicions and resentment of Milan and of the Venetians who were clamouring to put down their old rival :

O guerra o non guerra
Ferrara andrà per terra!
[War or no war, Ferrara shall be destroyed!]

Ercole walked the razor's edge – he sent his eldest son Alfonso to join Ludovico Sforza in the Italian League, while his second son remained in the pay of Charles. But vulnerable as Ferrara seemed, she succeeded, throughout Ariosto's lifetime, in holding up her head. On the invasion of Louis XII in 1499, and during the subsequent campaigns of Cesare Borgia, Ferrara's careful courting of French protection served her in good stead. She could not stand alone against France or the Empire, the Venetians or the Pope, but her friendship was always worth courting by the greater powers. The city was strongly fortified (one of the most heavily protected in Christendom, it was said) and her artillery was specially strong. If she could not resist the passage of strong hostile troops through her territory she could certainly add to the discomfiture of an engaged army.

The finances of the Ariosto family were probably strained throughout these years: Ludovico's father occupied various, often remunerative offices, but seldom held them for long and, when he retired to Ferrara for good, Ludovico took a post at court in order to make his contribution. When Nicolò died in 1500 his son suddenly found himself responsible for the education of his younger brothers and the care and provision of his unmarried sisters. The family had some property, a large house in Ferrara and various farms outside, but the income from these was not substantial and they involved the poet in trying lawsuits. Ludovico's studies and writing were certainly severely impeded. He was occupied at court in 1500 and 1501 and went to Canossa in 1502 as Captain of the garrison. A natural son, Giambattista, was born about this time; the mother, a certain 'Maria', may have been a family servant. Ludovico never took much interest in this child and did not legitimise him as he did a later natural child, Virginio, for whom he showed great affection.

In 1503 the poet's uncle died and Ludovico had to return to Ferrara to take care of his family. It was now that he began a period of service with Ercole's son, Cardinal Ippolito d'Este, whom he did not leave until 1517. Ippolito's brother, Alfonso, became Duke in 1505, on the death of Ercole, and the two brothers maintained prestigious households in Ferrara, between which there was considerable rivalry. Ippolito, Cardinal though he was, lived a thoroughly secular life, hunting, womanising and warring with great zest, but glad to have at his disposal, as Archbishop of Ferrara, numerous valuable benefices for which his courtiers vied. He has achieved some notoriety for his responsibility for a brutal attack on his brother Giulio, who was near-blinded by the Cardinal's men because, it is said with some plausibility, his 'beautiful eyes' had attracted a lady's praise and aroused Ippolito's jealousy. Ariosto had no specialised office: he was a 'famigliare' or 'cortigiano' whose job it was to make himself useful to his master – to undertake missions to other courts, accompany Ippolito on diplomatic journeys or on the battlefield, to oversee the preparation of meals, to buy clothes, to help in the administration of city and country property. In return he was provided with food for himself and his servant and a small stipend, which was not regularly paid. He was often in financial difficulties and his health was not good; he suffered from stomach troubles and probably should have had a special diet which he couldn't afford. He might have improved his fortunes had he been willing to take holy orders ('ordini sacerdotali') which would have opened up a richer field of ecclesiastical benefices – this he always refused; but he must have taken minor orders as he did enjoy certain benefices which involved him in some tedious legal disputes. He was also unwilling to absent himself for any length of time from Ferrara, partly for family reasons, partly because of his attachment, at least after 1513, to Alessandra Benucci.

During these years, then, he was closely involved in the political, social and cultural life of the court. Ferrara at this time was one of the most brilliant cities in Europe. Ercole had a passion for building and with his architect Biagio Rossetti he made substantial additions to the medieval city – the so-called 'Addizione Erculea' which more than doubled the area of building and earned Ferrara the reputation of 'the first modern city of Europe'. Much of the Ferrara of Ariosto's day is still standing : the Romano-Gothic cathedral, and Palazzo del Comune, which date from the thirteenth century; the huge Castello, begun in the fourteenth century, and still dominating the centre of the city; and the beautiful Palazzo Schifanoia, already built when Ercole came to power. Ercole rebuilt the church of S. Francesco, and added S. Maria in Vedo, and the Certosa, vast buildings in the characteristic Ferrarese brick; and also the Palazzo dei Diamanti and many fine street houses still inhabited today; and the high brick walls which he erected to contain his new buildings still guard the city with their massive ramparts cut here and there by the canals which in Renaissance times linked every part of Ferrara with the nearby Po.

Ercole's other notable achievement as a patron was his encouragement of the theatre. It was in Ferrara in the later fifteenth century that Plautus and Terence were translated and a succession of performances of their comedies gave a strong impetus to Italian drama. But in all aspects of the arts the Ferrara of Borso and Ercole could claim some distinction. Theatrical performances stimulated music and dance, particularly the 'intermedi', brief scenic interludes with music, which anticipated the melodrama. Famous foreign musicians were invited to the court, Josquin des Prés, Adriano Willaert and others, and among the Ferrarese were Francesco and Alfonso della Viola. The apogee of Ferrarese music came in the following century, under Alfonso II, with Monteverdi, Palestrina and Frescobaldi, but the tradition had been established earlier. So too in the visual arts a Ferrarese school developed in the fifteenth century with Cosme Tura, and Francesco Cossa whose magnificent frescoes are in the Schifanoia palace; and in the early sixteenth century some distinguished local painters were active in Ferrara, Lorenzo Costa, Dosso Dossi, and il Garofalo, alongside Venetian artists patronised by Alfonso I, Titian and Giovanni Bellini among them. Also in Ercole's circle was an active group of scholars and poets in Latin and the vernacular, the Strozzi, father and son, Antonio Tebaldeo, Niccolò da Correggio and Antonio Cammelli – and the authors of two outstanding romances, the blind Francesco Bello, who wrote his *Mambriano* in the same years that Boiardo was engaged on the *Orlando Innamorato;* and Pietro Bembo, the poet and linguistic authority, was a resident or frequent visitor to Ferrara after 1498, and became a lifelong friend of Ariosto.

The Estense court in Ariosto's lifetime was therefore a remarkable, a brilliant one. Apart from its cultural achievements it aroused comment for the splendour of its social life – its pageants and processions, balls, concerts, jousts and hunts, its glamorous costumes, and superb banquets. Contemporary chronicles report in elaborate detail the wonders of its festivities. They also report the squalor of the city – the poverty, famine, disease, violence: frequent flooding or severe frosts that wrecked the peasant economy; the plague; the havoc of war with its burning, killing and vandalism; and the violence of everyday life when no-one felt safe after dark and the Duke's officers were powerless to prevent looting and murder; the heavy mists that crept up from the marshes and the fevers that laid everyone low. Supporting the splendour of the glamorous court were the unsung peasants, subject to all the ills with few of the joys – a father is reported to have killed his children in 1504 rather than see them die of famine.

Ariosto was expected to undertake diplomatic and administrative duties like any other court official, but his fame as a poet soon helped to smooth his path. When sent to Mantua in 1507 to convey the court's congratulations on the birth of a son to the Marchioness Isabella Gonzaga, Ercole's daughter, he was warmly welcomed for

his account of 'the work which he is composing, which made these
two days pass extremely pleasantly'. The 'work' must have been the
Orlando Furioso which he probably began a year or two previously –
we have no clear evidence as to the precise date. The first edition
of forty cantos went to the printer in 1515 and was published the
following year. Its reception was favourable if not immediately
overwhelming – this edition of perhaps 1200 copies was sold out by
the end of 1520. There is a legend that Ippolito wanted to know
'Messer Ludovico, wherever did you find such a lot of nonsense?'
and to have sugegsted that he might have spent his time better on
his court duties. But the fame and fortune of the poem grew rapidly,
and it was to become the best-seller of its age. Ariosto was also much
occupied at court with the various theatrical performances staged in
the large hall in the Ducal palace. His five-act comedy *Cassaria* was
produced for the Carnival of 1508, and was very well received. *I
Suppositi* was staged the following year, and he prepared a production of *Il Negromante* for the carnival in 1510 but the political and
military crises at that time prevented its performance.

This was in fact the busiest and most worrying period of the poet's
life. Ferrarese internal and external affairs were tense and critical. In
1506 the conspiracy of Don Giulio d'Este, Ercole's bastard son,
to kill Alfonso and Ippolito was a particularly sordid event, and
Ariosto's eclogue on the subject, justifying the severe reaction of the
Duke, dismayed his biographer Catalano as 'perhaps the only real
blot on the reputation of our Poet'. Two years later in another
sordid episode a close friend of Ariosto's, Ercole Strozzi, was found
dead with twenty-two wounds in his body. Alfonso was suspected
of this murder.

Above all Ariosto's energies and skill were tested in supporting the
Estensi's diplomatic manœuvring between France and the Papacy
in the Italian wars in these years. In February 1507 the poet had
accompanied Ippolito on a visit to Milan, to pay their respects to
Louis XII, and Ippolito and Alfonso made a similar visit in May
1509. Julius II and Ferrara had joined the French in the League of
Cambrai against the Venetians in the spring of that year, but the
Pope was suspicious of Ferrarese intentions and Ariosto was sent to
Rome in December 1509 to reassure him and ask for help. But
Julius soon changed his mind and made peace with Venice early the
next year, in order to drive the French out of Italy. Ferrara decided
to maintain its alliance with France and pressed on with the war
against Venice: Alfonso won a number of encounters with the old

enemy, including one with the Venetian fleet in the Po, at Polesella
(1509), where fifteen Venetian galleys were captured, and in 1510,
he regained Rovigo, as well as other territories, such as Montagnana,
Este and Monselice. This further antagonised the Pope and Ariosto
was again sent to Rome to try to placate Julius. He remained in
Rome in June and July when the papal forces, under the Duke of
Urbino, attacked the Ferrarese, and the Pope excommunicated
Alfonso who refused to obey Julius' order for him to come to Rome,
but left the unhappy Ariosto to make his excuses. He then rejoined
Ippolito and during the following year accompanied him on his
travels, and he tells us that he witnessed the sack of Ravenna in 1512
by French troops who owed much, he says, to the Ferrarese artillery.
He then escorted the distinguished prisoner Fabrizio Colonna back
to Ferrara and participated in the festivities generously provided for
him. With the subsequent French defeats the Ferrarese were driven
back upon their capital. An attempt at reconciliation between
Alfonso and Julius in the summer of 1512 failed, and the Duke made
a dangerous escape from Rome during which Ariosto escorted him
on his flight to Florence 'with my heart in my mouth'.

   Then, in 1513, Julius died and Giovanni de' Medici became Pope,
as Leo X. The Ferrarese breathed a sigh of relief and Ariosto's hopes
rose. He and the new Pope were 'antiqui amici'; both had been
pupils of Gregorio da Spoleto and Ludovico had given proof of his
friendship for Giovanni on frequent occasions. He went to Rome,
expecting favours, but he got none; in his third satire he describes
his disappointment. Nor did the Pope show any favours to the
Estensi. When Francis I invaded Italy in 1515, Leo promised to restore Modena and Reggio to the Duke of Ferrara, but he never kept
this promise, and in 1519 Alfonso was warned of a papal plot to
seize Ferrara itself. During these years Ariosto continued to travel
with Ippolito or on his master's behalf, making several further visits
to Rome. Some years previously, probably while in Florence in June
1513, he had formed a serious attachment to the woman to whom
he was to be devoted for the rest of his life, Alessandra Benucci, the
wife of Tito Strozzi, a Florentine resident in Ferrara. Alessandra was
of Florentine origin but was born in Barletta. She was then about
30 years old; Ludovico was 38; Tito Strozzi, then about 45 years old,
died in 1515. There are no explicit allusions by the poet to Alessandra
before her husband's death and Ludovico may have known her for
some time before his visit to Florence in 1513. But his close connection with her seems to date from this period. We know very

little about it or about her: the one extant letter written by Alessandra suggests that she was a relatively uncultured woman.

In August 1517 Ippolito announced his intention of going to Hungary, and Ludovico as a member of his court was expected to accompany him. His first satire describes his reasons for refusing: his poor health, his need to look after his aged mother – perhaps really his love for Alessandra. He declined to go, and there was a break in his relations with Ippolito. As a result Ariosto lost not only his court stipend, but various benefices and properties as well.

He was fortunate to be taken into Alfonso's service, and from April 1518 he was included in the Duke's salaried staff with a somewhat better salary than his previous one, including an allowance 'for three servants and two horses'. He had a room in the palace which he shared with his friend Guido Silvestri. His duties were not very demanding, and he found the Duke a more congenial master than the Cardinal. During the years 1517–20 he wrote three satires, finished his comedy *Il Negromante* and started to revise the *Furioso*, the second edition of which came out in February 1521. The poem continued to be in great demand – there were seventeen editions between 1524 and 1531.

However, renewal of warfare between Ferrara and the Pope led to the suppression of his pay and in 1522 he was obliged to accept the post of Commissario of the Garfagnana. The inhabitants were quarrelsome and there were many bandits. Ariosto was supposed to keep order with a force of a dozen soldiers over the 300-odd square miles of mountain and some 83 villages. He hated the place and found the work beyond his powers. He tried to get a sort of militia together to support his soldiers, and he says he would have liked to bring the lawless priests to heel by destroying a few churches, but the Duke wouldn't let him. He wrote nothing for a year and then composed two satires which reflect his state of mind. He was desperate to get back to his beloved Ferrara and to Alessandra, and even refused the post of ambassador to the new Pope, Clement VII. He made several visits to Ferrara and at last was allowed to return for good in June 1525.

The remaining seven years of his life were moderately peaceful. He continued to fulfil his duties at court, and made visits to Florence, Venice, Mantua and elsewhere. In the campaigns of Francis I against the Imperial forces in 1521, as later in 1524, Ferrara had continued to support the French and to find the Papacy implacably hostile. Leo X held firmly on to Modena and Reggio and was set on seizing

Ferrara itself. By 1526 the alliances were reversed. Clement VII had joined Francis I in the League of Cognac against the Emperor, who was now supported by Ferrara. Charles V renewed Alfonso's investiture of the fiefs of Modena and Reggio and made him Captain-general of the Imperial troops in Italy – a timely change of alliance for Ferrara in view of the imminent collapse of French arms and the triumph of the Spanish. The historian Guicciardini, who had been Papal Governor of Modena and Reggio, accused Alfonso of urging on the troops that sacked Rome in 1527. By the Treaty of Barcelona of 1529 Alfonso was invested in all the disputed fiefs and Ferrara had ridden out the storm. Ariosto probably helped welcome Charles V to Modena in November 1529, and was entrusted with a mission to one of the Emperor's commanders, the Marquis Alfonso d'Avalos, in October 1531, to ensure Imperial support against the still hostile papacy. On this occasion he was granted an annual pension of 100 gold ducats by the Marquis – a generous gift which he did not live long enough to enjoy. His financial situation in any case was probably somewhat better than before: he had inherited several new properties and he gave up his father's house in 1528 to go and live in the house in the 'Addizione Erculea' which is still shown to visitors : *parva sed apta mihi* is the inscription over the door. But he was involved in frequent administrative and legal worries – a dispute with the Ducal administration lasted fifteen years and was still unresolved at the poet's death.

During these years he was able to take up his theatrical interests again. The tradition of court dramatic performances had been broken in 1509 because of the war, but was resumed in 1528 for the arrival of Ercole II and his French wife Renée de Valois. Ariosto's *La Lena* and his *Cassaria* were both performed at this time, and he translated the *Menaechmi* into Italian so that a French translator could then make a version for Renée. He was also much occupied with his revision of the *Furioso*, which was almost complete by June 1531. The third edition was eventually published in October 1532. A few weeks later he was in Mantua with Alfonso to welcome Charles V, whom Clement VII had invited to form an anti-French league. The Emperor is said to have crowned him with a laurel wreath in recognition of his poem, but there is no solid foundation for this legend.

At some stage during this final period in Ferrara, certainly between 1526 and 1530, Ludovico and Alessandra were married. The marriage was kept secret, probably so that Alessandra would not lose

her husband's inheritance and the care of her children, and the
couple continued to live separately even after the wedding. It would
seem on the surface to have been a cool relationship, but it must
nevertheless have been a devoted one. In support of this we have
both the allusions to Alessandra in Ludovico's poetry and the evidence of his life: his reluctance to be absent for long from Ferrara
was certainly to some extent motivated by Alessandra's presence
there. There is no evidence that she bore him any children.

Ariosto was now in his fifties and his health was not good. While
his financial circumstances had certainly improved he was not
sufficiently independent to be able to retire from court duties and
he was travelling a good deal in 1530-31, to Bologna, Florence,
Venice and elsewhere. He had several periods of illness now; he
complained of stomach trouble, chest pains, constipation, catarrh.
He fell severely ill in December 1532 and died in July 1533, with
Alessandra and Virginio by his bedside. His funeral was quiet and
passed almost unnoticed by the court from which he had withdrawn
increasingly during the past year; the lawsuit between the poet and
the Ducal authorities over Ariosto's property probably contributed
to the coolness between them at this stage.

What sort of a man was he in his everyday life? Such questions
are difficult to answer at a distance of almost 500 years. Biographers
tend to re-construct a poet's personality from his poetry, which
provides only a partial picture; and the legends that grow out of
the memories of his contemporaries are generally fictitious. Even
Ariosto's letters, which are not literary but practical, concerning
almost exclusively business matters, do not reveal much about the
writer. We have over 200 letters, two-thirds of which were
written from the Garfagnana in the years 1522-5. During this
period Ariosto's overriding concern was the administration of
justice and the establishment of peace and order in circumstances
that made this almost impossible. What is impressive is his con-
scientiousness and persistence in trying to do his job. He appeals *ad
nauseam* for the reasonable co-operation of the neighbouring authorities of Lucca and Florence; he pleads again and again for firmness
against evil-doers, and for the power and authority to act as he con-
siders just. He feels lonely and isolated, but he persists in his attempt
to do his duty.

His pity for the victims of poverty and violence produce moving
pleas for support : 'that place is subject to such tyranny and is in such
terror of these scoundrels, especially Moro's brother, the one called

Giuglianetto, who beats them, wounds them, robs, drives and
threatens them that eventually they'll be forced to abandon their
homes and go off wandering where they can. I myself, out of pity
for them ...' (Letter 92). There are several outbursts against the
priests, pardoned by their Bishop for atrocious crimes, and against
the right of sanctuary; and there are cries for severer penalties: 'It
would be enough to hang four or five people in this province ...'
(Letter 158). But we have no evidence that such stern measures were
taken – and frequently men accused by Ariosto were pardoned by
Alfonso, or not prosecuted by the Captain of Justice.

In general, however, Ariosto seems to have been too kindly to be
an effective officer: 'I confess quite openly that I'm not the right
man to govern others, because I'm too merciful, and I haven't the
heart to refuse what I'm asked' (Letter 46). He is conscious that he
is too inexpert, too humble and diffident to conduct difficult negotia-
tions with aggressive diplomats: he fears that his opponent will get
his way 'because he is more powerful and arrogant than I am'
(Letter 98). His pity for the underdogs, the poor, is tempered by his
exasperation at their tolerance of bandits, their failure to support the
authority that is protecting them. He comes to accept practical
Machiavellian politics: 'what we do out of kindness and the wish to
live in peace, they think we do because of cowardice'. He will see if
he can achieve 'by cunning, what I can't by force' (Letter 64).

These letters seem to support the picture that has come down from
his contemporaries of a kindly, well-meaning, conscientious man,
certainly no saint, too conscious of his own as well as of others'
weaknesses to be sanctimonious. His morals are those of his age and
his society: he lives as virtuously and as honestly as he reasonably
can: he has illegitimate children, a long attachment to a married
woman; he has to scramble like everyone else for benefices and
favours; he accepts and even supports the dubious conduct of his
patrons and superiors. But he is not malicious or grasping: he cares
conscientiously for his dependent family, and he is widely liked for
his wit and charm. He is not ambitious for wealth or honours – he
wants a quiet life, the company of his Alessandra and his friends, the
familiar streets of Ferrara, the leisure to read and to write. He lives
his life as one might expect the author of the *Furioso* to live it.

2. Minor Works

Apart from his letters, and various fragments associated with the *Furioso* (which we discuss later), Ariosto's 'minor works' comprise a collection of lyric poems in Latin and the vernacular, a small group of satires, and four comedies. The range and quantity are not large, evidence perhaps of the extent to which his creative energies were absorbed by the *Furioso*. Of the Latin lyrics some sixty survive, most of them short pieces of a few lines – epitaphs or epigrams – but there are also a number of more substantial poems too, such as the Epithalamium for the wedding of Alfonso d'Este and Lucrezia Borgia, which extends to some 150 lines. They were, many of them, occasional poems, closely related to court life: an inaugural oration, regularly delivered by a student, for the opening of the academic year at the University, or 'Studium', of Ferrara, in 1495; brief epitaphs for Ferdinand of Aragon, and 'De Raphael Urbinate', or longer laments for the deaths of his friends or their relations. The subjects are contemporary, the style classical. All of these poems are modelled closely on classical originals or borrow freely from them. Ariosto's son, Virginio, wrote of his father: 'He was not very studious and did not read many books: he liked Virgil, and Tibullus for his style; greatly admired Horace and Catullus, but not Propertius much'. But Ariosto's reading must have been quite extensive to judge from the echoes in his poetry of Cicero, Ovid, Statius, Terence, Seneca and many others; he seems to have shown comparatively little interest in the Latin poets of the Renaissance.

Ariosto's Latin lyrics belong very largely to a youthful period of his life, 1494–1503. One critic sees them as evidence of a phase in the poet's development marked by a sense of revulsion from the practical world. Ariosto refers in 'De diversis amoribus' to a time when his nature inclined him

> ... docto vitam producere cantu,
> per nemora illa, avidis non adeunda viris (LIV, 25–6)
> [to occupy my life with learned song, in woods remote from greedy men]

– an attitude reminiscent of Florentine neo-Platonism (with which

Ferrara had close contacts), in envisaging poetry as the gift of a
select few whom it consoles for the trials of everyday life. The Latin
lyrics are indeed learned and generally severe in style, and only a
few have attracted praise for their quality as poetry. There has been
a dangerous tendency to read as autobiography lyrics which owe at
least as much to Horatian originals as to the poet's own experience.
How far the poet's own feelings are involved it is impossible to say.
A contemporary event on which Ariosto meditates recalls a parallel
situation in a Latin poet – or is it that a reading of Horace sets
Ariosto thinking of his own situation, the invasion of Charles VIII
for example?

> Quid Galliarum navibus aut equis
> paret minatus Carolus ... (I, *1–2*)
> [What threat is Charles preparing with his Gallic ships and
> horses ...?]

What does the poet care, so long as he can be with his lady:

> me nulla tangat cura, sub arbuto
> iacentem aquae ad murmur cadentis ... (I, *5–6*)
> [let no thought of this trouble me as I lie under a tree by a
> murmuring waterfall ...]

In the reverence for antiquity which characterised Ariosto's age
many such poems were composed as though in response to the
question 'How might Horace have reacted to the invasion of
Charles VIII?' But imitate though he may, the poet's taste is apparent
in his selection of the source he wishes to follow. There are motifs here
which recur frequently in Ariosto's later writing; the anti-war protest,
seen in the two versions 'Ad Philiroen' and in his praise of Ercole I
as the peacemaker between Charles VIII and Ludovico il Moro (IV);
the dislike of the professional soldier (I bis); of political tyranny (I
bis,II,XV); the protest against the French, the 'hostis barbarus'
(V).

   In some of the love lyrics there is an insistence on the pangs of
jealousy which was to be a recurrent theme in the *Furioso*: to an
elegy of Bembo urging the lover to turn a blind eye on his lady's
lapses Ariosto replies indignantly:

> Me tacitum perferre meae peccata puellae? (VII, *1*)
> [Am I to tolerate in silence the transgressions of my lady?]

He is not one of those

> qui spectare suae valeat securus amicae
> non intellecta livida colla nota; (VII, *11–12*)
> [who can see, unperturbed, his mistress's neck blue with marks

that he does not recognise.]

Most of these poems are serious, literary, conventional, but there are some of lighter and more independent touch: the brief address to the graceful little Eulalia, so well trained by her mother that when the latter is too old to live by prostitution she can gain a livelihood as procuress for her daughter (XXIX). The poem which has been most admired, 'De diversis amoribus' (LIV), takes its cue from an elegy of Ovid but relates this to Ariosto's own experience, adopting a discursive, personal tone: the facetious mockery is aimed at a serious, typically Ariostesque target, human inconstancy, here his own:

Est mea nunc Glycere, mea nunc est cura Lycoris, ...
Non in amore modo mens haec, sed in omnibus impar ...

(LIV, 1, 11)

[First it is Glicera I care for, then Licori ... Not only in love is my nature like this, but it is inconstant in everything.]

He describes his giddy course from law student to poet to soldier, satisfied with none of these lives for long, just as he is with none or his ladies, constant only in the fire of his passions:

aut Glawan aut Glyceren, aut unam aut saepe ducentas
   depeream; igne tamen perpete semper amo. (LIV, <i>69–70</i>)

[Whether I die with passion for Glawa or Glicera, for one or two hundred, I always love in a perpetual blaze.]

*   *   *

ARIOSTO's vernacular lyrics in Caretti's edition comprise 5 *canzoni*, 41 sonnets, 12 madrigals, 2 eclogues and 27 *capitoli*. They are a miscellaneous and uneven collection, posing considerable problems of textual accuracy and attribution. They remained unpublished in the poet's lifetime, perhaps because Ariosto was not satisfied with them. When Marco Pio sent some of the drafts to Guidobaldo della Rovere he warned him: 'I am sending you these few poems of Ariosto which I have collected with difficulty, and against his wishes : he does not want them to be made public saying that they are faulty ('incorrette') and that he's ashamed for people to see them ...'. Most of these lyrics were composed after 1503, and it is generally accepted that Pietro Bembo was the formative influence. Bembo was in Ferrara from 1498 to 1500, and the first draft of his *Prose della Volgar Lingua* dates from this period, with its insistence on the supremacy of Petrarch as linguistic and stylistic model for the vernacular lyric poet. Bembo is said to have urged the youthful Ariosto to persist with his Latin lyrics which seemed to him more promising than

Ludovico's rather clumsy early Italian poems; but Ludovico is said
to have been unmoved.

It was certainly understandable that Ludovico should have been
drawn to the vernacular lyric when not only Bembo but so many
other contemporary poets were active in the genre – among those
writing in Ferrara were Antonio Tebaldeo, Ercole Strozzi, Niccolò
Lelio Cosmico, Niccolò Tossici and Gasparo Sardi, all caught up in
varying degrees in the fashion for the Petrarchan lyric – which was
not, however, as extreme in Ferrara as elsewhere. The occasional
composition of short poems in the Petrarchan style was in most cases
little more than a literary exercise, a cultured courtier's pastime, a
serious poet's apprenticeship. Ariosto's lyrics are frequently conventional – they treat the traditional Petrarchan amorous material as
well as current court subjects, political and social – the election of
Julius II (1503), the death of Eleonora d'Aragona, Ercole's wife
(1503), the battle of Ravenna (1512), the death of Giuliano de'
Medici (1516). There is a dramatic eclogue, a form much favoured
in Ferrara at this time, in which two shepherds discuss disapprov-
ingly the conspiracy of don Giulio and don Ferrante d'Este against
Alfonso (1506); and there is an anachronistic epic fragment in *terza
rima*, probably composed in the early years of the century, concerning the participation of an Estense ancestor, Obizzo, in the
war between Philip IV and Edward I of England – an interesting
if not very successful experiment in narrative style, moving to
and fro between a relatively prosaic diction and a lofty rhetorical
note:

> Canterò l'arme, canterò gli affanni
> d'amor, ch'un cavalier sostenne gravi
> peregrinando in terra e 'n mar molti anni ... (*Capitolo* II)
> [I'll sing the arms, I'll sing the grave trials of love which a
> knight suffered wandering by land and sea for many years.]

The love lyrics are more interesting. They repeat some of the
traditional Petrarchan themes: the poet's love and suffering, his
lady's indifference but occasional encouragement. They seem largely,
although not exclusively, to concern Alessandra Benucci and there
are traces of a *canzoniere* structure in a progression through the
lady's initial indifference, their happy meeting in Florence, the poet's
hopes, and his eventual triumph, bringing a happy phase punctu-
ated by occasional anxieties. The form and style are largely Petrarchan while the sentiments are often erotic or sensual in the manner
of the current Latin lyric. The less successful of these poems repeat

Petrarchan stylistic devices clumsily, or introduce Petrarchan reminiscences rather mechanically:

> ... e la mia Donna stassi
> lontan, forse con *gli occhi umidi e bassi* ... (Sonnet XXXV)

[my Lady is far away, perhaps with tearful, downcast eyes.]
Bembo may well have found some of these lyrics crude and harsh: they are often halting in rhythm and unduly complicated in syntax: long, involved sentences, with repeated relative clauses, build up to flat climaxes. The second and third *canzoni* offend particularly in this respect.

The best of the Petrarchan lyrics on the other hand show signs of Bembo's guiding influence: the language is polished, carefully chosen from Petrarch's lyrics – the opening of the first *canzone*, for example:

> Non so s'io potrò ben chiudere in rima
> quel che in parole sciolte
> fatica avrei di ricontarvi a pieno :
> come perdei mia libertà, che prima,
> Madonna, tante volte
> difesi, acciò non avesse altri il freno ...

[I do not know if I can record in verse what I should have difficulty in telling you in the language of prose : how I lost my liberty which before I so often defended so that no-one else should curb it]

– in which *chiudere in rima, ricontare, a pieno, perder la libertà*, and *avere il freno* are all to be found in Petrarch's *Rime*. In these poems rhetorical devices are used with restraint, and Petrarchan themes are modified to coincide more closely with the feelings and experience of Ariosto and his contemporaries. There are traces of current neo-Platonic philosophy, although these are rare: more frequently the note is down-to-earth, sensual and demanding. The third sonnet, 'O sicuro, secreto e fidel porto', is based on Petrarch's 'O cameretta che già fosti un porto', but Petrarch's suffering here gives way to Ariosto's hopes:

> ché tal mercé, cor mio, ti si prepara
> che appagarà quantunque servi e servi.

[for a reward, my heart, is being prepared for you such as will compensate you for your long service.]

The next sonnet stresses the lover's expectation that his lady should be totally compliant to his wishes : 'o nulla o vi convien tutta esser mia' ('you must be wholly mine, or not at all'). Another sonnet

(xxv), praises the lady's beauty with conventional hyperbole but
concludes :

... tutto è mirabil certo; nondimeno
non starò ch'io non dica arditamente
che più mirabil molto è la mia fede.
[all of you is wonderful indeed; but that shall not prevent me
from saying boldly that my constancy is even more wonderful.]

In Sonnet xxvi Alessandra copying an embroidery design is urged
instead to copy her lover's devotion. In Sonnet xiii he expects, like
Catullus, not suffering

ma benigne accoglienze, ma complessi
licenziosi, ma parole sciolte
da ogni fren, ma risi, vezzi e giochi;
ma dolci baci, dolcemente impressi
ben mille e mille e mille e mille volte;
e, se potran contarsi, anche fien pochi.
[but a warm welcome, embraces freely given, speech unrestrained, laughter, caresses, play, sweet kisses sweetly planted
many thousand times, and if they can be counted, then they are
too few.]

In the *capitoli* in particular the artifice recedes and the poet
lowers his tone. His use of the tercet here coincides with a shorter
sentence, a less elaborate syntax and a less contrived style. There is a
more realistic note, reminiscent of the satires – as in his absence from
his lady in the Garfagnana:

Mentre ch'io parlo, il turbid'austro prende
maggior possanza, e cresce il verno, e sciolto
da ruinosi balzi il liquor scende:
di sotto il fango, e quinci e quindi il folto
bosco mi tarda; e in tanto l'aspra pioggia
acuta più che stral mi fere il volto. (*Cap.* v)
[As I speak the turbid south wind grows stronger, the winter
deepens, the water comes pouring down from precipitous
crags; here and there thick forest delays me, and meanwhile a
harsh rain, sharper than arrows, strikes me in the face.]

The style is frequently discursive, in keeping with the less im-
passioned subjects. This is so even in the first *canzone*: when first
attracted to Alessandra he recognised the slimness of his chances and
turned his attention to other less discouraging ladies:

Quinci lo tenni e mesi ed anni escluso,
e dove più sicura

strada pensai, lo volsi ad altro corso;
credendo poi che più potesse l'uso
che 'l destin, di lui cura
non ebbi ...
[So for months and years I kept my love under restraint, and
turned it elsewhere along a safer path; thinking habit would be
stronger than fate I took no care of it.]
The style – and the sentiment – are closer to the *Furioso*. This is the
experience of Ricciardetto, who won his way to his lady's bed by a
trick, but claims a long-suppressed affection for her:

... e piacquer molto all'appetito mio
i suoi begli occhi e la polita guancia:
ma non lasciai fermarvisi il disio,
che l'amar senza speme è sogno e ciancia. (*O.F.* xxv, *49*)
[and her fair eyes and smooth cheek were much to my liking,
but I did not let my desire dwell there, for love without hope is
an empty dream.]

So the lyrics rehearse motifs closer to the sources of inspiration of
the *Furioso*, as in his memory of the festivities in Florence where he
met Alessandra:

Porte, finestre, vie, templi, teatri
vidi piene di donne
a giuochi, a pompe, a sacrifici intente, ... (*Canzone* I)
[I saw doorways, windows, streets, temples, theatres filled with
ladies busy with their games, their show,]
– which foreshadows Norandino's court in Damascus:

Adorna era ogni porta, ogni finestra
di finissimi drappi e di tapeti
ma più di belle e ben ornate donne ... (*O.F.* xvii, *20*)
[Each door, each window was decked out with the finest drapes
and fabrics, but even more with fair and finely dressed ladies.]
And one of the best lyric arias from the *Furioso*, Bradamante's im-
passioned declaration of her love for Ruggiero –

Ruggier, qual sempre fui, tal esser voglio
fin alla morte, e più, se più si puote.
O siami Amor benigno, o m'usi orgoglio ... (xliv, *61*)
[Ruggier, as I have always been, so will I be until I die, and
longer if that is possible. Whether Love is kind to me, or treats
me proudly ...]
– was an adaptation in octave rhyme of his *Capitolo* xiii:

Qual son, qual sempre fui, tal esser voglio,

alto o basso Fortuna che mi ruote,
o siami Amor benigno o m'usi orgoglio ...
[As I am, as I have always been, so will I be, whether Fortune's
wheel turn high or low, whether Love is kind to me, or treats
me proudly ...]
There is no room in Bradamante's words either for elaborate rhetorical ingenuity or for contrived Petrarchan parody: hers is a plea
which was to move its readers by its sincerity – *piazza* and *sala* were
meant to accept this without a smile, as we know that they did.
Bradamante's passion was warmly admired by sixteenth-century
readers all over Europe. In his lyrics Ariosto moves towards this
style, from the serious and learned Latin verse and the early artificial
love poems, checking the inflated epithets, the pedantic allusions,
the involved syntax. The most poetical and most characteristically
Ariostesque of these lyrics are those tending in this direction, particularly the *capitoli*, which are closest in style to the satires, the
form in which Ariosto was to make a really significant contribution.

*   *   *

ARIOSTO's seven satires were all written within a fairly short period
of his life, between October 1517 and April 1524, that is when he
was between the ages of 43 and 50, a mature poet, with the first
edition of the *Furioso* already published. They are all in *terzine;* all,
except the shorter final poem, are between 230 and 330 lines in
length; all have their point of departure in some contemporary
situation in which the poet was involved and which he uses to explain his conduct or his views and to criticise his society. They belong
therefore to a fairly precise literary convention: there is no doubt
that Ariosto had Horace and Juvenal as his guides: he borrow sa
fable from Horace's *Epistolae* in the first satire and he must have been
familiar with Juvenal who was well-known in Quattrocento Italy,
had been translated into *terzine* in 1480 and had inspired numerous
imitators. Ariosto's immediate predecessor was probably Antonio
Vinciguerra who wrote satires in *terzine*, not published, however, till
1527. Satirical verse in sonnet form is abundant in the Quattrocento
(Burchiello, Antonio Cammelli, Cariteo, etc.), and Dante had long
ago shown how effective the *terzina* could be for satirical purposes,
but the formal satire in *terzine* on the classical pattern, as we have
described Ariosto's, had not yet been established as an accepted literary genre. This was Ariosto's achievement and the later Renaissance
and seventeenth-century satirists looked consciously back to him

as the founder of their school. The satires were not published in
Ariosto's lifetime although he seems to have planned to publish
them. A manuscript collection survives with autograph corrections
by the poet, but a printed edition did not appear until 1534, the year
after his death.

Each of them, as I have said, is associated with some event or situation in the poet's life – the first with the break with the Cardinal in
1517, the second a visit to Rome to safeguard a benefice threatened
by a rival, the third his move to Alfonso's household, the fourth his
life in the Garfagnana, the fifth a friend's approaching marriage, the
sixth his search for a tutor for his son, the last his refusal of a post in
Rome. Each of them supplies the biographer with significant information about the poet's activities and movements, but they are
particularly revealing of his reactions and attitude to his environment; they show him considering the sort of practical problems
which face most men – whether to accept promotion and increased
responsibility or refuse it; to move elsewhere or to stay at home;
whether to take a wife or stay single; how to educate a child. In discussing these personal problems the poet tries to establish a personal
philosophy. What are his guide-lines for taking decisions in this
harassing world?

His philosophy, like his diet, is simple: knowing what he likes best:

   ... io meglio i miei
   casi de ogni altro intendo; (1, 31–2)

[I understand my own affairs better than anyone else.]

It seems largely to coincide with that of Horace (whether consciously or by chance who can say?): a simple life, with a simple
table and simple clothes: a quiet life, without show or ambition, free
from hazardous travelling, spent at home within sound of the bells
of the Duomo; a humble life without pretentious titles and trying
responsibilities; a free life not tied to capricious patrons or tyrannical
rulers; a stable domestic life close to the woman he loves.

'These being my tastes', Ariosto seems to say, 'how could I be
expected to go suddenly off to Hungary with the Cardinal, or to
govern the bandit-ridden Apennines, or to accept a permanent post
in Rome? It is, after all, reasonable and consistent, this attitude of
mine.' His attitude is determined by the way he is made, by the
society he lives in and the people he meets, so many of whom he
dislikes and, he shows us, dislikes with good reason. So the strictly
satirical components accompany the lyrical: he accuses others in
excusing himself. His targets are similar to Horace's: pretentious

people, hypocrites, flatterers, materialists of all sorts, social climbers, shady business-men. These are the people he dislikes at the courts, and in the Church, and he makes his dislike known, sometimes with the smiling irony of Horace, sometimes with an invective worthy of Juvenal.

The first satire was written in the autumn of 1517 at the time of Cardinal Ippolito d'Este's departure for Hungary. Ariosto did not want to leave Ferrara and went to see his master to ask to be excused: the Cardinal was offended, there was an angry scene, and Ippolito dismissed Ariosto from his service and threatened to deprive him of various sources of income. The poet did shortly after this lose his court stipend and some property that had been promised him. This was a serious blow for Ariosto, even though he was able to enter Alfonso's service the following year; but he had been with the Cardinal for some fourteen years and it was depressing, humiliating and embarrassing to be rejected in this way. His satire is addressed to two of his relatives who did go with Ippolito to Hungary, and it justifies the poet's decision, explaining his reasons – his health is poor, he needs a special diet, how could he stand Hungarian cuisine and those barbarous wines; and what would become of his aged mother and his unmarried sister? Rather than lose his liberty in this way he will give up his gifts and his court service; and he rounds off his poem with a version of Horace's fable of the fox that had to vomit up the corn it had eaten in order to squeeze out of the corn-bin.

This then is a poem of self-justification, written, I assume, to work off some of the frustration the poet felt in these circumstances – and partly to justify himself to his friends and colleagues who did go with Ippolito, some of them against their wishes. He cannot have intended it for Ippolito's eyes – he did not want a permanent rupture with the Cardinal; but the criticism of the court is quite harsh and there is little really conciliatory material or deference shown to his master – at most he imagines his friends making out his excuses to the Cardinal.

In these circumstances Ariosto is reminded of Horace and particularly of the Epistle of excuse written by Horace to Maecenas when the poet had offended his patron by over-staying his leave in the country; Horace justifies himself on the grounds of his health and insists, gently, on his personal independence with the fable of the fox. This surely explains why Ariosto, at this moment in his life turns suddenly to Horatian models. He recovers his dignity by this association of his own plight with that of Horace, and he finds in

Horace's tone and method a worthy means of justifying himself.
But here the tone is sharper than Horace's: Ariosto is still smarting
at his dismissal and he is heavily critical of court flattery. He resents
Ippolito's indifference to his poetry, and his sudden display of
hostility:

Pazzo chi al suo signor contradir vole ... (*10*)
[Mad is the man who contradicts his master.]

The verse provides a sting for his gibes at Ippolito, and it confers
dignity on his simple philosophy

Non feci mai tai cose e non so farne. (*145*)
[I have never done such things and I can't do them.]

It is also a vehicle for his irony which tones down the bitterness of
his criticism: he smiles imagining himself in Hungary, forced, because of his diet, to eat all his meals by himself like a monk:

solo a la mensa come un certosino. (*63*)

He recalls in mock-heroic tones his frenzied journeys for his master
through the mountains, 'playing with death', his facing 'la grande ira
di Secondo', the fury, that is, of Julius II who once threatened to
throw him into the Tiber to feed the fish. The occasional resort to a
mock-heroic diction serves to forestall criticism of his prosaic and unheroic self-defence: his old bones could never survive a journey to
Hungary, but for his younger brother it's another matter:

... tu che diciotto anni
dopo me indugiasti a uscir de l'alvo. (*221–2*)
[you who delayed 18 years after me in issuing from the womb.]

And in the final fable, in place of Horace's fox, he likens himself
ironically to

Uno asino ... ch'ogni osso e nervo
mostrava di magrezza ... (*247-8*)
[an ass showing every bone and sinew, so thin it was.]

The style, which is direct, lowly, largely conversational, is appropriate to the case he is making out to his friends: it is a dignified and
at the same time a modest message, in which rhetoric would be out
of place. Instead there are flashes of realistic observation which pinpoint the poet's frustration:

A chi nel Barco e in villa il segue, dona,
a chi lo veste e spoglia, o pona i fiaschi
nel pozzo per la sera in fresco a nona,
vegghi la notte, in sin che i Bergamaschi
se levino a far chiodi, sì che spesso
col torchio in mano addormentato caschi. (*100–5*)

[He has gifts for anyone who goes with him out into the country or to his villa; for those who dress and undress him, for those who go out at mid-day and put the wine-flasks in the well to cool them for the evening; for those who sit up at night with him till the Bergamasques (blacksmiths) get up to start hammering, so that they fall asleep with their torches in their hands.]

So Ariosto's fantasy works on the realities of court life, gathering the essence of Ippolito's patronage into a few colourful images – as he does the courtier's servitude, picturing himself sitting alone by the fireside 'where I shouldn't smell people's feet, or armpits or belches':

né piei, né ascelle odorerei, né rutti. (57)

Out of these blunt crudities emerges the poet's own dignified philosophy, his rejection of hypocrisy, his claim for liberty. A coarse, hard, everyday world no less than the imaginary world of chivalry can thus provide the material of his poetry.

The second satire (late 1517) seems to bear this out; the poet shirks neither crude realities nor legal niceties: it is as though he has set himself the task of putting into verse what it would take some skill to explain in a prose letter; 'I'm coming to Rome to rectify my failure to keep up payment of the taxes on a benefice which I expected to be made over to me by old Fusari when he dies, and which some-one else is now trying to get; unless I do, that some-one has a motive for getting rid of Fusari ...'

Sai ben che 'l vecchio, la riserva avendo,
inteso di un costì che la sua morte
bramava, e di velen perciò temendo,
mi pregò ch'a pigliar venissi in corte
la sua rinuncia ... (130–4)

[You know that the old man, who has the disposal of the office, hearing of some-one there who was eager for his death, and so being afraid of poison, asked me to come to court to take over the office he has renounced.]

So too the accommodation the poet will require in Rome is set out (not in telegraph code or the symbols of the guide-book) in *terza rima*:

Camera o buca ove a stanzar abbia io
che luminosa sia, che poco saglia
e da far fuoco commoda, desio ... (16–18)

[I want a room, or hole, where I can stay, that's light, has not too many stairs, and is convenient for lighting a fire.]

He thereby provides a picture not just of a room but of himself, and
the measured verse gives a quiet dignity to his actions – against
which he sets the ugly rapacity of the city *bonviveurs*:

    Unga il suo schidon pur o il suo tegame
    sin a l'orecchio a ser Vorano il muso
    venuto al mondo sol per far lattame. *(31–3)*
    [Let the chef's spit or pan smear Mr Glutton's snout right up to
    his ears, who's only in the world to create dung.]

So the poet establishes a contrast between his own hard life and the
luxury of the clerics, his own innocence and simple taste and the
treacherous world of ecclesiastical big business. The tone here is insistent, strongly abusive of the clergy and clerical corruption in Rome
– not mild irony but forthright denunciation of avarice and ambition. In lines worthy of Dante (he uses Dante's rhymes) and reminiscent of Machiavelli's blunt words in the *Prince*, he denounces the
wars of the Church, of Alexander VI, whose concern was to destroy,
not the Turks, but the rival families of the Colonna and the Orsini:

    E qual strozzato e qual col capo mozzo
    ne la Marca lasciando et in Romagna,
    trionferà, del crestian sangue sozzo. *(220–2)*
    [... leaving some strangled, some with their heads chopped off
    in the Marches and the Romagna, he'll stand triumphantly be-
    fouled with Christian blood.]

The third satire (1518) shares the theme of the first: service and
patronage. Service with Alfonso, he tells his cousin, is if anything
more congenial than that with Ippolito (he doesn't have to travel so
much), but he would prefer complete independence; he isn't sur-
prised that the new Pope, Leo X, an old friend, didn't produce any
special favours for him, and he tells a fable about a shepherd whose
prayers for water, in a time of drought, were rewarded and who
satisfied his own thirst first, then that of his wife, children, servants
and so on, so that a pet magpie at the end of the queue flew off to
look for water for itself. In any case the scramble for honour and
riches is never satisfied, and he illustrates this with another fable, of a
primitive people who climbed a mountain to try to reach the moon.
Ariosto's criticism is particularly aimed at a favourite target of his –
show, semblance, prestige, as contrasted with substance and real
worth:

    Il vero onor è ch'uom da ben te tenga
    ciascuno, e che tu sia; che, non essendo,
    forza è che la bugia tosto si spenga.

Che cavalliero o conte o reverendo
il populo te chiami, io non te onoro,
se meglio in te che 'l titol non comprendo. (*259–64*)
[True honour is to be held an honest man by everyone, and to
be it; for if you're not the lie must soon be exposed. That people
should call you knight or count or reverend brings you no
honour with me if I see nothing more in you than the title.]
This distinction between appearance and reality much concerned
Ariosto and his contemporaries: it recurs frequently in the *Furioso;*
it is a crucial factor in Castiglione's considerations on the *Cortegiano,*
and it is fundamental to Machiavelli's analysis of the *Principe* : 'C'è
qualcosa che sembra virtù, e non lo è'. [There is something which
seems to be virtue, but isn't.]

   This poem has been much admired by critics and there is much to
admire in it. It strikes quite effectively that 'tono medio' often found
in the *proemi* (the opening stanzas of each canto) of the *Furioso* – a
discursive, almost conversational style which is neither literary nor
prosaic; structurally too it seems to be skirting the conventions,
starting abruptly, inserting the two fables casually, and ending suddenly. And here perhaps are the best of Ariosto's fables, particularly
the strangely fascinating picture of the simple souls stretching up to
the moon :
   Quei ch'alti li vedean dai poggi bassi,
   credendo che toccassero la luna,
   dietro venian con frettolosi passi. (*226–8*)
   [Those who, from the lower hills, saw the others high above
   them, thinking they were touching the moon, came up behind
   with hurried steps.]
The *variabilità* of tone and material which characterises the *Furioso*
serves here to add a note of fantasy to the somewhat repetitive,
slightly nagging thesis of the simple life; the criticism of ambition
and materialism is not quite convincing on the lips of a man who is
so clearly disappointed that the new Pope has failed to reward his
old friend.

   The fourth satire (1522) expressing Ariosto's discontent with his
post in the Garfagnana returns to the theme of public repute and
real worth – spendthrifts, bloodsuckers and tyrants enjoy power or
public esteem :
   [il volgo] ... sovente
   titolo al vizio di virtù dato have (*56–7*)
   [[the crowd] ... often has given the label of virtue to vice]

– whereas the poet, to earn his living, is forced to administer these remote, bandit-ridden mountains, far away from his beloved Alessandra. This poem has a character and a flavour of its own: it contrasts vividly his present environment with his memory of happy days in the soft landscape of Reggio:

il lucido vivaio onde il giardino
si cinge intorno, il fresco rio che corre,
rigando l'erbe, ove poi fa il molino. (*121–3*)
[... the clear fish-pond that surrounds the garden, the fresh running stream that furrows the grass and then turns the mill.]

Hence his frustration, shut off from Alessandra, in the harshness of the mountains:

Vedendomi lontan cento e più miglia,
e da neve, alpe, selve e fiumi escluso
da chi tien del mio cor sola la briglia. (*22–4*)
[Finding myself a hundred miles and more away, shut off by snow and mountain, forests and rivers, from that lady who alone holds the reins of my heart.]

The Petrarchan sympathy did not extend apparently to a poetic expedition to a mountain top – mountains for Ariosto meant bandits and icy winds and precipitous rocky tracks.

The fifth satire (1523) is different from the others, being a letter of advice to a friend (Annibale Malegucci) about to marry and consisting largely of reflections on marriage. Much of this is conventional but there are some specifically Ariostesque touches – the distrust of youthful impetuosity in love, for example, which recurs in the *Furioso*; and it is interesting to see what the almost lifelong bachelor has to say in defence of marriage, for his verdict is positive:

ma fui di parer sempre, e così detto
l'ho più volte, che senza moglie a lato
non puote uomo in bontade esser perfetto. (*13–15*)
[... but I was always of the opinion, and I've said so a hundred times, that without a wife by his side, no man can be completely virtuous.]

However, what seems to be sincere encouragement to the prospective bridegroom is hedged about with reservations. In telling Annibale what to avoid Ariosto presents us with a gallery of *malmaritati*: old men married to young girls who deceive them; or old men who marry their servants or peasant girls in order to legitimise their bastards; wives who have been so spoilt as children that they are never satisfied with their new homes; pretty wives who cuckold you, ugly wives you tire of; pious wives for ever taking cakes to the priest; vain wives plastering their faces with filthy cosmetics. 'And don't think you can make her faithful if she doesn't want to be', he tells Annibale, and he relates a tale to show that there is only one way to prevent her betraying you – and the poem ends with a witty obscenity.

The last two satires have little of substance to add to what has been said before, except that the sixth, in which the poet seeks Bembo's advice on a tutor for his son, throws light on Ariosto's attitude to humanists and humanising poets – who are charged with sodomy, heresy and pedantry. There are some interesting biographical references to his enforced law studies, and his failure to seize his chance to study Greek. But the appeal for a teacher and his concern for his son's welfare do not blend well with the satirical passages on the vices of his times; the digressive references to his own youth are similarly disconnected and the poem as a whole sounds flat and un-inspired. The final satire is more consistent in tone and style but in explaining why he does not want an ambassadorship in Rome Ariosto only rehearses the arguments we have heard already – his reluctance to leave Ferrara and Alessandra, his scepticism of patronage, his humble needs, his dislike of the Garfagnana, his love of liberty. He himself sensed perhaps that he had no more to say in this form and he did not apparently write any further satires after 1524.

This little group of poems is, however, an impressive and important one in Renaissance literature : it had the character and the quality to establish a genre, and it signals an interesting moment and an interesting phase in Ariosto's poetic career. In the *Furioso* Ariosto used the conventional romance material as a vehicle of poetic expression, superimposing on it a spasmodic but insistent commentary on the society of his times; in the satires he reverses the position, using as his material the trite everyday world of lodgings and lawsuits, tax-gatherers and cuckolds, and he examines his own passage through this chaotic and unsavoury crowd from which he detaches himself, aiming his thoughts and his attitudes at a Horatian *serenitas*. Out of this he creates a poetic style which is different from that of his lyric poetry, and of his romance – a more discursive style close to prose and suggestive of conversation, yet rhythmical, rich in imagery and contrived in effects. His poetic vocabulary embraces crude, everyday terms, obscenities, technicalities, slang, dialect – which occur not frequently or obtrusively, but occasionally, moder-

ately, as the poem requires. He adopts frequently a conversational
note, as though speaking to the reader, imagining his replies, anticipating his interruptions; he is not infrequently casual about syntax,
uses the ellipses, repetition, emphases of the spoken language, and
popular idioms, especially proverbial expressions in current usage.
All this is interwoven into the traditional lyric and romance diction –
interspersed with the casual everyday expressions are wordy peri-
phrases, pithy dicta and classical allusions; there is a wealth of metaphor, a shrewd choice of detail and a contrived word-order. It is a
style, as has been said, reminiscent of the *proemi* to some of the
Cantos of the *Furioso* where the poet stands aside from his story and
comments to the reader about it, man to man. The stylistic experiment was not perhaps totally successful, and there is some uneven-
ness in the satires, but the attempt was an ambitious one and the
results for us very rewarding.

*   *   *

ARIOSTO is known to have written and produced four comedies for
the Ferrarese court. Some form of primitive stage presentations, referred to as 'comedie', had been given in Ferrara as early as the mid-
fourteenth century, and from early in the fifteenth century comedies
in Latin in imitation of classical comedy were performed in Rome
and Florence. A strong stimulus to the Ferrarese theatre came in 1471
with the succession of Ercole d'Este who encouraged both the *sacre
rappresentazioni* performed in the churches and in the piazza, and
also translations of classical comedy which were performed at court.
Plautus's *Menaechmi* was produced in 1486, his *Amphitryon* in 1487,
Terence's *Andria* in 1491, and there were many subsequent performances of these and other Roman comedies, given in the vulgar
tongue; and a number of original plays on the Roman pattern, by
Niccolò da Correggio, Ercole Strozzi and others, were also performed. Ferrara has therefore a good claim to being considered 'the
cradle of Italian comedy'.

Ariosto is known to have been a member of the company responsible for the presentation of these plays from the year 1493 although
we have no information about his precise duties. There were no performances between 1494 and 1498 owing to the political tensions
and disturbances of these years, but they were resumed in 1499. The
active support given to the theatre by Ercole and his court would
naturally have stimulated Ariosto's interest. He is known to have
made translations of Terence's *Phormio* and other Latin plays during

these years, but none of his versions survive. He wrote his first comedy, *La Cassaria*, in prose, for performance at the Carnival in 1508, and it was very well received; *I Suppositi*, also in prose, was performed in the following year, and Ariosto then began *Il Negromante*, in verse, intending it for the Carnival of 1510, but it was not then performed because of the outbreak of war.

The critical situation of Ferrara in the following years brought regular theatrical activities to a halt, and they were not resumed until the winter of 1528 when the court celebrated the arrival of Alfonso's son Ercole with his bride Renée, daughter of Louis XII. The first performance of a new play by Ariosto, *La Lena*, was given at this time; and also the first performance of *Il Negromante*, in a new version (Ariosto had completed an earlier draft in 1520 at the request of Leo X, but this had not been performed). Also at this time Ludovico wrote new versions, in blank verse, of his earlier prose comedies *La Cassaria* and *I Suppositi;* the former was performed several times in the period 1531–2, and there was also a further performance of *La Lena.* Another play, *I Studenti*, probably begun in 1518 or 1519, was left unfinished.

Ariosto's dramatic activity is therefore largely concentrated in two active periods of his life, 1508–10 and 1528–32, during which he was closely involved in the production and direction of the court theatre. Performances were normally given in the large hall of the Ducal Palace which was said to accommodate a large audience (several thousand according to Catalano!); most of Ariosto's plays were acted not by professional actors but by courtiers and other gentlemen of rank, and the author himself was closely involved in the production; he is generally credited with the construction of a permanent stage-set on the occasion of the performance of his *Cassaria* in 1531 – a notable advance on the flimsy temporary structures put up for the carnival. It was, according to a contemporary account, 'of wondrous beauty and so large that it looked like a small town with ground and upper-floor rooms, windows, balconies, shops and churches, and comedies were often performed there'. It survived only a very brief time, being destroyed by fire in December 1532.

Ariosto's small but much admired corpus of comedies, composed at a time when the secular theatre was in its infancy, has established for him a reputation as the 'founder of Italian comedy', possibly the leading comic dramatist of the Italian Renaissance, and for this reason alone his comedies deserve our close attention; they are also of considerable value to the student of the *Furioso* in throwing light on the interests of the poet at key moments in the composition of his major work. As with the *Furioso* we see Ariosto exploring a traditional genre of considerable popular appeal, drawing heavily on classical precedents not for the benefit of scholars and humanists, but for a broad audience of courtiers and people. His familiarity with Roman comedy and his indebtedness to it are apparent in all his plays and are referred to explicitly: 'e vi confessa l'autore avere in questo e Plauto e Terenzio seguitato' (Prologue, *I Suppositi*): but in none of the comedies does he follow closely any single source; he takes motifs from several plays and uses them in a new intrigue of his own making, with new characters and settings, contemporary in style and reflecting current interests and attitudes. And he is keen to emphasise his originality:

> Nova comedia v'appresento, piena
> Di varii giochi, che né mai latine
> Né greche lingue recitarno in scena. (*La Cassaria* (1), Prologue)
> [I present to you a new comedy, full of different wiles that no Greek or Latin tongue ever recited on the stage.]

– or he smiles at the ambitions of himself and his contemporaries in their search for originality:

> ... questi nostri, che quel che non fecero
> Gli antiqui loro, che molto più seppono
> Di noi in questa e in ogni altra scienzia
> Essi ardiscan di far. (*La Lena*, Prologue)
> [... our modern writers, who dare to do what the ancients never did, who knew far more than we do in this as in all other matters.]

Ariosto takes then as his starting-point the model of Roman comedy and adapts it to his Ferrarese sixteenth-century audience. Roman comedy is not too easily defined, the two major comic writers, Plautus and Terence, showing considerable differences from each other, but certain features stand out: stock characters such as youthful lovers, grasping old men, swindling and impudent slaves, braggart soldiers; love-intrigues involving trickery, disguise, misapprehension, discovery of unknown identities (*anagnorisis*) sudden reversals of fortune (*peripeteia*); frequent use of monologues, asides, eavesdropping, off-stage action (especially Terence); general observance of the unities; contemporary social allusion (Plautus); witty language and familiarity with the audience (Plautus); use of verse exclusively, a prologue, standard devices for ensuring suspense; dramatic irony. Much of this has become so famliar to us in

modern European comedy that we tend to overlook its classical
provenance.

Ariosto plays a key part in the transmission of this classical heritage
to the European theatre. His *Suppositi* for example was the model
for George Gascoigne's *The Supposes*, 'the first prose comedy of
English literature'. His plots present a series of variations on a fairly
standard basic theme: the young man in love, thwarted by his or
his lady's father, intriguing to win her, with the servants providing
most of the ideas for outwitting the guardians of chastity; once the
fortress has been invaded marriage follows easily; the old men not
only obstruct the young lovers' wishes but keep a tight hand on the
money, essential for oiling the palms of the servants; deception of
authority is achieved through disguise, lying, theft, concealment in
casks and chests. When these tricks are exposed other and more
elaborate ones are devised; indeed the sudden unforeseen twists in
events, the *peripezie*, are essential to the excitement of the play. The
resolution of an intrigue is aided sometimes by the sudden discovery
of the identity ('agnizione') of a long-lost relative, sometimes by the
sheer confession of the truth, sometimes even by the successful working of a servant's plan. The pattern of intrigue and discovery is highly
artificial, but when such patterns are skilfully contrived, as all these
are in varying degrees, we are prepared to suspend our disbelief. The
ingenuity and mental agility of the servants, in the Roman comic
tradition, is perhaps the most frequent source of comedy: lying and
deceit are not merely taken for granted, they are the very bread and
butter of the intrigue. So too is the assumption that the lover has the
right to enjoy his mistress, and the opportunity for a bawdy or
obscene double-entendre is rarely missed whether by a character or
by the author himself in his Prologue. With rare exceptions the
author treats his characters as outside of any moral scheme: the end
which is always virtuous (marriage), justifies the means which are
always unscrupulous, 'How will you get the money?'; one young
man is asked. 'My father might die' is the frank reply.

Is this then another Ariosto from the author of the satires and the
Furioso, with his concern for honesty and chastity and friendship?
It is true of course that each of the genres was a law unto itself, that
a Lorenzo could turn from an obscene 'Canto carnascialesco' to a
pious 'laude', and Ariosto's comedies are to be read as exercises in a
particular literary tradition and should not be searched too closely
for biographical evidence, whether practical or psychological. Yet
they do show us an attitude to his fellow men which seems consistent

with that of his other works. He accepts mostly without comment the
weakness and corruption of this society, harsh fathers, irresponsible
sons, treacherous servants, grasping officials: this is after all largely a
make-believe world like the world of the romances. But as in the
Furioso the fantastic and the realistic are sometimes juxtaposed, so here
the Latinate intrigue is conducted in a Ferrarese setting, with Ferrarese
customs, and the author steps out of the frame, so to speak, every now
and then to let us know what he thinks of it. There are elements of
social satire in all the comedies, the dilatoriness of the police, the corruption of the priests, the extortions of officials, the credulity of simple
people, the costliness of justice; Corbolo can get all the game his
master needs in spite of the severe penalties imposed by the Duke for
poaching:

> ... 'l Signor fa con tanta diligenzia
> E con gride e con pene sí terribili
> Guardar la sua campagna; e li medesimi
> Che n'hanno cura, son quei che la rubano. (*La Lena*, II, 3)
> [... the Master has his land guarded so carefully with decrees and
> terrible penalties; and the very men who guard it are the ones
> who rob him.]

A frequent complaint in the satires and in *Orlando Furioso* is that about
women's make-up, which recurs in *La Cassaria*, with an interesting
change between the 1508 and the 1531 versions. In the later version
Fulcio repeats his former denunciation of female vanity but now
extends his charges: the ladies of course want to look beautiful,

> ... Et è giustissimo
> Desir perché non hanno altro, levandone
> La beltà, che la faccia riguardevoli.
> Ma che diremo noi de' nostri gioveni
> Che per virtù s'avriano a far conoscere
> Et onorare? ... (*La Cassaria*, V, 3)
> [And that is a perfectly fair wish because, if you take their beauty
> away, they have nothing else to make themselves remarkable
> with. But what can we say of our young men who should make
> themselves known and honoured for their virtue?]

– and in a lengthy passage he goes on to denounce the perfumes and
padded clothes of modern men. There are times too when the
characters speak out against the traditionally corrupt habits of the
literary types – as when Corbolo comments on Lena:

> ... Porca! ch'ardere
> La possa il fuoco! Non ha conscienzia,

Di chi si fida in lei, la figlia vendere! (*La Lena*, I, 1)
[The swine! May she burn in hell fire! She's got no compunction
about selling the daughter of some-one who trusts her!]

La Lena centres on an idea probably suggested by Boccaccio's story
in the *Decameron* (VII, 2) where a young lover, caught by the unexpected return of his mistress's husband, hides in a wine-cask.
Boccaccio's incident is here elaborated so that the lover is actually
transported into his lady's house in a wine-cask on the instructions of
her husband. In Ariosto's comedy this happy action is the result, not
of any cleverly-laid plot by master or servant, but of chance, and it is
wittily and convincingly contrived in a series of scenes which rise to
a superb comic climax: the young Flavio, who is in love with Licinia,
is trying to bribe the go-between Lena to bring him and Licinia together; while visiting Lena he is trapped in her house by the sudden
arrival of Licinia's father, Fazio, who is Lena's lover. He hides in the
cask. But the cask is a borrowed one, and when the owner hears that
the bailiffs are about to descend on the house he goes to claim his
property. Bailiffs and owner are disputing in the street over the cask,
with Flavio trembling inside, when Fazio arrives and mediates in the
dispute; the result is that *he* takes the cask into safe-keeping and has it
carried into his house. So the father unwittingly introduces his
daughter's lover under his own roof. Licinia is thus compromised and
her father agrees to the marriage.

So the intriguing of Flavio and Lena, and the lies and trickery of the
servant Corbolo, the involvement of Pacifico, Lena's husband, of
money-lenders, and officials, all turn out to be futile; human ingenuity proves quite unnecessary where Fortune decides to lend a hand.
We are reminded of that frequent motif of the *Furioso*: 'O degli
uomini fallace speranza!' Yet the play provides some fine examples of
ingenuity and mental agility on the part of the servant, Corbolo, who
delights in the well-polished lie, and when that is exposed can lie
himself out of a tight corner. Ariosto achieves considerable comic
effect here as elsewhere in his comedies by exposing the servant's
trickery to his master and then watching his skill in wriggling off the
hook:

Ben succede l'impresa: avrà l'esercito
De la bugie, dopo tanti pericoli,
Dopo tanti travagli, al fin vittoria,
Malgrado di fortuna ... (V, 6)
[Our plan prospers: the army of lies, after so many dangers, so
much travail, shall at last triumph, in spite of Fortune.]

Corbolo finds Flavio's father, Ilario, a really difficult opponent, not
the conventional dupe of Latin comedy:

Ma che farò, che con un vecchio credulo
Non ho a far, qual a suo modo Terenzio
O Plauto suol Cremete o Simon fingere?
Ma quanto egli è più cauto, maggior gloria
Non è la mia, s'io lo piglio alla trappola? (III, 1)
[But what shall I do, having to deal not with a credulous old man
such as Terence or Plautus depict in their Cremete or Simon?
But the more cautious he is, isn't my glory the greater if I can
catch him in my trap?]

But in the end neither the intriguers nor the jealous guardians of
wealth and beauty can claim to have triumphed – the victors are the
young lovers with fortune on their side.

This twist of the conventional comic intrigue is, as I have said,
reminiscent of the *Furioso* where the traditional chivalrous motifs are
so often served up with new touches of realism and irony. The dish
is otherwise essentially much as before – young lover, intriguing
servants, obstructive parents, lies, exposure: although in line with the
more realistic treatment there are no disguises and no incredible
'agnizioni'. But it is not this intrigue, lively and original as it is, which
makes *La Lena* the most memorable of Ariosto's comedies, at least a
worthy companion to Machiavelli's *Mandragola*. The real human
interest is in the secondary characters created to establish the structure
for the intrigues – the fascinating triangle of Lena, her husband and
her lover. Lena as the go-between is unscrupulous, grasping, ready to
betray the confidence placed in her for the sake of 25 florins and the
satisfaction of cheating her mean lover; she knows what she wants,
trusts no-one, believes in no-one; she is for ever bad-tempered and
Menica tells her so in words that seem to supply the sub-plot:

Se tu perseverassi in questa colera,
Saresti, Lena, la più ingrata femina
Del mondo ... (V, 12)
[If you should persevere in this bad temper, Lena, you'd be the
most ungrateful woman in the world.]

Her husband, Pacifico, is a lazy good-for-nothing who grumbles at
her loose ways but is only too ready to exploit them; in fact it was he,
according to Lena, who pushed her into her life of prostitution, but
for which they would be penniless and without a roof over their
heads. The roof is supplied rent-free by Licinia's father, Fazio, a sharp,
miserly old man who in return for the house and an occasional present

for Lena gets a mistress for himself and a teacher for his daughter. Yet all three of these literary types, corrupt as they are, are presented sympathetically and thoughtfully: Lena for all her grasping ways has not profited much by them and we understand her discontent with her idle husband and her mean lover and she is genuinely fond of her young charge Licinia. Pacifico may have encouraged Lena in her loose life but perhaps he recognised that he would inevitably end up as a cuckold:

> Per viver teco in pace, proponevati
> Quel ch'io sapeva che t'era grandissima
> mente in piacere, e che vietar volendoti,
> Saria stato il durar teco impossible. (V, 11)

[In order to live in peace with you I proposed you should do what I knew was very much to your liking, and what would have been impossible to prevent you doing even if I'd wanted to.]

Who can say which is to blame, or indeed that either of them is to blame – they are what they are, penniless and unfortunate souls, 'dispreziati', who struggle with their poverty and have to take life as they find it. In the course of a jesting dialogue with Corbolo, Pacifico suddenly intrudes a note of sadness:

> CORB: Hai tu alcun'arme in casa?
> PACIF: Ne la camera
>   Dipinta ho nel camin l'arme di Fazio.
> CORB: Dico da offesa.
> PACIF: Assai n'ho che m'offendono:
>   La povertà, li pensieri, la rabbia di
>   Mia moglier, e 'l suo sempre dirmi ingiuria. (IV, 9)

[*Corb*: Have you any arms in the house? *Pacif*: I've got Fazio's coat of arms painted on the chimney-breast. *Corb* : I mean arms of offence. *Pacif*: I've got plenty of those to offend me – my poverty, my worries, my wife's temper, her always nagging at me.]

Even Fazio, with his money and his property and his mistress, appeals to us as another suffering mortal, who cannot trust his servants and is for ever nagged by Lena to whom he is really deeply attached – as his fit of jealousy reveals. How relieved he is to learn that the lady who has been seen embracing Flavio, is not his mistress but his daughter!

The second version of this play acknowledges the importance of the Lena-Pacifico-Fazio triangle by the addition of two scenes, after the conventional marriage arrangements of the previous finale. The later ending shows us Lena, Pacifico and a servant discussing their reactions to the events they have just been through; Lena's anger is calmed down and they settle back into the old corrupt pattern of life they had enjoyed, or suffered, before. The young lovers' lives may be changed by these incredible intrigues, but outside of the literary conventions this more credible situation continues on its inevitable course.

La Cassaria was judged later in the sixteenth century by Giraldi to be the best of Ariosto's comedies on the basis of its more involved plot, and indeed if one attaches weight to the *peripezie*, or the sudden developments in events which keep the audience guessing what is to happen next, then the *Cassaria* would rank high. The plot is essentially original although it draws on at least four Latin comedies for detailed situations or motifs. At the centre of the intrigue is the 'cassa', a valuable chest which has been deposited with Crisobolo for safe keeping. The chest is the instrument essential for the scheme devised by the servants Volpino and Fulcio to enable their young masters Erofilo (Crisobolo's son) and Caridoro to win the beautiful slave girls Eulalia and Corisca. Their owner, Lucrano, is driving too hard a bargain for the penniless young men, and the servants plan to seize the chest and offer it to him as security. Once the girls are secured the servants aim to charge Lucrano with theft and recover the chest. In this they are initially successful, but as Eulalia is led away to the waiting lovers, other servants, not in the know, 'rescue' her, and in the confusion the scheme for recovering the chest from Lucrano collapses. Volpino's excuses are seen through by the wily Crisobolo, but Fulcio now proves his ingenuity in contriving a solution. He gets rid of Lucrano by convincing him that he is about to be arrested, and then he deceives Crisobolo into thinking that his only way of getting the trunk back from Lucrano is to pay the price the latter had asked for Eulalia. So the young men get the girls, the servants get the money and the old men are duped.

The best comedy comes from the wit and ingenuity of the servants, whether successful (Fulcio) or unsuccessful (Volpino); for example, in the scenes where the servants' accomplice, Trappola, disguised as a merchant in Crisobolo's clothes, is discovered by Crisobolo in his house; Volpino builds up an elaborate story, with Trappola playing the deaf-mute, until Crisobolo frightens Trappola into a confession which brings the whole elaborate structure of lies crashing round the unfortunate Volpino's ears. 'Non riescono sempre i disegni'

comments Fulcio in the later version (v, 5) in a characteristic Ariostesque aside. The two old men are portraits of standard comic types –
the grasping Lucrano who thinks he can cheat the eager Erofilo, and
is cheated in his turn by the servant; and the mean Crisobolo who can
trust no-one and who is too astute to be taken in except by the really
skilful Fulcio. His lecture to his son describing the sort of son *he* was
is very convincing and it is not surprising that critics have thought it
a biographical reminiscence (v, 2).

La Cassaria contains a good deal of amusing satirical commentary,
particularly in the later verse text, where, for example, the procurer
Lucrano laments that in spite of much show and ostentation of wealth
in Ferrara – fine dress, carriages, retinues of servants – the Ferrarese
are really like 'scatole nuove di fuor pinte e dentro vacove' ['boxes
painted on the outside with nothing inside'] (I, 5); they have in other
words little money to spare for Lucrano's wares! They don't trade

> ... questi ogni exercizio stimano
> Vile né voglion che sia detto nobile
> Se non chi senza industria vive in ozio. (I, 5)

[they consider all occupations base, and will only call noble a
man who lives in idleness without working.]

There are complaints of the maltreatment of servants and a note of
sympathy for the unfortunate wretches at the very base of the social
pyramid:

> ... io che nacqui brutta et invecchiatami
> Son oggimai, non spero, anco volendomi
> Il patron dar in dono, non che vendere,
> Che mai si trovi chi voglia levarmigli. (III, 4)

[I, who was born ugly and have grown old now, I've no hope
that even if my master wanted to give me away, let alone sell me,
he'd find anyone prepared to take me off his hands.]

Il Negromante was written in verse from the beginning, but there
is a second version made later, also in verse, so that it is no surprise to
find a more conscious artistry here. The plot is indeed ingeniously
contrived: Cintio's secret marriage to his beloved Lavinia does not
prevent his guardian Massimo from marrying him officially to Emilia;
the young man feigns impotence in the hope of getting an annulment,
but a Negromante (Magician) is called in to cure him; the latter is
bribed by Emilia's lover, Camillo, to help him and arranges for
Camillo to be introduced into Emilia's room in a chest, alleged to
contain spirits for the curing of Cintio. The servant, fearing Cintio
will really be 'cured' against his will, has the chest taken instead to

Lavinia's room where the hidden Camillo witnesses the embraces of Cintio and his secret wife, and reports this to Massimo. But they then discover that Lavinia is really Massimo's long-lost daughter; so the old man is happy to have Cintio as a son-in-law and Emilia is free to marry Camillo. The Negromante who had aimed to cheat everybody is thwarted of his booty and has to make off in haste.

Again Ariosto shows his skill in devising intrigues, on the basis of classical conventions, with the concealed lover and the recognition scenes and cleverly laid plans which go wrong but end up happily. This provided the framework for the essentially Cinquecento figure of the Negromante whom his servant Nibbio portrays as a master in the arts of deception, a Spanish Jew claiming any origin but his own:

... e le vestigie
Sue tuttavia, dovunque passa, restano
Come de la lumaca ... (11) (11, 1)
[and wherever he goes he always leaves his traces behind him, like a snail.]

He is employed by Massimo to cure Cintio, but he accepts bribes from Cintio whom he plans to cheat too, and also from Camillo whom he pretends to help by shutting him in the chest whilst in fact he and Nibbio strip his house of its valuables. His astrology and necromancy are shown up as unmitigated fraud, and the credulity, not of the servants, but of the masters is ridiculed. The Negromante promises to get Camillo into Emilia's room that night, but how? He might turn him into a mouse, or make him invisible, but it would be quicker and more convenient, he says, to use a chest. The servants know better, not only Nibbio who is the accomplice, but Cintio's servant, Temolo:

Di questi spiriti, a dirvi il vero, pochissimo
Per me ne crederei; ma li grandi uomini
E principi e prelati, che vi credono,
Fanno col loro esempio ch'io, vilissimo
Fante, vi credo ancora. (11) (1, 3)
[To tell you the truth, I myself wouldn't really believe in these spirits; but important people, and princes and prelates who do believe in them set such an example that I, a humble servant, I believe too.]

Yet the satirical elements sound somehow out of key in this exaggerated picture, near caricature, with its artificial setting of *peripezie* and *agnizione*. A sort of sick comedy derives from the ludicrous success which attends this fraudulent astrologer almost until the end,

and his escape at the last cheats the play of its natural climax, leaving
Nibbio to supply an ironical comment:

    ... Or non curate se lo astrologo
    Restar vedete al fin de la comedia
    Poco contento; perché l'arte, ch'imita
    La natura, non pate ch'abbian l'opere
    D'un scelerato mai se non mal esito. (11) (v, 6)
[Now don't worry if at the end of the play you see the astrologer
end up unhappily; because art, which imitates nature, will not
permit the deeds of a rascal to be successful.]

    I shall comment only briefly on the other comedies. The unfinished
I Studenti repeats largely the method of the comedies already discussed. The story is derived substantially from classical patterns, with
characters in disguise, an action compounded of chance and intrigue,
and a final *agnizione*, but it has flashes of realistic observation and contemporary social satire. *I Suppositi* has similar components: a girl
pursued against her father's wishes; a poor lover disguised as his own
servant; a stranger waylaid and disguised as the lover's father, but then
confronted with the real father; a wealthy elderly rival whom everyone deceives but who happily discovers that the wily servant is his
long-lost son. The author declares that he took his material from
Terence's *Eunuch* and Plautus's *Captivi*, 'but so modestly, however,
that Terence and Plautus themselves, if they got to hear of it, wouldn't
object'. It is a lively, witty play, with some fine comic scenes that one
would expect to be highly successful on the stage. The elderly,
pedantic Cleandro in particular foreshadows many such figures of fun
in later Renaissance comedy, Machiavelli's Messer Nicia among
them:

    CLEAN: Io, Dio grazia, di mia etade ho assai buona vista e sento
        in me poca differenza da quel ch'io ero di venticinque o trenta
        anni.
    PASIF: E perché non? Sei tu forse vecchio?
    CLEAN: Io sono ne li cinquantasei anni.
    PASIF: (Ne dice dieci manco!)
    CLEAN: Che di' tu: dieci manco?
    PASIF: Dico che io ti stimavo di dieci manco ... (1) (1,ii)
    [*Clean*: 'For my age, thank heaven, I've very good sight, and I
    feel very little difference from twenty-five or thirty years ago.
    Pasif: Why not? Do you think you're an old man? *Clean*: I'm
    56. *Pasif*: (That's ten too few!) *Clean*: What do you say? Ten
    too few? *Pasif*: I say that I thought you were 10 years fewer.]

Of the four plays two exist as we have seen in both prose and verse versions, the prose versions belonging to the early period of composition 1508–9, and the verse to the later phase 1528–9. There are two different verse texts for *Il Negromante;* for *La Lena* we have essentially only one text, in verse, with, however, a later version with a different prologue and two additional scenes at the end. Revisions of substance occur in *La Cassaria* of which the later version has more emphasis on social satire, and there are some changes in this direction in *Il Negromante.* But the most significant changes are formal, notably those from prose to verse, and one wonders why Ariosto composed initially in prose and then changed to *endecasillabi sdruccioli* (blank verse with the stress on the antepenultimate syllable). Italian writers contemporary with Ariosto generally adopted prose for comedy – Machiavelli, Aretino, Bibbiena, and the anonymous author of *Gl'Ingannati* for example. Later in the century a number of playwrights preferred verse, Alamanni and D'Ambra for example; and Cecchi, like Ariosto, redrafted some of his prose comedies in verse. It has been suggested that regional differences are apparent here, the Tuscans generally using prose, the non-Tuscans often preferring verse – although there are some notable exceptions. One could understand that a non-Tuscan, sensitive to linguistic criticism, might prefer a medium less close to the spoken language. Linguistic factors may certainly have contributed to Ariosto's change to verse but he may well have felt that verse would confer greater weight to his comedies, bringing them closer into line with an established genre as exemplified in antiquity, and he may also have been attracted to the problem of finding a verse style appropriate for spoken dialogue – his *Satires* and his *Furioso* both reveal the author's interest in a 'tono medio', somewhere between the familiar and the high-flown. That he was concerned about linguistic problems is clear from the Prologues to *La Cassaria* and *Il Negromante.* In the former he admits that the vulgar tongue is inferior to Latin:

La vulgar lingua, di latino mista,
È barbara e mal culta; ma con giochi
Si può far una fabula men trista. (1) (Prologue)
[The vulgar tongue, with its mixture of Latin, is barbarous and unpolished; but with word-play one can brighten up a language.]

It was the deficiency of 'sali', of witty colloquial usage, for which the author of the 'Dialogo intorno alla lingua', normally attributed to Machiavelli, criticised Ariosto's *I Suppositi*, attributing this weakness to the poet's lack of familiarity with spoken Tuscan – and Ariosto

may well have felt at a disadvantage in attempting to produce a witty
dialogue which would be intelligible and acceptable outside Ferrara.
He says as much in the first version of *Il Negromante* : the Cremona
depicted here, he pretends, has made a long journey and her speech
has been influenced by other regions:

> Ma, se non vi parrà d'udire il proprio
> E consueto idioma del suo populo,
> Avete da pensar ch'alcun vocabolo
> Passando udì a Bologna, dove è il Studio;
> Il qual le piacque e lo tenne a memoria;
> A Fiorenza et a Siena poi diede opera,
> E per tutta Toscana, all'eleganzia
> Quanto poté più; ma in sì breve termine
> Tanto appreso non ha, che la pronunzia
> Lombarda possa totalmente ascondere. (1) (Prologue)

[But if you don't think you hear the normal speech of her
(Cremona's) own people, you must realise that she heard some
words at Bologna, where the University is; and she liked them
and remembered them. Then in Florence and Siena and all over
Tuscany she tried to acquire as much elegance as she could; but
in so short a time she hasn't learnt enough to hide completely her
Lombard pronunciation.]

This passage appears in the 1520 text, but is excluded from that of
1528, by which time Ariosto has made corrections in line with the
new linguistic practice he has evolved under the influence of Bembo,
whose *Prose della Volgar Lingua*, published in 1525, was a key influence in the revision of the *Furioso* for the 1532 edition.

When he writes prose it is realistic and down-to-earth, close to a
conversational style, with occasional dialect concessions, crude or
obscure words and double-entendres, local allusions and proverbial
expressions; but it is raised above the language of the real piazza, not
only in its rejection of dialect but in its occasional elaborate syntax,
inverted word-order and poetic inflections, so that whole sentences
can sometimes be dropped straight into the frame of the *endecasillabo*.
His verse is of course a stage further removed from conversational
usage but it struck his contemporaries as close to prose: 'Ariosto's
principal concern was to give his Comedy a style of verse as close as
possible to prose', commented Ludovico Dolce. What they particularly criticised was his *endecasillabo sdrucciolo*, a difficult metrical
form often causing artificial line endings (' ... credi tu/...'; 'rabbia
di/...') – it is said to have been motivated by the wish to reflect the

iambic senarius of the Roman comic writers, but it had been used before in popular or rustic contexts by Poliziano in his *Stanze* and by Sannazzaro for some of the eclogues in his *Arcadia*. While the later versions are more polished linguistically, they often lose the sparkle and pungency of the earlier prose texts which the modern reader tends to prefer: to give a single example, we should compare the witty burlesque by the servant of the Petrarchan language of his enamoured master:

EROF: Ah misero chi è servo d'amore!

VOLP: È più misero chi è servo de' servi d'amore. (*La Cassaria* (1) II, *1*)

[*Erof*: Ah, wretched is the man who is the servant of love! *Volp*: More wretched still the man who is the servant of the servants of love.]

– with the strained conceits of the verse equivalent:

CARID: – Deh, misero
Chi serve Amor!

VOLP: Noi che serviamo a miseri,
Servi sián, Fulcio doppiamente miseri. (*La Cassaria* (II) II, *3*)
[*Carid*: Ah, wretched is he who serves Love! *Volp*: We who serve wretches are, Fulcio, doubly wretched servants.]

3. The Literary Tradition

Ariosto's *Orlando Furioso* (1532) is the continuation of Boiardo's *Orlando Innamorato* (1495) which carries on the adventures of Orlando whose birth is described in the last Book of Andrea da Barberino's *Reali di Francia* (c. 1400). *The Reali di Francia* in its turn is a re-casting and re-ordering of a vast body of narrative prose and verse which had accumulated around the legends of Charlemagne and of his wars with the 'pagans', the origins of which are to be found in the French *chansons de geste*, and particularly in the eleventh century *Chanson de Roland*. This same Roland, whose tragic death at Roncevaux is described in the French poem, is the protagonist of Ariosto's poem more than four hundred years later; and essentially the same war is still being fought between Charles and Marsile, with Olivier (Uliviero), Turpin, Ogier (Ugiero) and the traitor Ganelon (Gano); and Roland's famous sword Durendal (Durindana) is as sharp as ever. This is a long life for a literary narrative and one may well wonder at the reasons for its popularity.

The characters and the legend have changed substantially by the sixteenth century. The *Chanson de Roland* is a serious, tragic poem with a strong patriotic and religious inspiration: its theme, the Christian defeat and the death of Roland, is clear-cut and coherent. In the later *chansons* the material is expanded to include other actions and characters: the twelfth-century *Chanson d'Aspremont*, for example, goes back to Roland's first deeds on the battlefield, at Aspramonte in Southern Italy; and another twelfth-century work, usually known as the *Pseudo-Turpin*, written in Latin prose, comprises an account of Charlemagne's exploits as if narrated by the Archbishop Turpin who is recorded in the *Chanson de Roland* as dying at Roncevaux. Both these works were drawn on widely by later writers, including Ariosto.

In the course of time not only the material but the tone of such narratives changed. The early chansons reflect the ethic of the society for which they were written, the chivalrous code of feudal France. They were sung or recited in the great halls on the occasion of feasts, marriages or other festivities, and the *jongleurs* carried them from town to town, to villages and fairs, adapting them to their different audiences. The poems get longer, the religious and patriotic inspiration weaker, as time goes on; and new material is added from another cycle of narratives, the Breton stories of King Arthur, which had evolved quite independently of the Carolingian poems. The Arthurian tales, which were best known in the twelfth-century versions of Chrétien de Troyes, are largely concerned with love, with individual acts of valour and adventure, with magic and fanciful inventions. In time they too grow longer, more digressive and relatively disjointed. So the *chansons* lose their original character as the society for which they are recited changes. The narratives become more popular, the material is brought down to earth; and the comic element is increased, sometimes to the point of parody.

Essentially the same process occurs in Italy. The French poems had made their way over the Alps as early as the twelfth century with the minstrels accompanying the bands of pilgrims along the valley of the Po, and their first home in Italy had been the cities of the northern plain, notably Ferrara and Venice, where Italian poets heard them and wrote down versions or adaptations in French or in a Franco-Venetian dialect – the late thirteenth-century *Entrée d'Espagne*, for example, written by an anonymous Paduan author, and recast in the following century in both prose and verse. As these versions multiplied in Italy the material was modified to Italian tastes: the serious, religious and patriotic note of the early French *chansons* became fainter in Italy as in France: the glories of France did not greatly appeal to Italian audiences, and the chivalrous conventions were less practised and not so widely admired as before. The material was Italianised: the renowned paladin Renault de Montauban (Rinaldo), who rebels against Imperial authority, came to appeal even more to Italian audiences than Orlando, the right hand of Charlemagne.

Meantime another current had joined the mainstream. The Arthurian tales were known of course to Dante's Italy, as Paolo and Francesca found to their cost; but their popularity was slower to gather force than that of the stories of Charlemagne. However, manuscripts in French of Arthurian tales are succeeded by Franco-Venetian and then Tuscan adaptations of French originals in the fourteenth century, in both prose and verse; the *Tristano*, *Tavola Ritonda*, *Storia di Merlino* and others. The loves and enchantments of Arthurian romance may have been less attractcive to the crowds in the *piazza*, but for the ladies and more cultured audiences at court they proved a welcome addition to the eternal duels and battles of the Carolingian tales; and, in the latter, amorous diversions and fanciful inventions came to play an increasing part.

The outstanding writer at the beginning of the fifteenth-century was the Tuscan, Andrea da Barberino, who wrote a number of prose romances based on these earlier Franco-Venetian narratives – *Guerrin meschino*, *Ugone d'Alvernia*, *Aspramonte* and others – but his most popular work was *I Reali di Francia*, which tells the story of the antecedents of Charlemagne from the time of Fiovo, the Emperor Constantine's son, up to the birth of Charlemagne's nephew, Orlando (here called Orlandino). This is a serious attempt to rationalise and clarify the confused romance material, and also to relate it more effectively to his fifteenth-century audience. In spite of its fanciful and supernatural elements there is a strong note of realism which brings the deeds of the knights down to earth. The love-stories, which are quite prominent, are narrated flatly, quite unromantically. Bovetto, caught kissing Feliciana by her cousin, kills the intruder: 'Feliciana was more afraid than sorry and said to him "Oh dear, what have you done to this gentleman? He is my father's nephew and my cousin, and how will you be able to avoid punishment?" Bovetto replied "I rely on you." She said to him "Put him under the bed ..."' The final chapters describe how Carlomagno's sister, Berta, falls in love with Milone and conceives a child by him: the Emperor banishes Berta, and Orlandino is born in poverty and exile in a cave 'per le bestie', a few miles from Rome; then Berta returns to Paris with Orlandino, riding on an old hack, to beg the Emperor's forgiveness: 'Berta begged for mercy and pardon. Carlo couldn't control his anger and lifted his right foot and gave her a great kick in the chest so that she fell over in the direction of Orlandino. ...' But then Carlo repents, bursts into tears, pardons his sister and adopts Orlando as his son.

The oral tradition of the romances was still strong. The *cantastorie* or *cantampanchi* or *canterino*, as he was variously called, recited or chanted the narrative by instalments, often in quite dramatic fashion with actions and gestures and appropriate musical accompaniment on a stringed instrument. Wherever a crowd assembled, whether in the *sala* of the court or in the *piazza* below, he might be found appealing for silence – beginning with a prayer, a recapitulation of his previous narrative, a promise of excitement to follow, and ending with a blessing, an invitation to his audience to hear the sequel on the following day, and passing his hat round for their contributions. The octave rhyme in which the *cantari* of the fourteenth and fifteenth centuries were composed was a particularly appropriate form for recitation, the rhyme jogging the *cantastorie's* memory and the stanza structure allowing pauses for him to recover his breath or strike a few notes, and for the audience to register their reaction. Before the time of printing, when manuscripts were rare and expensive, the oral performance was an essential part of the entertainment of rich and poor alike. The manuscript copies or notes owned by minstrels or patrons must have varied considerably in their degree of completeness and polish, and the performances too must have varied a great deal according to the culture of the minstrel and the nature of his audience.

Andrea da Barberino's prose tales and the *cantari* of the fifteenth century show the process of evolution of the romance from its medieval origins to the new society and culture of the Renaissance. Andrea raised the level of the romances, clarifying the narrative, improving the language and adapting the material to a more critical audience. Later in the century Luigi Pulci carried this process a stage further. Pulci, a friend of Lorenzo de' Medici, was a member of a middle-class Florentine business family without much literary culture. He was little influenced by the neo-Platonic humanism of Lorenzo's circle but he shared Lorenzo's interest in popular culture and the vernacular; and while Lorenzo was giving literary form to the popular lyric and Poliziano was transforming the vernacular drama, Pulci composed a very successful chivalrous romance, the *Morgante* (1483), out of two crude medieval poems. He followed his sources closely, almost transcribing them in places, but he brought a considerable degree of narrative skill to the clumsy, often obscure originals, and he intruded his own witty, contemporary commentary or interpretation. He wrote, it should be noted, after the introduction of printing, and his poem was published in 1482–3. Henceforth the romances were intended primarily for reading, although the *cantastorie* continued to recite to the audiences in the *piazza*, and a popular following persisted in some parts of Italy until very recent times. The Carolingian tales have been prominent in the repertoire of story-tellers, with their placards of coloured illustrations, in the twentieth century in Sicily; and the puppet theatres still present the battle between paladins and pagans.

Pulci's *Morgante*, a long poem of some 30,000 lines, retells the tale of the hatred of Gano for Orlando and the latter's death at Roncevaux. It acquired its title from the name of a very popular giant who has an elephant for breakfast and picks his teeth with a pine-tree. The

tone is down-to-earth and realistic, like the *Reali di Francia*, but
Pulci's racy Florentine with its wit and verve set the chivalrous
material in a new context. When Rinaldo sees a giant who has lost
his nose:

> Rinaldo guarda quel viso cagnozzo
> che non parea né d'uom né d'animali,
> e disse, 'Dove appicchi tu gli occhiali?
>   O con che fiuti tu l'anno le rose?
> Tu par bestia dimestica a vedere. ...'

[Rinaldo looks at that snoutlike face, which seems neither human
nor animal, and said : 'Tell me, where do you rest your spec-
tacles? Or what do you smell the roses in spring with? You
seem a very tame animal to me.']

In addition to this comic re-fashioning of his sources Pulci's poem
is remarkable for its reflection of its author's contemporary attitudes,
particularly his views on religion, which are irreverent and sceptical.
'I was destined for the turban rather than the cowl', he wrote and
his poem is coloured by his materialistic, often cynical philosophy.
There is some love interest in the *Morgante*: Rinaldo and even
Orlando have to be recalled to the path of duty from their flirtations
with pretty serving-maids:

> Per vagheggiare non venimmo in Levante.

[We did not come to the Levant to ogle women.]

But there is no sentimentality, and the love-episodes remain peripheral to the main interest in the poem, which is fighting. When
there is a call to arms the ladies are calmly abandoned or married off
to servants or vassals. They seem to expect this, and they accept it,
and the knights certainly shed no tears for them.

Pulci and his Florentine business friends didn't do so either, but at
Ferrara, where the Arthurian tales were well-known and much
admired, Boiardo entitled his poem *Orlando Innamorato* and introduced it as a story of arms and love:

> ... vederete i gesti smisurati,
> l'alta fatica e le mirabil prove
> che fece il franco Orlando per amore ...

[you will see the mighty deeds, the great labours and wondrous
feats performed by Orlando because of love.]

In making Orlando fall in love, Boiardo is often said to have fused
the Arthurian and Carolingian cycles. There is some exaggeration in
this, but it is true that, while keeping the characters and framework
of the Carolingian tradition, the war between Charlemagne and the

invading pagan armies, he enlarged and emphasised the Arthurian elements – the individual adventures of the knight-errant, the enchantments, and particularly the love interest, which now has a significant role, notably in the first Book.

Boiardo's is a long poem with a confused action, but it is so relevant to the *Furioso* that I will try to summarise it here. Each of the three Books seems to set out with a somewhat different intention. In the first, the Asian king Gradasso assembles a huge force to invade France in order to seize Orlando's sword, Durindana, which the author here imagines to have once belonged to Virgil's Hector. In this traditional setting Boiardo introduces a new character of his own invention, the pagan princess Angelica, whose beauty unsettles Christians and pagans alike. Orlando is furiously jealous when Angelica drinks from an enchanted fountain which makes her fall in love with Rinaldo, although Rinaldo has drunk from another fountain which has the opposite effect. In these circumstances Gradasso's army never comes into action against Carlomagno: the men on both sides stray through the forest, fighting giants and monsters, delivering ladies in distress or listening to long and complicated tales from chance acquaintances.

The second Book opens with a new pagan campaign against Carlomagno, called this time by Agramante to avenge his father's death and 'per aggrandir la legge di Macone' ('to extend Mahomet's law'). The war is a prominent feature of this Book, although the warriors on both sides are still distracted by beautiful girls, supernatural, allegorical and real. But a good deal of space is devoted to the search for the man who, it is predicted, will be the hero of the pagan campaign, Ruggiero. Angelica's part in this Book is small. She and Rinaldo again drink at different fountains, so that Rinaldo is now in love with Angelica and she has conceived a hatred of him. The rivalry between Orlando and Rinaldo is so intense that Carlomagno puts her in safe-keeping prior to the battle in the south of France, promising to each of the paladins not to let the other take her.

Book Three also begins with a new pagan offensive, this time mounted by Mandricardo, who is urged to avenge the death of his father Agricane at the hands of Orlando. With Ruggiero's help the pagan forces defeat the Christians, who retire in disorder to Paris, where a fierce battle follows, halted temporarily by a storm. Meanwhile Ruggiero has met Rinaldo's sister Bradamante, and the two have fallen in love: it is forecast that they will marry and engender a

famous line of heroes (the Estensi), but Bradamante is warned that
Ruggiero must be baptised a Christian. The poem then breaks off.

I have omitted numerous secondary characters and digressive episodes from this bare account of the narrative, which is very complex
and often disjointed. But the sheer profusion of Boiardo's characters, the rapid succession of incident, the variety of monsters and
enchantments win over the reader to a state of dazzled acceptance.
The author's approach to his material, whether military or amorous,
is often frankly amused. His knights engage in uproarious practical
jokes and chase eagerly through the woods like excited schoolboys;
there is a good deal of slap-stick comedy: one blow on the head
stuns Orlando, but the second brings him back to his senses:

> Io non saprebbi ben dir la cagione
> Ma il Conte alora uscì de stordigione. (i, xxvii, *10*)
> [The reason I could not explain to you/But then the Count
> quite suddenly came to.]

The poet sometimes smiles at his characters with a sly irony, but
more often he seems totally in sympathy with them, as though he is
out to enjoy the exuberance of jousting and love-making. Love is
like war, he says:

> L'uno e l'altro esercizio è giovanile
> nemico di riposo, atto all'affanno ... (ii, xii, *2*)
> [Both pursuits are youthful, alien to repose, favouring labour.]

There is no time for Petrarchan finesse and, in fact, in spite of its title
the main interest of *Orlando Innamorato* is not love, but arms. Boiardo
is preoccupied with fighting, and his second and third Books are
largely devoted to a sequence of jousts, duels and battles. He apolo-
gises at one point for a long absence from the battlefield:

> Già molto tempo m'han tenuto a bada
> Morgana, Alcina e le incantazioni,
> Nè vi ho mostrato un bel colpo di spada
> E pieno il ciel di lance e di tronconi ... (ii, xiv, *1*)
> [For a long time now I have been kept occupied with Morgana,
> Alcina and their enchantments, and I haven't shown you any
> fine sword-thrusts or the sky thick with lances and clubs.]

– and he promises that the canto that follows will have 'ferite e
fiamme e foco e ferro' [wounds, flames, fire and sword].

The first two books of the *Innamorato* had been published in 1483,
and the poet had not completed the third book when he died in
1494. The first edition of all three books appeared the following
year.

It was this poem, left unfinished by Boiardo in Book III, Canto ix, that Ariosto decided to 'continue' – this is the word he uses in a letter written in 1512: 'un mio libro al quale già molti dì (continuando la inventione del conte Matteo Maria Boiardo) io diedi principio' ['a book which I began many days ago, continuing the invention of Count M.M.Boiardo']. Ariosto takes over Boiardo's characters and the main action of his poem : the war, the love of Orlando, and the story of Ruggiero, as Boiardo had outlined them at the beginning of his third Book:

La gran battaglia e il trionfal onore
Vi conterò di Carlo, re di Franza,
E le prodezze fatte per amore
Del Conte Orlando e sua strema possanza;
Come Ruggier, che fu nel mondo un fiore,
Fosse tradito ... (III,i,3)

[I will tell you the great battle and the triumphal honour of Carlo, king of France, and the brave deeds achieved by Count Orlando because of love, and his great strength; how Ruggiero, the very flower of men, was betrayed ...]

Ariosto emphasises the same themes, and in the same sequence: 'i giovenil furori/d'Agramante' (1,1); 'Dirò d'Orlando ...' (1,2) and 'Voi sentirete ... ricordar quel Ruggier ...' (1,4). So he brings to a close the long struggle between Christians and pagans with the triumph of Carlomagno and the death of the pagan leaders. And Orlando from being 'innamorato' becomes mad with jealousy : when he discovers that Angelica has deserted him for an unknown Moorish soldier, Medoro, he runs berserk and is only cured when Astolfo goes to the moon and brings back his senses. Ariosto also completes the story of the courtship of Bradamante and Ruggiero, who fights for his African allies through most of the poem but is eventually baptised and marries Bradamante, so that their union may initiate the long line of Estense heroes. Ludovico also accepts responsibility for continuing the detailed adventures and situations of the earlier poem. Boiardo's 'serial' technique of breaking off one incident at an exciting point in order to continue another one interrupted earlier meant that some ten or twelve separate actions were left incomplete when he abandoned the poem in Book III, canto ix. Ariosto completed these, every one, inserting them carefully in his own complex narrative : the plight of Angelica, for example, who had been left awaiting the outcome of the earlier battle in the south of France and of whom we have had no news since the Christian defeat (resumed in Canto I of the *Furioso*); the battle for Paris, interrupted by a storm (resumed in Canto VIII), and so on down to the story of Ricciardetto and Fiordispina (which is not completed until Canto XXV of the *Furioso*). Ariosto dutifully accepts Boiardo's antecedents for his characters, and a good deal of their personalities: his poem was criticised later in the sixteenth century for lacking a beginning, for being only half a poem, and it is true that it does, so to speak, break into an action that is already going on. But this does not prevent it from being a unified, rounded work of art in its own right. In fact there is something very modern about this open-endedness of the *Furioso*, which not only opens with the action in full swing but ends before it is complete, with the forecast of Ruggiero's death by treachery hanging uneasily over the wedding celebrations – as though reflecting the continuum of real life.

But if we are to fault Ariosto for his loan of Boiardo's main action and characters, we should have to point out his debts to numerous other sources. He was an eager reader of chivalrous romance which he borrowed from the Estense library; and he makes especially frequent use of the *Aspramonte*, the *Spagna in Rima*, *Ancroia*, *Storia di Merlino*, and *Guerrin Meschino* as well as of his contemporary Francesco Bello's *Mambriano*. So of course did Boiardo, but Ariosto is differentiated from his predecessor by the extent of his debts to classical sources, to the *Aeneid*, the *Metamorphoses*, to Catullus, Statius, Horace and Lucan – the very title of his poem is taken from the *Hercules furens* of Seneca. If we add to these sources his frequent reminiscences of the 'tre corone', of Dante, Petrarch and Boccaccio, it soon becomes apparent that as far as the action and characters of his poem are concerned he really needed 'invent', in the formal sense, very little.

What, then, *was* Ariosto's contribution to the romance tradition? This is to some extent the theme of this book and will I hope appear in the succeeding chapters. Ariosto's 'invention' consists not in his creation of new characters or action but in the disposition, presentation and interpretation of the material he found in his sources, classical and medieval. His first great achievement was to create a structure in which this heterogeneous material could serve an artistic purpose. There is little conscious artistry in Pulci's disposition of his narrative, which follows stanza by stanza the sequence of his sources, naïve as these were. Boiardo goes his own way, borrowing and inventing as he chooses, but with very little forethought, letting his fantasy carry him on. This is of course part of his charm, as Byron

realised in *Don Juan* and J.H. Frere in his *Monks and Giants*, two
poems closely influenced by the Italian poets:

> I've finished now three hundred lines and more
>   And therefore I begin Canto the Second,
> Just like those wand'ring ancient Bards of yore;
>   They never laid a plan nor ever reckon'd
> What turning they should take the day before,
>   They follow'd where the lovely Muses beckon'd:
> The Muses led them up to Mount Parnassus,
>   And that's the reason that they all surpass us.
>
> (Frere, Canto II)

But Boiardo is led into all sorts of irrelevancies, repetitions, omissions,
ambiguities and the like by his lack of planning: and the result is often
tedious or disquieting: characters get lost, stories are not finished,
incidents are repeated. All this Ariosto avoids, but, more important,
he succeeds in controlling the complexity and variety of romance to
create a coherent, unified, harmonious effect. His poem exploits the
arts of the narrative in the true sense, taking the reader through a
sequence of actions so arranged that successive canti recall, echo,
illuminate or shade, parallel or contrast with each other, controlling
and guiding the reader's response, evoking an emotional reaction not
just by the poetry of its detailed components but by the relation of
those components to each other over a lengthy narrative.

If Ariosto then is a master of the art of narrative he is no less a great
poet. His is after all a narrative poem, not a prose romance or a novel,
and he gives expression to its complex and delicate subject through
the medium of verse, with its specialised linguistic and stylistic resources. For this Ariosto had to find an appropriate language, a major
preoccupation for Italian writers of his age when the vernacular
language was trying to free itself of the dominance of Latin and when
the spoken language varied so radically from one region to another.
Here too Ariosto's advance on Pulci and Boiardo is marked: Pulci's
language is often obscure, coloured as it is by current Florentine usage
and by its author's own whimsical humour, and Boiardo's vernacular
was heavily criticised for its local Emilian and Lombard flavour. Beset
as he was by the linguistic problems of his age and of his subject
(comprising an archaic material seen through Renaissance eyes) he
succeeded in creating a language and style which communicated at
once with readers all over Italy, and before long all over Europe.

I have also referred to Ariosto's originality in the interpretation of
his chivalrous material. To each of the main themes of the chivalrous

romance Ariosto brings his own rational and emotional reactions, conditioned as they are by his age and by his environment – and he lived at a critical time and in critical circumstances. While much of the apparatus of medieval chivalry and the ways of thinking associated with it still survived, a new Europe was emerging with new concepts of politics and of war. Machiavelli is Ariosto's contemporary. Italian humanism had encouraged new positive ways of considering society and man's role in the world, and yet while Ariosto wrote Italy was the victim of a devastating succession of wars and disasters. The crises of these years are reflected in the *Furioso* with the realistic and essentially humane philosophy of the poet. So, too, at a time when Florentine neo-Platonism had given a new direction to thinking on that sore subject of sexual love, Ariosto adapts the 'amori' of the romances to present a wide-ranging and moving interpretation of the relationship between the sexes.

In all this the literary tradition is of fundamental importance for an understanding of the *Furioso*, and not just because the poem is, as we have shown, conditioned by that tradition. But more than that, the literary tradition is in some sense the *subject* of the poem. The *Furioso* is indeed a poem about the real, contemporary world of Ariosto, but it is also a poem about the past, not the real, historical past of Charlemagne and Paris but the past as described by poets and envisaged by their audiences, the past of knights-errant and beautiful princesses and dragons. Like so many of his contemporaries Ariosto had been caught up in the appeal of that world – he had devoured the treasures of the Estense library and his imagination had responded to its warmth and colour. And he succeeds in conveying that appeal in his poem – we too enter the world of medieval romance. But another part of Ariosto looked more critically, with the eye of a humanist and a realist, and he recognised the dichotomy between literature and life – and the exaggerations of the minstrels and the credulity of their public are enfolded within his narrative. Cervantes was indeed Ariosto's successor, and crowned his work when he depicted that most credulous of all readers, Don Quixote, who actually lost his sanity in the world of the romances. It was Ariosto's achievement to conceive a poem in which the subtle balance is reflected between the worlds of the imagination and of practical experience, between the ideals of courage, courtesy, loyalty, friendship, love, and the reality of fear, lust, cruelty, treachery, envy, which one met every day. That hinterland of human experience, where the imaginative and the practical worlds meet is a constant source of inspiration of his poetry.

4. The Theme of Love

Ariosto, in a letter, described the *Furioso* as a 'work which deals with pleasant and entertaining matters concerning arms and love', and these are the two themes presented in the first line of his poem. 'Le donne' are given pride of place, as though advertising the originality of the poet's approach, which is underlined in the following octave:

Dirò d'Orlando in un medesmo tratto
cosa non detta in prosa mai né in rima:
che per amor venne in furore e matto,
d'uom che sì saggio era stimato prima. (1, 2)

[At the same time I shall tell something about Orlando that has never been told before in prose or verse – how a man who had previously been thought so wise, went raging mad because of love.]

This advertisement of the novelty of the poet's wares is a romance convention (Boiardo too had invited his audience to 'Cose dilettose e nove') but the treatment of 'amori' in the *Furioso* does indeed constitute a new departure in Italian romance. It is not merely the love of Orlando that is unusual; the love affairs of paladins and pagans and of many of those that they meet, wayfarers, inn-keepers, damsels in distress, are recounted so frequently and at such length that the poem comes to resemble an anthology of love stories.

Readers and critics have long been aware of this and have interpreted it in their different ways. One of the most extreme views was put forward some forty years ago by M. Chini who saw the whole poem as reflecting the poet's own relationship with Alessandra Benucci: the *Furioso* was a love treatise in octave rhyme reflecting the progression of Ariosto's earthly love to a worldly perfected platonic love with the guidance of Alessandra. More recently N. Cappellani has reminded us that Ariosto wrote with an unsatisfied passion for Alessandra whose husband died only in 1515, the year the poem was completed, and suggests that Ariosto essentially repeated the Petrarchan theme of unreciprocated love, using the narrative in place of the lyric form. Another view of the poem, which eschews the dubious autobiographical approach, sees Ariosto as the heir, not of Petrarch, but of

Boccaccio, in creating an anthology of love stories extremely varied
in their origins, nature and intention, but unified in exploring the
essence of the relationship between the sexes. The analogy with
Boccaccio is more convincing than that with Petrarch – but one could
round off the reminders of Ariosto's medieval heritage by pointing
out that his distracted Orlando is only restored to the path of Christian
duty thanks to a journey into the underworld and up to the moon,
and that the first and last lines of the *Furioso* are in fact reminiscences
of the *Divina Commedia*.

The autobiographical thesis merits perhaps an initial note of explanation. It is true that explicit allusions to the poet's own love life
are scattered throughout the poem, from the very first stanzas where
Ariosto declares he will be able to write about Orlando's love and
madness only if allowed to do so by the lady who has nearly reduced
him to the same state ('che tal quasi m'ha fatto'). Yet the number of
such allusions is very restrained in relation to the length of the poem,
and most of these are ironical in tone. Several of the personal allusions
are blatant literary reminiscences introduced ironically, as the Petrarchan:

> Ben mi si potria dir: Frate, tu vai
> l'altrui mostrando, e non vedi il tuo fallo, (xxiv, 3)
> [People might well say to me – Brother, you keep pointing out
> other people's faults and don't see your own]

– coupled with a reference to the 'lucido intervallo' that has allowed
him a clear and penetrating look at the effects of love. It seems likely
that these allusions refer to Alessandra, as well as the serious tribute
paid to 'una gran donna … di … sublime aspetto …' (xLII, 93). But one
cannot attribute unreservedly any of the allusions in the *Furioso* to
Alessandra Benucci, and in any case they are so generic, conventional
and lighthearted that one would learn little of his relationship with
Alessandra from them. And, on the other side, we know too little
about the poet's real-life relationship with Alessandra or other
women to be able to trace their reflection in his poem. What *is* clear
is what the poet tells us, that he too has known the pains and joys of
love, and that out of his own experience he can project the feelings of
the lovers whose tales he takes from a wide range of literary sources.

The love material is indeed largely literary in origin and the sources
are generally known and indisputable. Very little can have been truly
invented by Ariosto, or even based on contemporary situations,
although commentators have been tempted into finding court
intrigues in the 'amori' of the poem. But rarely are the sources

followed at all closely, and the modifications in Ariosto's versions are what really constitute his 'invention', and show us his attitude or his 'theory' or 'philosophy' of love – and here it is far more difficult to pinpoint his sources. He lived at a time when literary and social circles were preoccupied with discussions about love, which had been given a great new impetus by the writings of Marsilio Ficino and the neo-Platonic Academy: the lyrics of Lorenzo and Poliziano, and many of the Cinquecento Petrarchisti show the effects of this, and so do the discussions in Castiglione's *Cortegiano* and Bembo's *Asolani* – not to mention the paintings of Botticelli and others. Yet neo-Platonism leaves very little mark on the *Furioso*, which is anything but an academic treatise on love. Ariosto's attitudes reflect, as we should expect, the sources on which he draws for his material: *stil novisti* concepts of *gentilezza* and courtesy; Petrarchan niceties of unreciprocated passion; Boccaccesque acceptance of the gratification of the senses; or the medieval belief in the *aegritudo amoris*, love as a sickness, confounding body and soul. But the choice and treatment of the material exemplifies no coherent and explicit philosophy of love, certainly not the reigning neo-Platonic fashion. Such philosophy as emerges, is a personal one, a human, humane and common-sense acceptance of love as a power for good or evil in men's lives.

This is something that the poet sets out consciously to demonstrate. He does more than assemble and co-ordinate a collection of interesting love stories: he selects his material, he adapts it and he provides it with a commentary – all of this with the intention of conveying a point of view. His attitude is moral but one cannot truly contend with Chini that his aim is 'to punish wicked and exalt virtuous love'. There is no general equation in the *Furioso* between virtue and happiness in love: it is true that Orlando's unsuitable passion for the enemy of his faith and his country is punished by God who deprives him of his senses for a while; and that Bradamante's devotion to Ruggiero, who is converted to Christianity and brought into Charlemagne's camp, is rewarded with marriage and the founding of a long and successful lineage. However, devoted and innocent women suffer (Isabella, Drusilla) together with the wicked ones; the flirts (Angelica, Doralice) and the wanton (Fiordispina) not only go unpunished but live happily ever after; there is no compensation for the devoted Alceste, driven to his death by Lidia, or for Grifone harried by the treacherous Gabrina. Love implies suffering, even for the chaste devoted reciprocal lovers (Ariodante and Ginevra, Isabella and Zerbino). The happy lovers owe their happiness to luck as often as to

virtue: Medoro, Mandricardo and Ricciardetto could all fairly be said
to be lucky in love, and hardly to have earned their good fortune by
their conduct with their respective ladies. Yet if the poet has no
general moral lesson to teach in the poem as a whole it is abundantly
clear that the individual love situations serve to show something more
than their own particular chain of incidents: they are examples of
types of love. This is made explicit frequently in the poet's commentary, and it was certainly regarded as patently obvious by his
Cinquecento commentators and others. But what do they exemplify?

Despite much juggling with the twenty or so important relationships no one has yet fitted them into any very clear pattern. There are
certain themes with variations, or, to change the metaphor, a few
groups of interlocking themes, which themselves fail to interlock
with other groups, and the reason is perhaps not far to seek. Love, no
less than fighting, is subject to the capricious hand of Fortune which
recognises no patterns or simple guidelines. It is part of Ariosto's
essentially down-to-earth and anti-humanistic frame of mind to see
man not as the master of his circumstances but as their often very
insignificant plaything. Love, so often personified as a capricious goddess or Cupid, delights in making havoc of human hopes:

> Ingiustissimo Amor, perché sì raro
> corrispondenti fai nostri desiri? (11, 1)
> [Most unjust Love, why do you so rarely make our desires
> correspond?]

Love is indeed coupled with Fortune as subjecting its victims to un-
predictable woes:

> Misera Olimpia! a cui dopo lo scorno
> che gli fe' Amore, anco Fortuna cruda
> mandò i corsari ... (x1, 55)
> [Unhappy Olimpia, to whom after the rebuff that Love
> delivered, cruel Fortune sent the pirates ...]

Isabella's misfortunes are the fault of Love ('colpa d'Amor', x111, 4):
her eye first alights on the valorous Zerbino, perhaps because of
Zerbino's courage but perhaps because that tyrannical *Amor* pointed
him out:

> Fra gli altri (o sia ch'Amor così mi mostre,
> o che virtù pur se stessa palesi)
> mi parve da lodar Zerbino solo ... (x111, 6)
> [Among all others (whether because Love showed me, or
> because virtue makes itself apparent) I thought only Zerbino
> worthy of praise ...)

Love therefore, like Fortune, is alien to rational explanation or
analysis: it is the enemy of man's reason:

Quivi il crudo tiranno Amor, che sempre
d'ogni promessa sua fu disleale,
e sempre guarda come involva e stempre
ogni nostro disegno razionale,
mutò con triste e disoneste tempre
mio conforto in dolor, mio bene in male. (XIII, *20*)

[Then the cruel tyrant Love, who never kept a promise, and is
always searching for ways of confusing and spoiling all our
rational plans, wickedly changed my happiness into suffering,
my blessing into misfortune.]

The romance material is not therefore analysed and grouped in any
really logical manner, as, for example, in the *Faerie Queene*; yet it is
not fortuitous or capricious in its selection or arrangement. Ariosto
seems concerned to present us with a balanced picture of the relationship between the sexes as he saw it in sixteenth-century Italy; his
selection of material seems made with the intention of providing a
wide range of lovers and loves, virtuous and vicious, successful and
unsuccessful, happy and miserable. Within the framework of this
large canvas the love situations are sited with a good deal of apparent
disorder: lovers meet and are separated, are wooed, won, betrayed
and abandoned after the capricious fashion of Fortune. But the guiding hand of the artist is behind the disorder, and it is his aesthetic
judgment which is responsible for the final effect. Out of the vast
range of classical and medieval sources at his disposal his selection is
made in order to provide a balanced range of emotional situations and
a succession of poetic impressions or effects which together will constitute the poem he has in his head, each canto, each episode, carrying
the echo of its predecessor, and echoing forward to its successor.

Of the love relationships in the *Furioso* the large majority are contained within the space of one or two cantos and are then forgotten,
but a few enjoy a protracted life over a considerable portion of the
poem. Orlando's and also Rinaldo's infatuation with Angelica are
examples of this, and so is the love between Ruggiero and Bradamante. They show us a conflict between the claims of love and of
duty: Orlando and Rinaldo are Christian paladins who neglect their
obligations to Charlemagne because of their infatuation with a
Saracen princess; and Bradamante too is distracted by her passion for
an enemy of her country and her faith. The loves of Orlando and
Rinaldo, though chaste, are strictly improper and immoral – both

have wives already – and they both fail, causing considerable suffering. The love of Bradamante and Ruggiero, however, though beset by difficulties, ends in a happy marriage and the conversion of Ruggiero to the Christian faith: Bradamante insists that her African lover accept her religion and ask her hand formally in marriage from her father.

In the simplest terms Ariosto seems to say that the conflict of love and duty can be resolved if the love is a right one. Orlando's love for Angelica is a foolish infatuation with a pretty face and for his dereliction of duty he is punished by God by the loss of his senses. St John explains to Astolfo that Orlando's invulnerability and superhuman strength were given him by God for the defence of the true faith, and that by his 'unchaste love' for Angelica he has betrayed his divine task:

> E Dio per questo fa ch'egli va folle,
> e mostra nudo il ventre, il petto e il fianco. (xxxiv, 65)
> [And for this reason God makes him go about mad, showing his
> bare belly and chest and hips.]

Only with the aid of St John are Orlando's senses restored and is he freed from his wicked obsession. And Rinaldo, the second knight in all Christendom, is also seduced from his duty to country and faith by the charms of the capricious Angelica, but in his case an enchanted fountain has drugged him. He, like Orlando, becomes intensely jealous, but with some assistance he succeeds in fighting and conquering his passion, and he returns to his Emperor and his family.

In these cases the claims of love and duty are irreconcilable, but in the Bradamante-Ruggiero relationship a solution is found. Both the lovers are tempted by their passion to neglect their obligations to their leaders: Bradamante in particular is so deeply in love that she refuses a call for help to defend Marseilles, for which she is responsible, in order to carry on her search for Ruggiero (II, 65); but she does not lose her head, in spite of her jealousy, and she sticks firmly to her aims, a legal marriage with a Christian husband: she is

> ... disposta di far tutti
> i piaceri che far vergine saggia
> debbia ad un suo amator ... (xxii, 34)
> [prepared to give all the satisfaction that a wise virgin should to
> her lover,]

and she wins through in the end. Ruggiero, however, is the outstanding example of the dilemma posed by the conflict of love and duty, and the question is raised so insistently that we feel it is taken in all

seriousness by the poet. While the Saracen forces are threatening
Paris he is ready to go off with Bradamante to be baptised, but once
his lord is in danger he feels obliged to support him:

Ora, essendo Agramante che gli pose
la spada al fianco, farebbe opra rea
dandogli morte, e saria traditore;
che già tolto l'avea per suo signore. (xxxvi, 80)
[Now, as it was Agramante who fastened his sword to his side,
he would be doing a wicked thing in killing him, and he would
make himself a traitor, having once taken him as his lord.]

Ruggiero, therefore, is not distracted from his loyalty to his lord – nor
later does he let his love for Bradamante distract him from his honour-
able obligation to Leone; here, in the supreme test of love and honour,
he fights on behalf of his rival against the woman he loves, so that
Leone may have her.

These two extended love relationships serve to exemplify a moral
theme, which is underlined explicitly by the poet. Yet this moral
pattern is not obtrusive, and certainly it is not any such moral lesson
which gives these situations the vitality they possess. The essence of
the Orlando-Angelica relationship is not the conflict of love and duty,
and St John's revelation of the divine origin of Orlando's madness,
coming as it does late in the poem (xxxiv), strikes us as irrelevant.

Orlando's madness is the result of his uncontrollable jealousy, and
it was this surely which attracted Ariosto's attention and which holds
our interest. He envisaged the effects of a thwarted passion in a man of
Orlando's temperament, a soldier, a man of action rather than words,
a powerful, dominant fighter frustrated by a capricious flirt and a poor
unknown Moorish soldier. It was around this situation that Ariosto
built this relationship, and the scene in which the lonely Orlando
gradually discovers the evidence of Angelica's love for Medoro is one
of the most moving in the *Furioso*; from his first glimpse of their
carved names on the trees to the account given him by the shepherd
in whose cottage they had slept, the dreadful truth is borne in on
his resisting mind, and from suspicion to fear to certain knowledge,
despair and rage he reaches madness.

The effectiveness of this scene of mounting frustration is increased
by (is dependent on) the incidents we have just witnessed in those
same woods, that same cottage, with Angelica and Medoro – an idyll
of romantic love. It is one of Ariosto's most effective ironies that the
lovely Angelica, who has the greatest leaders of Europe and Africa at
her feet and who only uses them for her own interest, should at last

herself be struck by love's arrow, and that her passion should be roused for a helpless unknown soldier. And it is one of Love's tricks that a capricious self-centred princess should be linked with the brave and loyal soldier who has just risked his life to bring back the body of his wounded king. So we witness a succession of vividly imagined scenes: the young boy, standing at bay over the body of his king before the threatening Scots soldiers, treacherously wounded by them, and found alone, near dying, by the passing Angelica who hastens to his rescue and is strangely touched with pity for the handsome, helpless youth. Their love is a sudden rapidly rising passion, without hesitation or restraint, and in spite of the warnings elsewhere in the poem about youthful passion and desire they are allowed to enjoy their idyllic passion without ever a hint of trouble present or future. The storm clouds that follow this sunny interlude do not touch them: it is Orlando in his helpless rage who suffers the aftermath of their passion.

Orlando's jealous infatuation is itself a madness, in keeping with his obsessive belief in his role as protector of Angelica's maidenhood. He is simply deluded about Angelica, deluded that she cares about him, and deluded that she equates with the chaste and beautiful ideal which he has long been pursuing. Angelica, after so many adventures in the wild woods, swears she is a virgin, although Ariosto has his doubts:

Forse era ver, ma non però credibile
a chi del senso suo fosse signore; (I, 56)
[Perhaps it was true, but it wouldn't have been credible to any-one in his right senses.]

Angelica perhaps is hardly a real person: she is the sort of woman no man can resist, so beautiful and desirable that no-one ever finds out her real nature: she exists in her lovers' imaginations, and to the lucky Medoro she is certainly a virgin:

Angelica a Medor la prima rosa
coglier lasciò, non ancor tocca inante. (XIX, 33)
[Angelica let Medoro pluck the first rose, never touched before.]

Their passion and Orlando's jealousy strike us as totally true-to-life, yet they have a fairy-tale quality about them – the idyllic romantic love and the tragic jealous despair.

These two extended love relationships form as it were a major theme on which the numerous lesser affairs are as variations. They have a movement of their own within the poem and complement each other – Ruggiero is progressively purified by his love for Brada-

mante and the poem ends with their marriage, while Orlando sinks
further and further into the mire and is lost from the scene, until
Astolfo recovers his senses and cures him of his mad passion. The one
love ripens while the other dies. The poem begins therefore with the
two passions which are set moving on their respective courses before
the first set of variations is introduced – but between Canto IV and
Canto XI three new love stories are told which have much in common
with each other, and which throw light on the destructive passion
which has now overtaken the main protagonists. The new episodes
are those concerning Ariodante and Ginevra, Ruggiero and Alcina,
and Olimpia and Bireno, and each of them merits far more than the
very brief attention we can give them here.

The first is one of the most subtle and attractive episodes in the
whole poem. It is the tale the unhappy serving-maid Dalinda tells
Rinaldo (IV) when he saves her from her lover Polinesso's servants
who have been ordered to kill her. Polinesso had persuaded the infatuated Dalinda to dress in her mistress Ginevra's clothes and receive
him on her balcony at night so that Ginevra's faithful lover, Ariodante, watching the incident, was persuaded of his lady's infidelity
and went off to hurl himself into the sea. Ariodante's brother, Lur-
canio, then charged Ginevra with unchastity and by the 'aspra legge
di Scozia' ('the harsh Scots law') she must die unless someone comes
forward to proclaim her innocence. Rinaldo, hearing all this from
Dalinda, hurries to the court and finds that an unknown champion has
presented himself – but Rinaldo himself reveals the truth and challenges the wicked Polinesso who is defeated and admits his guilt on his
death-bed. Then the unknown defender reveals himself as Ariodante
who did throw himself into the sea but swam out and returned to
save the lady he believed had betrayed him. The lovers are happily reunited and Dalinda retires to a nunnery. It is the story later taken up by
Bandello, by Spenser, and by Shakespeare in *Much Ado about Nothing*.

It is essentially, like *Much Ado*, a story of deception in love. Dalinda
is so infatuated with Polinesso that she cannot see through the lies he
tells her in order to win her co-operation for the conquest of her
mistress. He asks her to press his claims on Ginevra so that he can
marry the princess but keep his true love, the serving-maid, as his
mistress; and when that fails he persuades her to dress up in Ginevra's
clothes so that he can rid himself of his obsession for Ginevra by
making love to Dalinda in the pretence that she is her mistress. Spenser
provided a more plausible excuse by having the lover pretend he
wanted to see the maid looking as beautiful as the mistress, in *her*

clothes. But it is essential to Ariosto's theme that Polinesso's story is a
patently false one; only an infatuated lover like Dalinda could fail to
see through it. Love makes us prone to deception; we can no longer
trust our senses. Ariodante is convinced that he has seen Polinesso
making love to Ginevra because he is in such an emotional state that
he does not stop to question the evidence of his eyes. In the Spanish
source the lovers quickly establish the truth of the matter themselves.
Ariosto's episode thus comprises a dual deception: Dalinda believes
her lover is true when he is really faithless; Ariodante believes his
lady is faithless when she is really true. But deception can be for good
as well as ill, and Ariodante returns in disguise to save his lady. The
true and chaste love of Ginevra wins its reward, the devoted but sensuous and illicit love of Dalinda brings her misery.

The high point in the story is, I think, the balcony scene when
Ariodante, who has every reason to believe that Ginevra reciprocated
his love, is suddenly confronted with the apparently clear-cut evidence of her falseness. What happens to a man in a situation such as
that? Ariosto imagines one such scene and in so doing he anticipates
another such confrontation later in the poem, when Orlando discovers the (true) evidence of Angelica's love for Medoro. This is one
of a number of studies of the effects of jealousy, and the narrative is
poised delicately between tragedy and comedy, with the despairing
Ariodante flinging himself from a rock, but recovering his senses in
the water and swimming out to safety. It is the only real touch of
irony in the story and it is characteristic of Ariosto to stop for a
moment and smile at this romantic lover and bring him back to
human proportions. It is also noteworthy that the villain of Ariosto's
piece is a man, rather than the scheming and treacherous female of his
source.

The Alcina episode follows immediately after the Dalinda story
(xi) and it provides another variation on the theme of deception in
love. Alcina is an ugly old hag, toothless and half bald, but she is an
enchantress and to those under her spell she appears very different,
highly seductive with her 'dainty limbs', her blonde hair, black eyes,
full bosom and white skin. Ruggiero is warned of her wickedness and
her magic powers by Astolfo, a previous lover now turned into a
myrtle, but Astolfo has never seen Alcina in her true shape and his
description of his voluptuous amour with her is not sufficient to safeguard Ruggiero when the real test comes, and he in his turn is soon a
victim of her charms, a willing participant in the sensual paradise of
Alcina's kingdom.

The central appeal of the episode is certainly the 'locus amoenus' itself, the sensuous garden of literary tradition which poet and reader enter without any sense of sin, where the emphasis is on the delights of the senses, not their viciousness. The whole is heavily dependent on literary sources, classical and modern, but the sources are assimilated at least in the erotic idyll, if not so successfully in the allegorical apparatus accompanying it. An atmosphere of natural sensuous beauty lulls Ruggiero's resolution:

> Per le cime dei pini e degli allori,
> degli alti faggi e degl'irsuti abeti,
> volan scherzando i pargoletti Amori: (vi, 75)
> [Through the tips of the pines and the laurels, the tall beech trees
> and the shaggy firs the tiny Cupids flit and play ...]

Once he sees the seductive Alcina he is immediately ensnared and is convinced that Astolfo's report of her capricious treachery is itself a lie. He forgets Bradamante, Ariosto tells us, because Alcina uses enchantment to wash her from his memory, but the real enchantment is something else:

> Bianca nieve è il bel collo, e 'l petto latte;
> il collo è tondo, il petto colmo e largo:
> due pome acerbe, e pur d'avorio fatte,
> vengono e van come onda al primo margo,
> quando piacevole aura il mar combatte. (vii, 14)
> [Her lovely neck is white snow, her breast milk: her neck is
> round, her breast full and swelling: two fresh apples, made of
> ivory, come and go like a wave on the water's edge when a soft
> breeze strikes the sea.]

In this stylised literary setting Ariosto places the very real Ruggiero, waiting for Alcina to come to his bed, leaping to the door at every sound in an agony of impatience.

Yet for all its attractions this entirely sensual passion is shown to be vicious and dangerous, and it is set in an allegorical framework more elaborate than any other in the poem. Alcina and her sister Morgana are 'piene d'ogni vizio infame e brutto'; they have usurped the territory of their virtuous sister Logistilla; Alcina's beauty is a fraud and her love, being merely sensual, is capricious and volatile. And Ruggiero's love for her, which is also for the senses, Alcina having no other worthy qualities, is selfish and corrupt. When Melissa, in the guise of his guardian, Atlante, puts the ring of reason on his finger she tells him how this passion has made him a slave, and that he has forgotten all sense of honour and duty. Warned in this way of his danger, and equipped with the magic ring, he sees Alcina as she really is, abandons her and makes his way to the kingdom of her virtuous sister.

The central inspiration is the poet's image of a sensual love, treated with a psychological acumen which gives it a deep human truth. The traditional motif seems to relate to a local setting : the seduction of Ruggiero is achieved thanks to a party-game well known at the Estense court, and the diversions of the two lovers are all those of the court circle – parties, jousts, plays, dances, hunting, bathing, fishing. Yet at the same time the episode is removed from real life by the use of magic and allegorical machinery which blur the edges of this Renaissance love affair and turn it into a court dream. There is thus a strange blending of fantasy and reality, of seriousness and irony which explains, I think, the charm of this incident. The poet part creates, part inherits, this fantastic scene and puts into it a serious, deeply-felt human situation; but he smiles at himself for doing so, and at his readers for joining him. The ignorant crowd won't believe this, but he appeals to those who have travelled:

A voi so ben che non parrà menzogna ... (VII, 2)
[I know this won't seem untruthful to you.]

And Ruggiero's role as progenitor of the Estense line itself comes in for some gentle bantering, in Melissa's rebuke:

Questo è ben veramente alto principio
onde si può sperar che tu sia presto
a farti un Alessandro, un Iulio, un Scipio! (VII, 59)
[This is a truly fine beginning to let us hope that you will soon become an Alexander, a Julius, a Scipio!]

However, while Ruggiero is still pressing on through great difficulties to the kingdom of the virtuous Logistilla, Ariosto presents us with a new situation, the love of Olimpia and Bireno, which extends over the next three cantos (IX–XI) – part of the new material added in the 1532 edition. It is a further example of deception in love, but it goes further than either of the previous instances. Olimpia, who has lost everything for love of Bireno – territory, possessions, money, father, brothers – is eventually enabled to marry her lover, but after this long and romantic courtship she is abandoned, not quite at the altar, but on the honeymoon, by her bridegroom, who sails away with another young girl, leaving Olimpia on a desert island to lament her misfortune. Olimpia by her constancy should have earned a lifelong devotion in return, but she was deceived as so many have been by lovers' promises:

L'amante, per aver quel che desia,
senza guardar che Dio tutto ode e vede,
aviluppa promesse e giuramenti,
che tutti spargon poi per l'aria i venti. (x, 5)
[Lovers, to get what they want, not considering that God sees
and hears everything, weave promises and oaths which are later
all scattered by the winds.]

But Bireno, no less than Olimpia, has participated in this arduous
courtship. He has to fight the forces of the rival contestant for
Olimpia's hand and in so doing he is captured and imprisoned. We
have no reason to believe that he deliberately deceives Olimpia from
the first; he falls in love with her, fights for her and marries her. But
then his eye lights on the pretty 14-year-old daughter of his defeated
opponent and he cannot resist her. He too, then, is deceived about his
own love, which is a youthful passion, not to be trusted, as the poet
warns his lady readers:

Guardatevi da questi che sul fiore
de' lor begli anni il viso han sì polito;
che presto nasce in loro e presto muore,
quasi un foco di paglia, ogni appetito. (x, 7)
[Beware of those who in the flush of youth have such smooth
faces; their every desire is swiftly born and swiftly dies, like a
straw fire.]

And so a new passion quickly blazes up for his young protégée – and
the poet, no longer young himself, banteringly advises the ladies to
address themselves to rather more mature men! It is not just the lovers
themselves who are deceived by these straw-fires: Bireno's paternal
attentions to his pretty young ward are misjudged by everyone:

Oh sommo Dio, come i giudicii umani
spesso offuscati son da un nembo oscuro! (x, 15)
[Almighty God, how men's judgements are often obscured by a
dark cloud!]

There is a gulf, as we have been reminded before, between appearances and reality. Here is a fairytale romantic love that does not
end happily ever after.

Yet the Olimpia story is not allowed to end in disaster and as so
often in the *Furioso* the tragedy is averted, or turns into tragi-comedy.
Olimpia is captured and exposed on a rock as an offering to a sea-
monster, from which Orlando rescues her. Orlando's chivalrous
treatment of the beautiful naked girl is in marked contrast with
Ruggiero's attitude to the monster's previous victim, Angelica. When

Ruggiero makes off with his naked lady he at once forgets the lessons he should have learnt with Alcina and brings the hippogriff down to a quiet meadow in order to enjoy his prey. But in his impatience he so fumbles with the fastening of his armour that Angelica is allowed to escape. The insertion of the Olimpia episode allows Ariosto to underline Orlando's chivalrous chastity by contrast with Ruggiero's selfish lust – and it links in its two halves the theme of love and duty (here chivalrous honour) with that of deception in love.

It also enriches the poem with two superb scenes, first the abandonment of Olimpia, and then her exposure to the monster and rescue by Orlando. Both were favourite Renaissance motifs in literature and the visual arts – the exposure on the rock, in the Andromeda style (with Perseus flying in to the rescue), afforded painters a dramatic nude subject, and Ariosto's bravura description of the naked Olimpia fully justifies his repetition of a scene he has just shown us with Angelica. The abandonment of Olimpia, which recalls that of Dido, also reflects the Renaissance interest in the Ariadne legend and even a contemporary interpolation of a rival for Ariadne (a sister whom Theseus was to have offered to his son). Both these scenes are dramatic and moving, essentially serious in treatment but balanced delicately between the pathos of abandonment and then terror, and an ironical incredulity and conscious exaggeration. Olimpia is no helpless, tearful maid of romance but a truly militant lover, really a mate for Orlando, and Bireno might well have taken fright at her rigorous devotion. She had pretended to accept the husband forced on her by her victorious enemy, but had him killed by her servant with an axe-blow delivered from behind the wedding-bed, a blow which, she says,

... gli levò la vita e la parola:
io saltai presta, e gli segai la gola. (IX, 41)
[... deprived him of life and speech; I quickly leaped forward and cut his throat.]

The pathos of her abandonment is toned down by our memory of her ruthlessness, by the account of her indecorous groping in the bed for her missing husband, and by the stylised form of her despair in the wake of Ovid and Petrarch:

Or si ferma s'un sasso, e guarda il mare;
né men d'un vero sasso, un sasso pare. (X, 34)
[Now she stops on a rock and gazes at the sea, and seems no less a rock than the rock itself.]

– which serves the purpose of detaching the reader from too close an identification with Olimpia's situation. We have a long journey to

travel across the range of human passions and we must steel ourselves
to accept misfortune as part of our lot.

Olimpia does so after all, when she goes off with Oberto, the king
of Ibernia, whom she is to marry, thus bringing her romantic story
to a prudent conclusion; and in the following canto Ariosto reverts
to the two main love stories with which his poem had begun:
Orlando continues his pursuit of Angelica, Ruggiero his of Bradamante, both unsuccessfully. The latter relationship is to extend
throughout the poem and provide a suitable climax at the end, but
Orlando's madness cannot be long delayed, as a long train of adventures is to accompany Astolfo's recovery of Orlando's senses. The
next major love story (that of Isabella and Zerbino) fits logically into
this context. Orlando is closely involved in their adventures and witnesses one more example of female devotion to contrast immediately
after with his own 'faithless' Angelica : and the themes underlying the
new episode are particularly appropriate to Orlando's own situation.
Angelica, in his view is *his* lady, bound to him by her long acceptance
of his protection and devotion, by her encouragement and perhaps
her promises; her love for Medoro is an act not only of ingratitude
but of broken faith:

> la sua donna ingratissima l'ha ucciso :
> sì, mancando di fé, gli ha fatto guerra. (xxiii, *128*)
> [His most ungrateful lady has killed him, making war on him
> with her broken faith.]

– and the episode of Zerbino and Isabella, with the interconnected
story of Gabrina and Filandro, is closely concerned with this same
theme, the keeping of faith, with trust and friendship and their part
in the lover's conduct.

Isabella's and Zerbino's is a romantic love, beset by obstacles, but
true and loyal. They are of different beliefs (he is Christian, she
Moorish), and Isabella loses her possessions, and her family, in her
loyal devotion to her lover : Zerbino has to entrust to his friend
Odorico the task of bringing his bride home,

> sperando che la fede che nel resto
> sempre avea avuta, avesse ancora in questo. (xxiv, *16*)
> [hoping that the good faith he had always kept in all else, he
> would also keep in this.]

– but Odorico proves 'traditore' and 'disleal', tries to rape his charge
and is only prevented by the arrival of a band of brigands. The lovers
are finally united by Orlando's chivalrous efforts but their happy love
is broken by Zerbino's death and Isabella is left alone to face the perils

of the woods – confronted with the lustful Algerian king Rodomonte,
she persuades him to spare her in return for a magic potion which
she pretends will protect him from all wounds; then she makes him
test it on her own neck and dies with Zerbino's name on her lips – and
with Ariosto's blessing:

> Vattene in pace alla superna sede,
> e lascia all'altre esempio di tua fede. (XXIX, 27)
> [Depart in peace to your resting place above, and leave for others
> the example of your fidelity.]

Rodomonte is amazed, all the more so because he had had no intention of keeping his side of the agreement: 'pensa poi di non tenere il
patto' (XXIX, 18).

The insertion of Gabrina and Ermonide into this tale is interesting.
Both stories are from the same romance source but Ariosto pulls them
together in this one episode, clearly I think as interlocking tales of faith
and friendship. Zerbino, while still searching for Isabella, meets the old
hag Gabrina who had been Isabella's guardian in the brigands' cave.
By a foolish indiscretion he binds himself to protect her and having
given his word he must abide by it, as Ariosto insists in his *proemio*:

> La fede unqua non debbe esser corrotta,
> o data a un solo, o data insieme a mille. (XXI, 2)
> [Faith must never be broken, whether given to one person, or a
> thousand.]

The treacherous Gabrina enjoys the benefit of this, as she has previously unscrupulously taken advantage of Filandro, close friend of
her husband Argeo. Gabrina had tried to seduce Filandro but he had
remained faithful to his friend through every temptation, and only
when she treacherously exploits this faith (tricking him into killing
the man she pretends is attempting to betray her husband, but who is
really Argeo) is he forced into submitting to her. She then has Filandro murdered, and Filandro's brother, Ermonide, pursues her and
ultimately finds her in Zerbino's unwilling charge. The two branches
of the story thus come together: Zerbino is obliged by his plighted
word to defend the treacherous woman who betrays him too, but
with a fine sense of justice he hands her over as the charge of his former
friend Odorico, who had tried to betray him with Isabella, and has
now fallen into his hands. This is to be Odorico's punishment and he
has to swear to protect the old crone, who meets her deserts the next
day when Odorico hangs her

> contra ogni patto et ogni fede data (XXIV, 45)
> [in violation of his explicit word and faith.]

The two incidents are thus complementary examples of the conflict of love and friendship: love, or lust, leads Odorico to betray
Zerbino, but Filandro remains loyal to Argeo despite Gabrina's lustful pursuit. But Love upsets all their lives – Isabella's dramatic change
of fortune from rich and happy to poor and miserable is 'Colpa
d'Amor' (xiii, 4) and Odorico's treachery is similarly 'colpa d'Amor'
which has 'turned his senses upside down'. Yet through all this confusion of lust and treachery, the true love and loyal devotion of
Isabella and Zerbino shine out like a guiding light. Melodramatic and
contrived as the Filandro story seems, it serves to heighten the intensity of this one beautiful and moving passion, epitomised in Isabella's
tragic death, but even more in the scene where Orlando brings the
long-separated lovers together. Isabella does not at first recognise
Zerbino because of his armour, and he hesitates to approach her for
fear she has become Orlando's mistress; but when Zerbino removes
his helmet and Isabella recognises her lover she rushes towards him
in an impulse of unrestrained affection:

> Vede la donna il suo amatore in fronte,
> e di subito gaudio si scolora;
> poi torna come fiore umido suole
> dopo gran pioggia all'apparir del sole.
>
> E senza indugio e senza altro rispetto
> corre al suo caro amante, e il collo abbraccia;
> e non può trar parola fuor del petto,
> ma di lacrime il sen bagna e la faccia. (xxiii, 67–8)
>
> [The lady sees her lover's face and turns pale with sudden joy:
> then she changes as a flower that is wet with heavy rain does when
> the sun appears; and without delay or any restraint she runs to
> her dear lover and throws her arms round his neck; and she
> cannot utter a word, but tears run down her face and breast.]

It is a moment of unabashed sentimentality, free of irony and prepares
us for the pathetic scene between the lovers in the following canto as
Zerbino is dying. In his treatment of Isabella's death at the hands of
Rodomonte later, Ariosto seems anxious that this scene shall not
strain our credulity excessively, and he embroiders his source (the
early fifteenth-century *De re uxoria* of Francesco Barbaro) by sug-
gesting that Rodomonte may have been intoxicated ('vinto anco dal
vino forse', xxix, 25) when he let fall such a blow. The passage is
literary and stylised but the conscious Petrarchan, Biblical and classical
reminiscences serve not to diminish the pathos of Isabella's devotion

to Zerbino's memory, but rather to mute the tragic note; and the serious tone of the episode is underlined by the tribute to Isabella d'Este which follows.

The Isabella episode extends over a considerable portion of the middle of the poem (XIII–XXIX), and during this time other love adventures are progressing. The most notable is the idyll of Angelica and Medoro, which destroys Orlando's reason: it is significant that he should have witnessed Isabella's spontaneous outburst of affection for Zerbino immediately prior to his discovery of the evidence of Angelica's 'infidelity'. But three other 'amori' are introduced also before Orlando's madness, Doralice and Mandricardo, Orrigille and Martano, Norandino and Lucina, and we are led to wonder what is their significance here. Each is a colourful adventure story, rich in dramatic effect, and it may well be that no particular thematic significance is to be read into their grouping at this point in the poem. Two of them, the Norandino and Orrigille stories, continue and complete episodes begun but left unfinished by Boiardo, the link between these two being already established in the *Innamorato*.

Norandino's story (XVII) is clearly an *exemplum* of devoted love. His attachment to Lucina had been described by Boiardo who also exposed the lady to the orc, from which she was rescued by Gradasso and Mandricardo; the story was therefore virtually complete but for the reuniting of Lucina with Norandino, who was far away during her adventure. It was left to Ariosto to exploit the Homeric and Virgilian precedents by bringing Norandino on to the scene and making him scheme an escape for Lucina from the blind orc's cave in the guise of a goat (the plan fails: all escape except Lucina who is discovered by the orc, perhaps, we are told, in an ambiguous and characteristic enquiry into the female mind, because she was too squeamish to grease herself properly). Norandino thus exposes himself constantly to danger, remaining in the herd even after his companions have escaped in order to be near Lucina. And in due course his 'lunga pruova' is rewarded, when she escapes with Gradasso, as in the *Innamorato*.

Grifone hears this story when he comes to a tourney arranged to celebrate Norandino and Lucina's delivery (XVIII–XIX). He too is a devoted lover, but had been separated from Orrigille, who had conceived a sudden passion for him in the *Innamorato* but had been prevented from accompanying him to the tourney. Ariosto brings the two together, but, remembering Orrigille's treacherous character in the *Innamorato*, he equips her with a lover, Martano, whom she hastily passes off as her brother when she meets Grifone. Now Grifone's constancy is tested when the false brother proves a coward at the tourney and then schemes with Orrigille to make Grifone take the blame. Grifone, like Norandino, rises superior to all the ills endured because of love, but his devotion is wasted on a fickle and deceitful woman. Yet even after this transparent act of treachery he cannot bring himself to condemn Orrigille when she is brought for punishment with Martano.

The Doralice story is introduced in Canto xiv shortly before the Orrigille episode, although not concluded until Canto xxvii, and it provides a further example of the incomprehensibility of the female heart. Doralice's acceptance of a new escort, Mandricardo, thrust on her by chance in spite of her plighted troth to Rodomonte, is parallel in many ways to Orrigille's preference for Martano over Grifone. In each case the accepted lover and the superior soldier is rejected. Orrigille prefers the cowardly and treacherous Martano to the brave and loyal Grifone; Doralice prefers the far less impressive newcomer to her famous Rodomonte. It is a bad time for the leading knights – Orlando has only just been rejected for Medoro. Doralice's progressive acceptance of Mandricardo, who establishes his claim on her by force but consolidates it by shrewd and tactful wooing is described with masterly insight; and the account of Doralice's choice between them is a superb piece of story-telling. When the aggressive and blustering Rodomonte comes to claim his rightful bride, and Agramante allows Doralice to choose between them, both lovers are confident of their success – Rodomonte because no knight could have performed better on the battlefield or the tourney on her behalf, and the crowd think Mandricardo foolish to agree to the pact: but the latter relies on his recent experience with her 'mentre il sol stava sotterra' ('while the sun was down') and can ignore the poor odds given him by public opinion. And indeed, with downcast eyes, Doralice says she prefers Mandricardo – and Rodomonte, who had agreed to leave the choice to the lady, raves and wants to fight and settle the matter by the sword,

> e non l'arbitrio di femina lieve
> che sempre inchina a quel che men far deve. (xxvii, *108*)
> [and not by the judgement of a fickle woman who is always inclined to do the last thing she should.]

And he goes off cursing the fickleness of woman – until he chances on the lovely Isabella, weeping for her dead Zerbino, and promptly forgets Doralice in the pursuit of an even lovelier prize!

These three episodes dealing broadly with the theme of constancy and inconstancy in love are grouped around the central motif of

Orlando's madness, caused by the supreme 'inconstancy' of Angelica, and they provide greater depth to this key episode which alone might seem stark and even naïve. Orlando's desertion is no longer an isolated freak, but essentially a common experience shared with lesser mortals. It is a sad fact of life, and we may well begin to think that the facts of life *are* sad with all these desertions and betrayals, murders and suicides which love brings in its wake. The mood of the poem is beginning to grow more serious: Orlando's lost senses will involve an epic journey of recovery, and Ruggiero will have to leave his wild oats behind him in order to prove himself a worthy founder of the Estense family. It seems reasonable to suppose, therefore, that the Ricciardetto-Fiordispina story which follows after Orlando's madness was intended as a touch of light relief and had no ulterior motive. It is the only love story in the poem which is not equipped with some moralising comment from the author: it is on the contrary a totally amoral, if not immoral, bawdy tale. That Fiordispina should suddenly be caught in a great blaze of desire for the handsome knight who unfortunately turns out to be a woman, Bradamante, seems excusable; but that Ricciardetto, Bradamante's identical twin brother, should exploit this passion and pass himself off as his own sister on whom Love has performed a very fortunate anatomical miracle, seems unworthy of a noble Christian paladin. Ariosto (and we) have no qualms about the credibility of his story which is simply a very funny bawdy joke, but he cannot resist a word in defence of Ricciardetto who is conceived as having formerly admired the lovely Fiordispina from afar but restrained his desire. The new opportunity re-awakens his love, which is shown thus to be capable of infinite flexibility!

Echoes of this bawdy laughter carry down to the Fiammetta story three cantos later, but the Fiammetta episode is something more than a hilarious and bawdy farce: it is the first of four stories spread over the latter half of the poem dealing with jealous husbands and marital infidelity (Fiammetta, XXVIII, the Rocca di Tristano, XXXII, and Melissa, and Adonio, XLIII) and I should like to treat it together with them. It occurs early in the latter half, probably because the poet wished to maintain a more serious and dignified tone in the conclusion of the poem where the love stories abandon the light-hearted ironical note of the earlier cantos, appropriately in accordance with the increasingly epic note that characterises the rest of the material.

Apart from these four stories there are two significant love episodes occurring in this third quarter of the poem, both hinging on the interaction of passionate love and honour. Lidia's tale (xxxiv) is an inset *novella* which she herself relates to Astolfo from the flames of hell where she is punished: she describes the torment to which she submitted her lover in a black and white picture of constancy and cruelty. It has some interest psychologically as a story of the imperious and heartless beauty, and it comes appositely perhaps at the point where Astolfo is searching for the senses of Orlando, lost thanks to the cruelty of Angelica. It is one of the least successful episodes artistically proceeding in Lidia's words in a dull monochrome, and set awkwardly in an unhappy framework of Dante parody. But it is linked to the Marganorre story in showing how a violent and ill-directed passion can drive a man to abandon his honour: Alceste, at Lidia's bidding, shamelessly changes his allegiance and kills the king for whom he has been fighting.

The Marganorre episode, which was introduced only in the 1532 edition, is a serious and pondered study in this same aspect of the love sickness. There are two components; Marganorre's own story, the growth of his misogynism (discussed in the next chapter) and those of his two sons, each of whom met a violent death as a result of his passion for a married woman. Ariosto emphasises from the beginning that Cilandro and Tanacro were chivalrous, generous and well-mannered young men, both formally enrolled in a chivalrous order, noble and hospitable to their guests who always left their house charmed by the 'alta cortesia' of their hosts. Their misfortune was that they were 'distracted from the right path' by uncontrolled illicit passions: Cilandro attempts to seize a lady guest by force and is killed by her husband. Tanacro, who falls in love with another married woman, Drusilla, resolves not to risk his brother's fate and ambushes the lady and her husband, killing the latter. Drusilla pretends to accept his proposal of marriage but tricks him into drinking poison with her at their wedding and dies cursing him. The two men, because of love, are led to violate the basic principles of the code which has until now regulated their conduct: they assault their guests. Tanacro does so treacherously in an ambush:

Tosto s'estingue in lui, non pur si scema
quella virtù su che solea star sorto. (xxxvii, 54)
[Soon that virtue on which his conduct was based, not only wanes but is quite extinguished.]

We have seen the conflict of love and duty in Orlando and Ruggiero, of love and friendship in Odorico and Filandro; here is a deeper conflict between love and honour or self-respect.

These two tales are not, however, among the more memorable of
Ariosto's love stories. They are, as we have said, a late addition and
they share something of the general characteristics of most of
Ariosto's later work. The stories are contrived and mechanical, but
so are some of Ariosto's successful episodes. What is lacking here is
above all the slightly detached ironical note and that sensitive variation in tone in which even the more serious of the earlier tales are told:
the Marganorre stories are deadly serious, even grim; the material is
brutal, crude; Drusilla maims herself cruelly in her first attempt to
commit suicide, and Marganorre vents his spite on her dead body; he
later maltreats all women, forcing 'them to expose what Nature and
decency hides', and flays their men-folk. All this is treated without a
touch of irony: Ariosto is serious and earnest, he has no time to pause
and pace his narrative; he presses on in a forthright, generally prosaic
style, covering the action quickly and unceremoniously:

Andò la vecchia, e apparecchiò il veneno,
et acconciollo, e ritornò al palagio. (XXXVII, 67)
[The old woman went away, and got the poison ready, and
dressed it up and returned to the palace.]

Drusilla's dying words are lacking in any sensitivity; they are a harsh,
strident, nagging denunciation of Tanacro:

E che merti esser puon maggior di questi,
spenger sì brutte e abominose pesti? (XXXVII, 74)
[What greater merit could there be than this, to destroy such
ugly and abominable pests?]

A more serious, sad and even bitter note characterises several of the
later love stories and we are conscious of an over-all change or development of tone from the uncomplicated pursuit of Angelica in the
early cantos to the earnest and murky passions of the later ones. It is
noteworthy also that whereas the love stories in the first half of the
poem are largely concerned with bachelor knights and unwedded
maidens, or at least with wooing, falling in love and the first flush of
love or desire, the later cantos present us with a succession of married
women and especially men, no longer concerned to win their lovers
but preoccupied with keeping those incipient horns from their
worried heads. Apart from the married women of the Marganorre
episode, coveted by young lovers, and the newly wedded Olimpia,
abandoned by her husband (another late addition, be it noted) the
four late episodes to which we have referred (Fiammetta, the Rocca
di Tristano, Melissa, and Adonio) are all stories of married couples,
and are concerned with problems of marital fidelity.

The first of these is the extremely light-hearted and bawdy tale of
Fiammetta. It occurs (xxviii) well before the Marganorre episode
and arises directly out of the unhappy experience of Rodomonte,
jilted by Doralice. Rodomonte, brave and powerful fighter though
he may be, is emotionally and sexually immature and Ariosto is certainly not inclined to waste any tears over these starry-eyed idealists who expect women to conform to their visions. His picture
of the smarting Rodomonte is heavily ironical ('Di cocenti sospir
l'aria accendea' [with burning sighs he set the air ablaze], xxvii,
117, etc.), and the poet smilingly dissociates himself from Rodomonte's denunciation of the female sex: it is true that he himself
has not yet found a faithful woman but he hasn't stopped trying
(122–4).

The following canto, in which the inn-keeper tells a tale to prove to
Rodomonte that women are never chaste, is prefaced by an ironical
apology advising ladies to skip this canto – it is only included because
it is in the source. The story itself, in which the two most handsome
men in the world, Iocondo and Astolfo, find they are cuckolded by
their wives and set off to get their revenge, is a superb example of
Ariosto's narrative skill. It is beautifully paced, pausing where the
interest lies or where a mood can be created, rarely overstating or
straining for a laugh; and the atmosphere is delicately poised between
fantasy and reality. It is clearly a fairy story – the handsome king who
admires his own beauty in the mirror and is irritated to learn that
there is a man at least his equal, and the fantastic events (the queen and
the dwarf (an Ariostesque embroidery on his source), and Fiammetta's ingenious tricking of her two lovers) remove this from the
world of reality and tone down the attack on female virtue, as of
course does the ironical style. The old man at the end is right to protest that it proves nothing, being a fictitious tale, but the poet succeeds in convincing us that it is more than this. The realistic details
(Iocondo going back for his wife's parting gift which he had left
under his pillow) and the contemporary allusions (the reference to
Gian Francesco Valerio from whom the host got the story) bring it
back into the real world. As so often with Ariosto there is a marked
theatrical note, particularly in the final bedroom farce, where the
young lover's progress through the dark to the lady's bed has a
burlesque echo of Dante's hesitating steps up the hill of virtue!

Fa lunghi i passi, e sempre in quel di dietro
tutto si ferma, e l'altro par che muova
a guisa che di dar tema nel vetro. (xxviii, 63)

[He takes long steps and always pauses on his hindmost foot, and moves the other as though afraid of knocking into glass with it.]

Fiammetta's success in cuckolding her two lovers while they lay on either side of her provoked not an outburst of wounded pride but a roar of laughter from the two men who came to see their own situation and that of all married men in a more reasonable light. How foolish to lament over a universal misfortune! And they return satisfied to their wives. Fantastic the story may be but it suggests that a sense of humour and of moderation can prevent the scenes of miserable jealousy which recur so often in the poem. Wasn't Orlando indeed mad to lose his head over Angelica's very questionable virginity? And isn't Rodomonte a fool to rave about Doralice's lover? Astolfo's and Iocondo's return to their wives marks the triumph of common-sense over romantic idealism – and so did Olimpia's acceptance of another husband when she lost Bireno.

The 'rocca di Tristano' (XXXII) provides a variation on the motif of the jealous husband. Bradamante, herself needlessly jealous of Ruggiero and the Indian queen, Marfisa, comes to a castle where a chivalrous convention has been established by a jealous knight. Clodione's possessiveness and suspicion of his wife had caused him to bar all visitors from his house, and his discourtesy was denounced by Tristan who challenged, defeated and then punished him by playing on his jealousy – he had to spend the night outside his castle while his lady was inside, safely, with Tristan. Bradamante accepts Clodione's convention that hospitality in his castle is granted only on a competitive basis for the most valorous knights and the fairest ladies, and she wins a place for the night on both counts. It is a strange incident and Ariosto does not add very clearly here to his other statements on the theme of jealousy. He is more interested in another subject, the debate about women's rights, which we discuss later (pp. 116–20). The jealous husband is a figure of fun, but not so obviously a fool (Tristan after all was under a spell so as not to be attracted to other ladies, and the woods were full of less enchanted potential rivals). Ariosto doesn't pursue the theme here; Spenser did so in his version of Ariosto's story, showing how this possessiveness might positively induce a betrayal (*Faerie Queene*, III, ix).

Ariosto's more serious enquiry into marital fidelity is made in the two stories told to Rinaldo in Canto XLIII. In the first, Rinaldo refuses to try the magic cup which will reveal the truth about his wife's fidelity and hears of the misfortune that befell its owner,

who was persuaded by the witch Melissa to put his wife to the test by
disguising himself as her former lover and bribing her to accept
him; she does so and is so outraged when she discovers her husband's treachery that she leaves him and goes to live with the lover
(unlike the accommodating Procris in his source who accepted her
husband's apologies). In the second tale the jealous husband, Adonio,
whose wife's infidelity is forecast correctly by an astrologer, is exposed to similar temptation and caught out by his wife, and the two
are reconciled.

Two special motifs appear in these stories. One is the fragility of
marital fidelity in conflict with avarice. All the seductions are made
with the lure of wealth: money is the great corrupter – as the *proemio*
to the canto stresses – not merely of married women but of young
girls who sell themselves to rich old men : it is Avarice that

in un dì, senza amor (chi fia che 'l creda?)
a un vecchio, a un brutto, a un mostro le dà in preda (XLIII, 4)
[makes them a prey in a single day, and without love (who
would believe it?) to an old man, an ugly wretch, a monster.]

The other new concept is the danger of the prying search for truth in
love relationships. Both the husbands are sorely tormented by the
desire to know absolutely and unhesitatingly if their wives are faithful; they have no grounds for suspecting them, but their jealous
curiosity drives them on and leads to their downfall. Rinaldo refuses
to test his wife's fidelity, not because of his faith in her, but essentially
because of lack of faith:

Mia donna è donna, et ogni donna è molle (XLIII, 6)
[My wife is a woman, and all women are weak.]

His attitude is that there are some things about which it is best for us
not to have certain knowledge:

Potria poco giovare e nuocer molto;
che 'l tentar qualche volta Idio disdegna. (7)
[It might do little good and a lot of harm, for God sometimes
shows his scorn for those who tempt others.]

The appeal of certainty seems obvious in a world where appearances
and reality do not coincide, but Rinaldo is shown as clearly sensible in
not putting his illusions to the test.

The second story follows naturally from the first. The first tale
ends with Rinaldo's observation that not only women but men too
will do anything for gold, and he tells the husband :

Se te altretanto avesse ella tentato,
non so se tu più saldo fossi stato. (49)

[if she had tempted you as much, I don't know if you would have
been firmer.]
– in words that echo Cephalus' admission of this in the *Metamorphoses*.
The Adonio tale shows the temptation of the husband and his corruption. In both stories the mood is pro-feminist, anti-male. Two faithful
wives are exposed to unfair testing: their weakness is mitigated by
Ariosto's introduction of lovers (or in one case the appearance of a
lover) who have some claim on the wives' affections. The disguised
husband is the villain of the first story and gets his deserts when his
wife leaves him. He lacked trust. The husband's offence in the second
story is more serious than his wife's : she yielded to an admirable and
devoted lover and a very tempting bribe. Her husband was corrupted
by a far less attractive offer from an ugly Moor, and one of his own
sex (a further Ariostesque addition to his source).

Yet the latter tale, perhaps because of Ariosto's eagerness to con-
trive convincing proof of the injustice of male sexual attitudes, lacks
the finesse of many of the earlier tales, and even of the Melissa story
itself. There is much use of magic in both, but in the latter episode a
fairy disguised as a snake, a dog that produces gold, a Moor with his
enchanted castle, clash unhappily with the underlying psychological
truth of the human relationships, the topical allusions, the precise
geographical setting, and the autobiographical hints. In spite of the
happy conclusion the story leaves a bitter taste. There is little irony
here, or in the Melissa tale, which is told by a sad defeated man who
has lost his wife through his own foolishness.

Gone are the romps after Angelica! All this jousting for the ladies
and wooing beneath their balconies, this swearing of eternal love,
this raising of armies, these elopements and youthful passions end
with anxious husbands consulting fidelity-cups and astrologers. But
through all the infidelities and disappointments, a few happy pairs
have weathered the storms – the determined ones, or the lucky ones ?
The love of Ruggiero and Bradamante has stood the test and in the
end, despite the lady's fears and jealousy, and her lover's occasional
indiscretion, they come together and are legally married. The final
note is triumphant and in spite of the suffering the general tone is
cautiously optimistic. In several passages the poet speaks out positively
in praise of love: in spite of the dangers of betrayal or desertion a lady
should not renounce love: without a lover she is like an untrained
vine with no pole to support it (x, 9); and a man, however much he
may suffer, should not regret his passion provided it is for a worthy
lady (xvi, 2).

Ruggiero and Bradamante are not alone in enjoying the rewards of reciprocal love: Angelica and Medoro, Norandino and Lucina, Olimpia and Oberto, Ariodante and Ginevra, Ricciardetto and Fiordispina, survive their misfortunes. Love is a sickness, but not a universal disaster.

5. The Theme of Arms

Ariosto's declared themes in the *Furioso* are twofold: arms and love. The opening line of the poem,

Le donne, i cavallier, l'arme, gli amori,

was a corrected version of that in the first edition:

Di donne e cavallier li antiqui amori

– and the substitution of the line containing 'l'arme' represents at once a raising of the tone with the Virgilian reminiscence and an accentuation of the serious, military nature of the material. The war is mentioned at once in the following lines:

... che furo al tempo che passaro i Mori
d'Africa il mare, e in Francia nocquer tanto,
[of the time when the Moors crossed the sea from Africa and wrought such havoc in France.]

The mad love of Orlando follows in the second stanza.

The war was traditional: Andrea da Barberino in *I Reali di Francia* had sketched out its origins in the death of the king of Biserta, Barbante, at the hands of Carlomagno, and the first invasion of Calabria by Barbante's son Agolante, defeated by the Emperor at Aspromonte, where Agolante's son Troiano was killed by Orlando. The war left unfinished by Boiardo in the *Innamorato* was the war of revenge undertaken by Agramante, Troiano's son, who assembled a vast army of African forces, invaded France and carried the attack up to the walls of Paris. Ariosto carries on the war, but he goes back to the battle in the south of France where the Christian defeat puts Paris in danger; in so doing he gives the war a more central function in his poem; we are given the antecedents of the siege of Paris which is to be the main military action and which is not finally relieved until Canto XXXI. Thereafter Agramante's forces are driven successfully from France, Africa and the Mediterranean but the tension in the conflict has gone after the saving of Paris and the mopping-up operations barely hold our interest.

However, the outcome of the war is now made dependent on a series of duels between individual knights – first a single combat between Ruggiero and Rinaldo, then a triple contest between Orlando,

Brandimarte and Oliviero on the one side, and Gradasso, Agramante and Sobrino on the other, and here our interest revives. Throughout the poem a series of individual duels keep the arms in constant use; chivalrous challenges, punitive attacks on malefactors and local tyrants, dangerous assaults on enchanted monsters. The variety of encounter is great, and it is part of Ariosto's narrative skill that, while lacking the exuberant inventiveness of Boiardo, he avoids repetition in the fifty-odd 'passages of arms' scattered through the poem – which Boiardo does not. The duel itself is generally not much particularised (although there are some notable exceptions) but the contexts nearly always are – origins, motive, preliminary argument, oaths, outcome, reaction to victory or defeat. And when the poet has nothing really to say about an encounter and his interest is in its outcome, rather than its progress, as is often the case, he speeds up the narrative and concludes the affair very summarily: Bradamante despatches the three knights at the Rocca di Tristano in the space of four lines. The abruptness of the encounter elsewhere is a startling reminder of the fragility of human existence :

> che ne lo scontro il principe d'Anglante
> lo fe' cader per mezzo il cor passato. (xii, 75)
> [for in the clash the prince of Anglante brought him down
> pierced through the heart.]

– or the capriciousness of Fortune, as when Zerbino, in two lines, is unseated from his horse and suddenly no longer the mocker of Gabrina but her enforced guard (xx, 126).

What part then does the war play artistically in the poem? Is it really an accident (an enforced heritage from Boiardo) – or a structural convenience (a framework for the adventures of individuals) – or is it a source of poetic inspiration in its own right? I think that elements of all three of these explanations are relevant. Boiardo, while acknowledging the war as a primary theme of his poem nevertheless forgets it for long periods – and so apparently does Ariosto. But in continuing and completing the war Ariosto gives it a prominence and importance it lacked in the *Innamorato*. His poem begins with the defeat of the Christians in Canto i, and the last flicker of Saracen resistance is not extinguished until the death of Rodomonte in the last stanza. The siege of Paris occupies the centre of the stage for long periods between Cantos viii and xxxi and is treated with a seriousness, even a grandeur, appropriate to the epic: the troops are reviewed,

> Chi può contar l'escercito che mosso
> questo dì contra Carlo ha 'l re Agramante,

conterà ancora in su l'ombroso dosso
del silvoso Apennin tutte le piante; (xiv, *99*)
[He who could count the army which Agramante assembled
this day against Charles could count every tree on the shady
ridge of the woody Apennines.]

The individual leaders on each side are enumerated; the preparations
of besieged and besiegers are described; God beholds from on high
the Christian danger and sends off the Angel Michael in search of
Silence and Discord, the former to help reinforcements enter the city
safely, the latter to confuse the Saracen ranks. The seriousness of the
war is reinforced by its equation with the defence not merely of
France but of the Christian faith. In answer to Charles' prayers God
sends rain to save the Christians from the pagan attack, and the final
success is contrived by St John, who advises Astolfo how to create
and equip an army by miracle. Before the attack on Biserta Astolfo
and Rinaldo order a period of fasting and prayer. All of this is serious,
even if it fails to convince us that the war really matters; but the siege
itself, particularly the impetuous assault of Rodomonte and his scaling
the walls, is dramatic and exciting. In this and in a number of other
incidents – the duel of Rinaldo and Dardinello (xviii), the sortie of
Medoro and Cloridano (xviii–xix), the combat of Lipadusa (xli–
xlii), the final duel of Ruggiero and Rodomote (xlvi) – in each of
these scenes Ariosto has in mind a classical epic precedent and his
account takes on something of the serious epic tones of his original.
A whole series of impetuous and fearless classical figures echo behind
Ariosto's warriors – Anteus, Capaneus, Nembrotte, Hannibal, Attila
etc. Rodomonte's violent onslaught is based on Pyrrhus' assault on
Priam's palace in the *Aeneid* (ii, 470 ff.). When Rodomonte, alone
within the walls of Paris, is at last forced to retreat after a heroic
stand, he does so in the style of Ajax and of Turnus, in a passage of
clear epic pretensions:

Qual per le selve nomade o massile
cacciata va la generosa belva,
ch'ancor fuggendo mostra il cor gentile,
e minacciosa e lenta si rinselva;
tal Rodomonte, in nessun atto vile,
da strana circondato e fiera selva
d'aste e di spade e di volanti dardi,
si tira al fiume a passi lunghi e tardi. (xviii, *22*)

[As a courageous beast, hunted through the woods of Numidia
or Massilia, retreats still showing its noble heart, and withdraws

slow and threatening into the forest; so Rodomonte, cowardly never, encircled by a grim and strange forest of lances, swords and flying arrows, draws back to the river with slow and tardy steps.]

The sortie of Medoro and Cloridano is based on those of Euryalus and Nisus in the *Aeneid*, and on Statius's Opleo and Dymas, and has at its centre of inspiration the brave but helpless defence by the young Dymas of his prince's body. Medoro, surrounded by Zerbino's men, stands over his king's body with the same epic grandeur:

L'ha riposato al fin su l'erba, quando
regger nol puote, e gli va intorno errando ...
come orsa, che l'alpestre cacciatore
ne la pietrosa tana assalita abbia (xix, 6-7)

[He rests it at last on the grass when he can carry it no longer, and circles round it, like a bear attacked by the hunter in its rocky mountain lair.]

Fighting therefore is a serious matter and occasions much serious and moving poetry in the *Furioso*. There is no doubt that Ariosto intended his readers to take it seriously, and in fact they did so. The early commentators saw the poem not as an ironical or burlesque satire of the romances but as an improvement on these in the direction of increased gravity, polish and dignity – and in his co-ordination of the individual exploits with the central war Ariosto showed a serious attempt to give his poem something of the cohesion and the wide sweep of the classical epic. The individual knights, Christian and Saracen, are not oblivious to the course of the war, except when completely infatuated with amorous passion: and their love passions are in fact closely linked with the war itself. It is the war which has brought Angelica into the Christian camp, and has brought Ruggiero into Bradamante's life; and the course of the war is closely affected by the movements of the paladins. The arrival of Rinaldo with reinforcements from Britain, saves Paris from Rodomonte; the departure of Orlando and Rinaldo brings on the Christian danger, which is only relieved by the return of Rinaldo; and the final success of the Christians has to await the curing of Orlando who brings victory at Lipadusa.

Ariosto uses the war therefore with some degree of epic pretension: it helps to unify his narrative and it provides an occasion for genuinely poetical expression of the epic motifs of bravery, energy, ambition, patriotism, religious faith. Yet the tone is muted: for all its classical derivations (and they are many) the *Furioso* clearly does not belong with the *Iliad* or the *Aeneid*: it is not an epic, but a romance employing the material and the methods of its Italian predecessors. Ariosto steps only marginally out of the framework established in the romances and the *Innamorato* – partly because this was the framework he knew, and he was not an innovator or a radical; partly because his own mood, and that of his society was ill-attuned to the classical epic. And Trissino, Giraldi and others who attempted shortly after him to give Italy a true epic failed lamentably to do so.

In the *Furioso*, then, while treating a theme not inappropriate to epic and reminding us intermittently of its epic potentiality, the poet adopts the structure and the style of romance. The war is forgotten for long sections of the poem while the knights attend to their personal affairs. Rinaldo, when sent to Britain to recruit reinforcements, asks the first people he meets if there are any good adventures to be had in the vicinity (IV, 55). Bradamante firmly rejects the plea for help she has from Carlomagno in Canto II and continues her pursuit of Ruggiero. Both Orlando and Rinaldo desert Paris in its hour of need in order to pursue Angelica. But then how seriously need they take the war? Is it really a holy war in defence of the faith? Its origin is a personal spite ('l'ire e i giovenil furori') of Agramante against Orlando. The religious connotation of the war is significantly not mentioned in the opening stanzas explaining the poem's scope: and Rinaldo in exhorting British reinforcements before battle, suggests that their motives will be first to save their own king and the emperor, then to secure Paris and those under attack in France, and only finally to defend the Christian religion. Furthermore, the characterisation of the pagans as brave, loyal and mainly chivalrous fighters, not infrequently joining hands with the Christians in defence of the weak and oppressed, takes something of the partisan nature out of the war. The real hero, father of the Estense line, does not, after all, become a Christian until late in the poem.

The unwillingness of paladins and saracens to take the war seriously is paralleled by the poet's reluctance, even in the moments of greatest epic endeavour, to commit himself unreservedly to an epic tone. The troop-reviews, the siege, the earnest combats in the final cantos reveal in varying degrees of intensity an ironic use of hyperbole which reminds us that this is a literary fiction. Rodomonte's heroic assault on the walls of Paris, which draws so heavily on classical precedent for epic grandeur, is also given the wild exaggerations of the romances – he leaps thirty feet over the walls (XIV, *130*) and pulls down houses with his hands. At the height of the assault we find a drunken contemporary of Ariosto's, Antonio Magnanino (Moschino), flung into

the moat and lightening with his misfortune the grim seriousness of
the battle:

> Getta da' merli Andropono e Moschino
> giù ne la fossa: il primo è sacerdote;
> non adora il secondo altro che 'l vino,
> e le bigonce a un sorso n'ha già vuote.
> Come veneno e sangue viperino
> l'acque fuggia quanto fuggir si puote:
> or quivi muore; e quel che più l'annoia,
> e 'l sentir che ne l'acqua se ne muoia. (XIV, *124*)

[He hurls Andropono and Moschino down from the battle-
ments into the moat: the former is a priest, the latter worships
only wine and has emptied buckets with one gulp; water he
shunned with all his might as though it was poison or viper's
blood; now he dies in it, and what most annoys him is knowing
that it's water he is dying in.]

It is a characteristic touch, this bringing of his audience into his
narrative, this consciousness of his public for whom after all the
defence of Paris was unlikely to evoke much serious concern when
the sack of Rome was accepted so passively (XXXIII, 55).

Ariosto's comments on the great calamity of his age are remarkably
calm, but it is significant that it finds a place in his poem together with
the invasions of the French and the great battles of his day, Agnadello,
Novara, Fornovo, Pavia, Ravenna. Indeed the poet's account of the
war between Carlomagno and Agramante is provided with a frequent commentary on the contemporary Italian military scene. The
situation of the Saracens in France who, despite their successes, had
suffered heavy losses, is deliberately compared to the recent battle of
Ravenna where so many French captains were killed (XIV, 2). Many
such allusions are acts of deference to Alfonso and recent Ferrarese
successes – the capture of Bastia by the Ferrarese from the Spanish
garrison in January 1512, the battle of Ravenna (April 1512) where
an adroit move of the Ferrarese artillery played an important part in
the outcome of the battle (II, 55). There are five separate references to
the battle of Polesella (1509) in which a Venetian fleet in the Po was
routed by a numerically inferior Ferrarese force and fifteen Venetian
galleys captured. The link here, as elsewhere, between the romance
fiction and contemporary reality is effected by a casual, conversational style in which the Ferrarese audience is reminded of their recent
experience. In describing the defeat of Agramante's fleet by the forces
of Astolfo and Orlando, the poet refers to the recent battle on the Po:

he himself was not present, having been sent for help to Julius II, but anyone who was there will understand the situation of the Saracens (XL, 5).

The contemporary military allusions, however, are not exclusively flattering reminders of Estense brilliance. War is a bloody and ugly business and was particularly so in Italy in the early sixteenth century with the increased frequency and scale of fighting, and there are moments in the poem when we are reminded of its brutality, sometimes implicitly in a particularly forthright description, free of hyperbole or irony – Carlomagno finding his men in disorder, cut up by a Saracen attack:

> e vede a molti il viso o il petto fesso,
> ad altri insanguinare o il capo o il gozzo,
> alcun tornar con mano o braccio mozzo. –
> Giunge più inanzi, e ne ritrova molti
> giacere in terra, anzi in vermiglio lago
> nel proprio sangue orribilmente involti. (XXVII, 20-21)

[he sees many with their faces or chests split open, some with their head or throat bleeding, some coming back with a hand or arm lopped off. He goes on and finds many lying on the ground, or horribly immersed in a red pool of their own blood.]

In the war everyone suffers, simple inhabitants of towns and farms, nuns in their convents, and the soldiers, capable of rape and plunder, but themselves often at the mercy of their brutal commanders. Agramante has the gates of the besieged Arles shut and the bridges over the Rhône cut, and so the inhabitants have no escape:

> ... Ah sfortunata plebe,
> che dove del tiranno utile appare,
> sempro è in conto di pecore e di zebe! (XXXIX, 71)

[Unfortunate people, always treated like sheep or goats when it suits the tyrant's book.]

The campaign thus throws light on the problems of leadership: Rinaldo who (like Alfonso) is secure in the affection of his men (XXXI, 57; XV, 2) contrasts with Rodomonte who drives his soldiers into the ditch where they are burned to death (XV, 3), and with Agramante the tyrant who is secretly hated but remains ignorant of his men's attitudes from which he is insulated by flatterers:

> ... non vede
> mai visi se non finti, e mai non ode
> se non adulazion, menzogne e frode. (XXXIX, 76)

[he sees only false faces, and hears only flattery, lies and fraud.]

Elsewhere the poet explicitly condemns the brutality of modern military manners, particularly the sacking of towns and the treatment of prisoners. There is little pulling of punches here; all come in for their share of criticism, the French who need new captains to punish the troops which raped and plundered the victims of Ravenna; the Spanish and Jewish mercenaries who killed the defeated governor of Bastia; the Ferrarese who in their turn slaughtered the Spanish garrison there; and the Venetian mercenaries who executed the young Ercole Cantelmo, captured at the siege of Padua in November 1509. The latter in particular occasions an outburst of indignation from the poet comparing the 'cortesia' and 'gentilezza' of ancient times with the cruelty of the present:

> Schiavon crudele, onde hai tu il modo appreso
> de la milizia? In qual Scizia s'intende
> ch'uccider si debba un, poi che gli è preso,
> che rende l'arme, e più non si difende? (xxxvi, 8)
>
> [Cruel Schiavon [Venetian mercenary], where did you learn your way of fighting? In what Scythia [barbarous land] does one learn to kill a captive, who has surrendered his arms and cannot defend himself?]

To the horrors of war modern military techniques have contributed, in the poet's view – notably the invention of firearms. His protest is not merely a digression from his romance theme, but is worked into the texture of the poem with a good deal of artifice: in the war waged by Olimpia's suitor and his father, the King of Frisa, against his own father's forces, whom Orlando helps, the wicked Cimosco uses the arquebus first to destroy Olimpia's forces, then in an act of treachery and cowardice to ambush the gallant Orlando. He fails and Orlando captures the accursed weapon and hurls it in the sea. There it lay for many years, Ariosto tells us, until the devil who invented it, revealed its presence only recently to a necromancer; and the poet proceeds to curse the 'arcobugio' in a passage that has become famous:

> Come trovasti, o scelerata e brutta
> invenzion, mai loco in uman core?
> Per te la militar gloria è distrutta,
> per te il mestier de l'arme è senza onore;
> per te è il valore e la virtù ridutta,
> che spesso par del buono il rio migliore. (xi, 26)
>
> [O ugly, cursed invention, however did you find a place in the heart of man? Because of you military glory has been destroyed,

because of you the profession of arms is dishonoured; because
of you valour and virtue have declined, and the bad often seem
better than the good.]

Ariosto's objection – part of the Renaissance 'chorus of disapproval
which accompanied the use of guns' (J. R. Hale) – would seem to be
more emotional than rational; his outburst would be relevant almost
as well to all 'armi da tiro' (missile weapons) (the bow in particular),
which usurp the role of 'armi bianche' – weapons of close combat.
Olimpia complains how her father was killed 'di lontan' ('from a
distance'); and Ferrarese strength was based essentially on its artillery,
perhaps the best in Europe, which had earned Alfonso his success
at Ravenna, so highly lauded elsewhere in the poem! – and didn't
Titian paint Alfonso with his hand resting on the muzzle of a cannon?
New missile weapons have provoked criticism from the time when
the King of Sparta, seeing the first catapult, cried 'This is the tomb of
bravery.' What a headache the poet might have had a few years later
when missile weapons were used on a large scale by *cavalry* – as in
Roman times! However, the 'archibugio' certainly appears very
appositely in his poem at this time, when it had just begun to prove
its worth on the battlefields of Italy, and the ability of some feeble
footsoldier, by releasing a spring (IX, *29*), to bring to the ground a
noble knight and his superb mount, seemed indeed to drive the last
nail into the coffin of chivalry. Cimosco's shot at Orlando strikes us
as a brilliant imaginative dramatisation of a moment in history when
men stood, or felt that they stood, on the brink of a precipice.

Much of the fighting in the *Furioso*, however, is quite unrelated to
the war; the 'audaci imprese' of the knights are the traditional chivalrous encounters of the romances, chivalrous challenges issued and
accepted in order to prove one's worth or to rescue a damsel in distress
or to amend some local injustice. Chivalrous ideals and practices thus
loom largely in the poem and it is no easy matter to assess their
over-all significance and effect. Ariosto's attitude towards medieval
chivalry is complex: he is dealing of course with a code of conduct
largely antiquated. Not only is the knight-errant an anachronism
in sixteenth-century Italy, the very foundations of chivalry had
crumbled long ago as a result of social, economic and military change.
Already in the fourteenth century Sacchetti had complained that
chivalry was dead, destroyed by the raising to knighthood of
mechanics, artisans and sedentary lawyers. In a military sense the
knight on horseback suffered a series of set-backs from this time on-
wards: while in the twelfth and thirteenth centuries the heavy feudal

cavalry was master of the battlefields of Europe, its supremacy was
soon challenged by the cross-bow which could pierce light armour
at a distance and later by gunpowder which could penetrate the
heavier, and much costlier, armour the cavalry were forced to develop. And in the fifteenth century the Swiss infantry showed how
the well-trained infantry formation equipped with pikes could master
cavalry, and henceforth the knight on horseback played only a subordinate role to the infantry, artillery and musketeers. With the increased expense of equipment, and the greater continuity of military
operations, fewer and fewer nobles had been prepared or able to
assume the responsibilities of knighthood, as Villani observed in the
fourteenth century, noting a serious decline in the numbers of 'cavalieri di corredo' (élite cavalry). The serious business of fighting was entrusted therefore to the professional captain, and the knights became
courtiers, wielding the pen rather than the sword, practising only the
externals of chivalry, the title, dress and ceremony. The courts adopt
the chivalrous tourneys and jousts as normal accompaniments to
social and political occasions, but these are increasingly hedged in by
rules and become progressively elaborate games and pageants, accompanied by dancing and feasting, and remote from their original
military connotations. Outdated as much of the chivalrous apparatus
seemed, however, it continued to accompany Renaissance man – he
lived with it, as has been aptly suggested, just as he lived with the
architecture of several centuries past. Even on the battlefield the
influence of 'outdated' chivalrous conventions continued to be felt
(– as when an officer at Pavia fought with his left arm bare for love of
his lady, or Francis I proposed a single combat to resolve his dispute
with Charles V). Yet medieval chivalry implied something more than
a set of military practices and social conventions: it embodied a code
of conduct based on certain beliefs which were not so easily de-
molished by pikes and gunpowder: beliefs in certain virtues such as
courtesy, generosity, loyalty and trust. With the decline in the role
and status of the knight went a decline in the acceptance of chivalrous
ideals which was noted all over Europe. Boccaccio had satirised the
carpet-knights of his time, and the Paduan author of the *Entrée
d'Espagne* wrote, he said

> por vouloir castoier li coarz e li van
> e fer an cortoisie retourner les vilains.

Caxton in the 1480s asked 'Oh ye knights of England, where is the
custom and usage of noble chivalry that was used in those days?', and
he published Malory's *Morte Arthure* with the specific aim that 'noble

men may see and learn the noble acts of chivalry'. Yet while in
England men such as Caxton and Stephen Hawes were calling for
a revival of chivalric culture, few Italians by this time could seriously believe that this was a possible solution to their misfortunes. To
many these qualities seemed hopelessly inappropriate to the times:
to Machiavelli, for example, who wastes no time trying to revive
cavalry or chivalry but asserted that the 'verità effettuale' (or real
truth of the matter) was that generosity and trustworthiness might
turn out not to be virtues at all in sixteenth-century Italy. The
humanists brought another culture and laughed, many of them at the
naïve credulity of the masses who worshipped the fantastic heroes of
the romances.

The chivalrous ideals therefore inspired a complex set of reactions
among Renaissance readers, varying considerably according to their
personal experience, native culture and their political and social situation, and the chivalrous romance in the sixteenth century reflects this
complexity. For if medieval chivalry was a waning force throughout
Europe, chivalrous literature continued to enjoy widespread favour.
The chivalrous romances, remote as they seemed from the experience
of sixteenth-century Italy, retained a great hold on the imagination of
the Italians; first Boiardo's and then Ariosto's poem enjoyed an
enormous success and the *Furioso* continued to be read throughout
the Cinquecento. What is the explanation? The literature of escape?
A.B.Ferguson, examining the vogue of chivalrous literature in
England in the fifteenth and sixteenth centuries, suggests simply that
literature here parts company with reality. 'The ideals and ideas connected with knighthood, once given a fictitious substance in the
chronicles and in romances of chivalry and a substance more accurately to be described as meretricious in the pageantry of the court,
could maintain a life of their own largely independent of the facts of
actual life.' I am sure that this is true, but it needs perhaps to be supplemented by another view, that is that long after the facts of life had
relegated chivalry into literature there remained in people's minds
and imaginations a nostalgia for the 'golden age' of chivalry, which
continued to influence conduct; parallel perhaps in some way to the
appeal of another past age, that of the ancient Romans, which the
Italians were for ever recalling in despair.

All of these factors I think help to explain the function of chivalry
in Ariosto's poem, which is not merely a butt for his facetious wit.
Ariosto chose to adopt the material of the earlier chivalrous romances,
with its knights-errant and ladies, its adventures and enchantments,

because they continued to appeal seriously to his imagination, and it would be highly exaggerated to say that such material is constantly represented ironically. On the contrary, chivalrous pursuits are depicted extensively in the same spirit of frank enjoyment and admiration which we find in his predecessor Boiardo's poem. Ariosto's paladins with their bravery and skill are not mere comic anachronisms; we admire their strength and their courage; but more significantly we are made to respect their courtesy and generosity which are the true sign of their essential humanity : repeatedly they seek for fair conditions of fighting; they will not strike an opponent's horse; they remove their helmet, get down from their horse, etc., if their opponent is at a disadvantage ; having given their word, they keep it : even the undisciplined Saracen Rodomonte fulfils his vow not to wear arms for a year, a month and a day because he has been defeated by a woman; they are generous to defeated opponents; Astolfo cannot bring himself to kill Caligorante who is caught in a net; Orlando, passing through the Saracen camp at night, will not kill the sleeping soldiers.

In these and many other similar instances Ariosto repeats the motifs and the spirit of the 'cavalieri antiqui', sometimes ironically, but often sincerely, even labouring his point as though didactically. The seriousness of this sympathetic portrayal of chivalry is particularly apparent in the last cantos of the poem, added for the final edition, where Ruggiero, the antecedent of the Estense family, is given added stature by his meticulous observance of the chivalrous code in fighting for his rival in love to whom he owes a debt of gratitude. Courtesy, generosity, trustworthiness, sense of honour and loyalty to one's lord – all these are shown us as clearly admirable qualities in the *Furioso*. They create around the action of the poem a sort of moral climate, poetical and appealing, recalling the times of 'li antiqui amori'.

One aspect in particular of the chivalrous passage of arms which is particularly evocative for Ariosto is the atmosphere of the 'show': the fine clothes, beautiful ladies, bedecked horses; the processions, the assembling of the spectators, the taking of positions, the sounding of trumpets – the atmosphere of a Renaissance court, in fact when a tourney was arranged for a visiting diplomat :

> Di trombe, di tambur, di suon de corni
> il popul risonar fa cielo e terra, ... (xx, *83*)
> [The people make heaven and earth resound with trumpets,
> drums and the ring of horns.]
> Le vaghe donne gettano dai palchi

sopra i giostranti fior vermigli e gialli,
mentre essi fanno a suon degli oricalchi
levare assalti et aggirar cavalli. (XVII, *81*)
[From their boxes the lovely ladies throw down red and yellow
flowers to the jousters, and they to the sound of orichalcs make
their horses leap and wheel.]

There is a keen sense of the drama of the occasion, of an audience
reacting to the events enacted before them – as when they mock the
cowardly Martano, or are taken aback by the dashing Grifone:

Il batter de le mani, il grido intorno
se gli levò del populazzo tutto, (XVII, *91*)
Ognun maravigliando in piè si leva;
che 'l contrario di ciò tutto attendeva. (XVII, *93*)
[A clapping and shouting broke out all around him from the
mob . . . Everyone jumps to his feet in surprise because they
expected quite the opposite.]

Ariosto knew of course that chivalry was an anachronism and that
the chivalrous romances had lost contact with reality: they had
appealed largely to a naïve and uncultured public who seemed to
swallow with extraordinary credulity the wildest and most fanciful
exaggerations. Ariosto repeats many of the fantastic achievements of
the paladins with an amused satire of the exaggerations of the 'can-
terini' and the credulity of their audiences:

Il cavallier d'Anglante, ove più spesse
vide le genti e l'arme, abbassò l'asta;
et uno in quella e poscia un altro messe,
e un altro e un altro, che sembràr di pasta;
e fin a sei ve n'infilzò, e li resse
tutti una lancia: e perch'ella non basta
a più capir, lasciò il settimo fuore
ferito sì, che di quel colpo muore. (IX, *68*)
[The Knight of Anglante lowered his lance to where he saw the
densest throng of people and arms; and on that lance he caught
up first one then another, and another and another as though
they were made of dough; as many as six he ran through and he
lifted them all on one lance; and because there isn't room for any
more, he left the seventh one off, though he was so wounded
that he died from the blow.]

A single knight will take on an army in this world with every chance
of success; Orlando frequently does this, and in case you doubt it,
says Ariosto ironically, we have Turpin's authority for it (XXIII, *62*).

It is thus the chivalrous romance which is often the butt of Ariosto's humour, not the knight-errant himself, although he too gets some of the backwash – Orlando has to fight the vast sea-monster which demands a human victim daily; he rows his boat into its mouth, and secures its jaws open with his anchor. It is a superb burlesque of the chivalrous romance in which the hero resembles the Mickey Mouse of an animated cartoon, triumphant over some gigantic beast:

> Da un amo all'altro l'àncora è tanto alta,
> che non v'arriva Orlando, se non salta. (xi, *38*)
> [From one barb to the other the anchor is so high that Orlando can't reach it without jumping.]

– and then making a hasty escape

> Sentendo l'acqua il cavallier di Francia,
> che troppo abonda, a nuoto fuor ne viene. (xi, *40*)
> [The knight of France, finding the water too plentiful, comes swimming out.]

The magic of the romances is a particular source of amusement to Ariosto who dutifully equips his knights with all the traditional enchantments – magic swords, lances, shields, helmets, invulnerable skin, enchanted horses. How can they ever fail? And how does one reconcile their inordinate bravery, strength and skill with this eternal reliance on supernatural aids? Ariosto never makes this point explicitly, but he presents us for example with two paragons of might – Ferraù who is only vulnerable in his navel, and Orlando on the soles of his feet:

> Duro era il resto lor più che diamante
> (se la fama dal ver non si diparte);
> e l'uno e l'altro andò, più per ornato
> che per bisogno, alle sue imprese armato. (xii, *49*)
> [The rest of them was as hard as diamond (if repute coincides with truth) and both of them went into battle armed for the sake of appearance rather than because they needed to.]

Their duel promises to be something extraordinary, or as we read between the lines, a real nonsense!

> Non eran in tutto 'l mondo un altro paro
> che più di questo avessi ad accopiarsi:
> pari eran di vigor, pari d'ardire;
> né l'un né l'altro si potea ferire (xii, *47*)
> [There was not in the whole world another couple that could be matched like these: equal in strength, and equal in daring, and neither could wound the other.]

The knights' confusion over the use of their magic weapons is often
apparent: Ruggiero has a magic shield he is reluctant to use on
Alcina's island 'because he wanted to use virtue and not fraud' but he
does in fact use it to save Angelica from the sea-monster and later
when it accidentally becomes uncovered and enables him to defeat
Sansonetto he is covered in shame and hurls it into the pool, to the
accompaniment of Ariosto's mock-serious applause (xxii, 93). It is
akin to Orlando's throwing the accursed 'archibugio' in the sea (ix,
90) for what is essentially the same reason, the threat it poses to 'la
militar gloria'. The magic weapons are thus looked at ironically
through the eyes of the smiling poet who plays many variations on
this fruitful theme, all essentially dependent on the conscious rap-
prochement of the fantasy of the romances with the reality of the
modern world. How can feeble mortals handle these fantastic inventions? – flying horses that fly when you don't want them to, magic
weapons which bring you success you hadn't expected, the magic
horn which Astolfo proudly uses to frighten the hostile Amazon
women but which drives friends as well as foe away in panic as soon
as he blows it?

A further, perhaps more searching, variant on the chivalrous theme
is provided by the continual conflict between chivalrous duty and
self-interest. The knights' long training and experience in the bearing of arms in the service of others has not provided them with the
discipline to banish their envy, jealousy and lust. Frequently their
motives are sadly mixed as they wield their power in apparently
purely chivalrous causes: Ruggiero bravely rescues Angelica from
the orc, only to try to ravish her himself; Grifone who has been
thoroughly betrayed by his lady Orrigille with Martano, generously
offers to pardon them both because, says Ariosto in parenthesis, he
can't very well pardon just Orrigille (xviii, 92). Most effective of all
these dilemmas where men are caught between the cross-fire of duty
and desire is the famous scene at the beginning of the poem and which
sets the tone for so much of what is to follow. Rinaldo and the pagan
Ferraù are fighting for Angelica and she seizes the opportunity
afforded by their preoccupation with their duel to make her escape
on Rinaldo's horse. They suddenly notice her disappearance and stop
to consider their reaction: why fight for a prize you have lost?
Rinaldo proposes a truce in order to pursue and recapture Angelica
and the pagan agrees: but Rinaldo has lost his horse and Ferraù
generously offers him a ride on his! and off they go together:

   Oh gran bontà de' cavallieri antiqui!

Eran rivali, eran di fé diversi,
e si sentian degli aspri colpi iniqui
per tutta la persona anco dolersi;
e pur per selve oscure e calli obliqui
insieme van senza sospetto aversi. (I, 22)
[Oh the great goodness of the knights of old! They were rivals,
of different faiths, and they could still feel their whole bodies
aching from the harsh and cruel blows they had given each
other, and yet through dark woods and tortuous paths they ride
together without suspicion.]

The chivalrous code therefore does not provide a convincing set
of answers to the problems of living – indeed it seems to raise as many
problems as it solves, and we are left in no doubt that these simple
old-fashioned ideals could never really work in a world of flesh-and-
blood human beings. The nostalgia for a golden age of chivalry is
overlaid by an awareness of the complexity of human nature. For
example, there is an equation in the chivalrous world between
bravery and beauty: only the brave deserve the fair, the top men get
the prettiest girls. The knight who has bludgeoned his opponent into
submission will naturally make off with his opponent's lady, unless
his own is more beautiful. This naïve romantic world where no-one
stops to consult the lady and rarely to enquire as to the defeated
knight's reaction is explored a little further by Ariosto. *Do* the ladies
mechanically fall for the victorious heavy-weights? Not the most
desirable one of them all, Angelica, who prefers the humble, unknown Moorish soldier, Medoro, to Orlando and Rinaldo and all the
finest knights in Christendom; nor does Rodomonte's superior claims
in terms of long devotion and overwhelming strength persuade Doralice to prefer him to Mandricardo (XXVII, *107*). Indeed some ladies
are so perverse as to prefer the coward: Orrigille's lover is the miserable Martano who flees at the sight of danger in the tourney, and for
him she betrays the brave, successful, courteous Grifone (XVII, *107*).
On two occasions the ladies, in a charmingly lady-like way, intervene
to stop the senseless slaughter of their obstinate men-folk. Fiordiligi
implores the farouche Rodomonte to drag her half-drowned lover
out of the water where he is imprisoned under his fallen horse (XXXI,
73); and when Isabella sees her beloved Zerbino struggling for his
life against Mandricardo, she takes Mandricardo's lady, Doralice, to
one side and begs her to stop the fight, and Doralice, no less anxious
for *her* lover, readily does so (XXIV, *72*).

The chivalrous formulae are not only inadequate in that they fail to take account of the human emotions and interests which are coerced within them. They fail, with their over-elaborate conventions and rigid rules, to fit the harsh realities of life; and the knights in faithfully fulfilling the code they are sworn to, may commit blunders and injustices. Ariosto does not generally question the shrewdness of the paladins in espousing the right causes, but in one episode he burlesques the chivalrous paraphernalia with a wit worthy of Cervantes. Gabrina is an ugly old hag used by a gang of rogues to guard Isabella, whom they have captured; when Orlando frees Isabella the hag manages to attach herself to Marfisa for protection: she is fearful for her life because of her wicked past, having been responsible for the death of her husband and her lover; she has been treacherous and malicious, cunning and lustful and she is the antithesis of the type of lady served by 'li cavalieri antiqui'. But Marfisa who does not know this and to whom Gabrina is a complete stranger, accepts her chivalrous obligation to protect the old woman. When therefore a haughty young lady laughs at Gabrina, Marfisa avenges the affront and proves that the old hag is more beautiful than the lady by the simple means of knocking down her defender, Pinabello. She then decks out Gabrina in the lady's fine clothes and proceeds on her way. They meet Zerbino who cannot resist laughing at the hag and mocking Marfisa. Marfisa is now committed by the chivalrous convention to declare black is white and prove it to Zerbino:

... Mia donna è bella,
per Dio, via più che tu non sei cortese; (xx, *121*)
[My lady is more beautiful, by God, than you are courteous.]
But Zerbino has no wish to fight Marfisa for the old woman:
O brutta o bella sia, restisi teco:
non vo' partir tanta amicizia vostra.
Ben vi sète accoppiati: io giurerei,
com'ella è bella, tu gagliardo sei. (xx, *123*)
[Whether she's ugly or beautiful you can keep her: I don't want to break up your fine friendship. You're a good pair: I'll bet that you're as valiant as she is beautiful.]
– and after a brief dialogue they agree to duel but on special terms – the loser shall have to accompany the hag. So the chivalrous code is parodied: Zerbino is defeated and goes off cursing his misfortune. The hag, finding Zerbino is Isabella's lover, tortures him with false tales of her infidelity to him, and far from showing chivalrous gallantry to her he is soon threatening to cut her throat. However, he is tied to his chivalrous oath and even finds himself obliged to unhorse

Ermonide, brother of the man Gabrina has betrayed. When he hears
Ermonide's story, Zerbino's lame apologies underline the whole non-
sensical futility of the chivalrous code:

Zerbin col cavallier fece sua scusa
che gl'increscea d'averli fatto offesa;
ma, come pur tra cavallieri s'usa,
colei che venìa seco avea difesa:
ch'altrimente sua fé saria confusa; (xxi, 68)

[Zerbino made his excuses to the knight saying that he was sorry
to have wronged him, but as is the custom among knights he
had defended the lady who was with him: otherwise his reputation would have been tarnished.]

Eventually Zerbino gets rid of Gabrina by passing her on to his false
friend, Odorico, who within a day breaks his promise and hangs her
from an elm tree. (xxiv, 45)

The problem here is that the generous, courteous, high-souled
knights have to live in a world of cunning, hypocritical and treacherous rogues and their rigid ideals are not fitted to meet them.
(Machiavelli's discussion of the prince's moral obligations faces precisely this problem.) The dilemma is often acute in the duel where
one's opponent doesn't respect the rules: the Saracens often don't
and the Christians are sorely tried to keep their chivalrous standards:
Bradamante is determined not to abate her principles:

... Tua villania
non vo' che men cortese far mi possa, (xxxv, 70)

[I will not let your rudeness make me any less courteous.]

– but when her jealousy is aroused she and Marfisa forget their
dignity, and punch and kick each other (xxxvi, 50). Ruggiero
although attacked when on foot by Rodomonte from his horse, will
not strike his opponent's mount (xlvi, 126); but Sacripante's brutality in attacking Rinaldo from the latter's horse, seems to free Rinaldo
of any constraints: when the enamoured knights hear that Angelica
has gone off to Paris with Orlando Rinaldo seizes his horse and makes
off without further ado:

E dove aspetta il suo Baiardo, passa,
e sopra vi si lancia, e via galoppa,
né al cavallier, ch'a piè nel bosco lassa,
pur dice a Dio, non che lo 'nviti in groppa. (ii, 19)

[And he goes to where Baiardo is waiting, jumps on and gallops
away, and he doesn't even say goodbye to the knight he is
leaving in the woods, let alone offer him a lift.]

– whereas Ferraù had previously taken his Christian opponent with him. So the reaction of knights and others to the chivalrous code becomes a paradigm for a much wider social problem: the interaction of principles and self-interest, of means and ends, of ideals and reality. Within the fictitious and artificial community of the chivalrous romance and covered with the glow of that 'golden age' is a great complex of human dilemmas, dilemmas for Ariosto's own society and which others of his contemporaries found equally disturbing – Castiglione, for example, wondering how relevant his ideal courtier was in an Italy torn by foreign invasions.

The theme of arms therefore, while motivating some moving poetry of bravery, loyalty and chivalry in its widest sense, is integrated into the contemporary scene of the Renaissance court and acquires a new subtlety. It helps to convey some of Ariosto's deeply felt beliefs on the relationships between human beings. But it is interesting to note further how it is integrated artistically into the structure of the poem. Fighting is of interest both because it shows us something about the way people treat each other, but also because it changes people's lives – it may of course end their lives, but it may also change the course of their life, their conduct, their possessions, their attitudes. The encounter between two knights or two bands of knights, which recurs constantly in the earlier romances, is often there an isolated combat, a test of strength, skills and bravery, undertaken essentially for the knight's honour and self-satisfaction, in which his opponents lack individuality and his protégés remain colourless pawns. The interest, even in Boiardo, to whom these comments are less apt than to his predecessors, is in the fighting itself, the thumping and hammering, the heads flying, the lances shattering – and interesting as this is, up to a point, like so much literature of sport, it soon palls.

The isolated chivalrous encounter, in which knight singly meets knight, fights and goes his way, is rare in the *Furioso*. It comes near to being parodied in the first canto where Sacripante hears the loud noise of an approaching knight – and how noisy that sylvan paradise must have been with these mountains of armour and muscle forcing their way through the undergrowth! – whom he immediately challenges, like some aggressive dog which knows no other reaction to his fellows than to attack them – and has no other means of communication. The hapless Sacripante is sent flying from his horse and when he looks around his opponent is clattering off into the distance, having already forgotten him. How futile it all seems, but not in the

context of Ariosto's poem, where the defeated Saracen's self-esteem
has to be restored by Angelica (whom he is supposed to be protecting)
who consoles him that it was the fault of his horse.
  In the *Furioso* fighting is rarely of interest for its own sake. The
interest is in the men behind the armour, and the encounter of words
which invariably precedes that of arms is nearly always the more
interesting of the two. It is this clash of two personalities or attitudes
which is often the real fight. Consider for example the lively dialogue
between Orlando and Mandricardo in Canto XXIII, 71 ff.; the Saracen looks Orlando up and down without knowing who he is and tells
him he has been searching him out for ten days in order to avenge
the death of his friends: he is sure now he has found his enemy.
Orlando is courteous and offers first to remove his helmet and show
his face. The Saracen, however, is eager to fight but Orlando sees he
has no weapons other than his lance and asks what he will do if this
fails. Mandricardo is increasingly impatient: he has sworn never to
wear a sword till he has recovered Durindana from Orlando, who,
he says, has treacherously killed his father, Agricane. Orlando's blood
rises and in a dramatic outburst he gives Mandricardo the lie:
  Il conte più non tacque, e gridò forte:
  – E tu e qualunque il dice, se ne mente.
  Ma quel che cerchi t'è venuto in sorte:
  io sono Orlando. ... (XXIII, *80*)
  [The Count was silent no longer and shouted out loud: You,
  and anyone else who says that is lying. But your destiny has
  brought you the man you are looking for: I am Orlando.]
  The fight itself is then part of a larger whole and fits into a larger
context: it sometimes seems like one act in a drama – the first perhaps,
which leads us into an interesting situation: Ruggiero meets a band of
men about to execute a youth (XXV): he thinks it is Bradamante and
dashingly wields his sword to effect a rescue; having routed the
executioners he hears the youth's story: it is Ricciardetto, Bradamante's twin brother and the reason for his present predicament is
that ... Sometimes the fighting is the middle act in the play: it causes
a new development in the situation. The stirring duel between
Mandricardo and Zerbino (XXIV) is an intermediate act in the story
of Zerbino and Isabella; following their long courtship, her abduction
and attempted rape by Zerbino's friend, she is rescued by Orlando
(whose sword here too is the means whereby the deadlock in her tale
is resolved) and united with her lover: the duel with Mandricardo,
in which Zerbino is mortally wounded, prepares the way for the

climax of the episode, Isabella's heroic suicide rather than submit to
Rodomonte. The same point could be made in relation to Orlando's
battle with the king of Frisa's forces (IX) which is a turning point in
the story of Olimpia and Bireno. Elsewhere the duel or combat is
the last act in the play; it resolves a situation which has built up, as a
complex, not of military factors, but of human emotional conflicts –
the Ginevra-Ariodante story, for example, where Rinaldo's lance both
confirms and punishes Polinesso's treachery. The Marganorre episode
is a further example of this.

The dramatic nature of the duel or combat is apparent in a series
of episodes where something like a comedy of intrigue develops, the
various *peripezie* resulting not from some unforeseen act of over-
hearing or misunderstanding, but from the success or otherwise of
men with lances and swords; and the armour, which can so easily
conceal identity, prepares the *agnizione* – as in the vivid sequence of
scenes where the cowardly Martano passes himself off as the victor
in a tourney (XVII–XVIII). Ariosto has many other variations on the
tedious contests of hacking and charging of the romances: the duel
between Ruggiero and Bradamante for example (XXXVI), both
anxious not to hurt the other, and the fight for Orlando's helmet
(XI), where the invisible Angelica plays tricks on the sweating
combatants.

Elsewhere arms are essentially an instrument of tragedy. The combat on the island of Lampedusa in which the three Saracen kings meet
the three Christian knights in a battle to decide the outcome of the
war, is very reminiscent of the theatre in the interplay and conflict of
the six men, each of them bringing his separate temperament and
experience which affect his approach to the combat, but each of them
subject to the chance play of events: the Saracens are desperate: from
the beginning they use foul means – three times they savage the
Christians' horses – and at last Brandimarte is killed by a blow
delivered by Gradasso, who has come up on him unawares; misfortune and foul play endanger the Christians but in the end it is
Orlando's righteous anger at the death of Brandimarte which decides
the issue. In his fury he cuts down Agricane, and Gradasso, seeing the
death of his leader, trembles before the approach of the paladin:

tremò nel core e si smarrì nel viso;
e all'arrivar del cavallier d'Anglante,
presago del suo mal, parve conquiso.
Per schermo suo partito alcun non prese,
quando il colpo mortal sopra gli scese. (XLII, *10*)

[he trembled in his heart and his face fell, and he seemed already beaten, anticipating his fate, when the knight of Anglante came up. He made no move to protect himself when the mortal blow descended upon him.]

So we are left, as in the last act of a tragedy, the stage littered with the bodies of the dead and wounded, and the grim Orlando lamenting the fate of his beloved Brandimarte.

The Christians are triumphant; the infidel threat is finally destroyed and faith is triumphant over unbelief, virtue over vice. Valour also is triumphant over Fortune; in the end the resolution of Carlomagno's warriors overcomes the continual hazards to which men are exposed by their destiny. This latter theme, the power of Fortune, which runs all through the *Furioso*, is particularly emphasised in the numerous duels and battles in the poem. The fighting does not always turn out as expected – indeed the very confidence of two opponents who each fights expecting to win, cannot be justified on both sides. Although various procedures for stalemate and truces are adopted at various times, one side usually has to lose. Ricciardetto preparing to charge Guidon Selvaggio is quite confident he will unhorse his opponent,

ma contrario al pensier seguì l'effetto: (xxxi, 9)

[but the outcome was contrary to his expectations.]

Alcina spurs on her fleet determined to capture the fleeing Ruggiero but her ships are routed:

Oh di quante battaglie il fin successe
diverso a quel che si credette inante! (x, 54)

[In how many battles the result turned out differently from what was expected beforehand!]

Such is the nature of war and fighting, and Ariosto drives the point home repeatedly throughout the poem. Agramante's plan to retrieve his fortunes at the end of the campaign comes to nought when his fleet is defeated by Astolfo's: this is shown to be characteristic of modern warfare no less than of ancient: Francis I captured at Pavia, the French army besieging Naples struck by plague:

Ecco Fortuna come cangia voglie,
sin qui a' Francesi sì propizia stata; (xxxiii, 57)

[See how the will of Fortune changes who up till now had been favourable to the French.]

– indeed Fortune had changed since the earlier edition of the poem in which Francis I had been credited with 'la fortuna d'Alessandro' (xxvi, 47).

The theme of arms thus illustrates, no less than that of love, the

underlying mood of the poem; the Christians when their determination is aroused, with the courage of their convictions and the intervention of their God, repel the infidel invasion – but only just; and
the Christian knights with their greater skill and courtesy and generosity are generally victorious over their individual opponents – but not
always. Man is not master of the battlefield – he shares it uneasily
with Fortune, as he does every other field of human endeavour. So
the war, with its conflict of personalities and creeds, is a testing-
ground not only of military strengths and skills but of men's inner-
most characters, and the knight on horseback is no cardboard hero
but a moving, poetical figure, subject to a complex interplay of
motives and influences: his determination and his fortune, his ideals
and his self-interest, his hostility to evil and aggression and his love
and respect for his fellow men. Boiardo's simple explanation of
loving and fighting ('L'uno e l'altro esercizio è giovanile ...' – see
above, p. 52) no longer seems to apply.

6. Dynastic, Political and Other Themes

The *Furioso* as we have seen is very largely devoted to the two themes of love and arms advertised in the first lines and elaborated in the first two stanzas, but there is another theme alluded to in the following stanzas:

Voi sentirete fra i più degni eroi,
che nominar con laude m'apparecchio,
ricordar quel Ruggier, che fu di voi
e de' vostri avi illustri il ceppo vecchio. (1, 4)
[Among the worthiest heroes whose names I intend to praise you will hear Ruggiero mentioned, who was the ancient stock of your illustrious forefathers.]

Ruggiero and Bradamante, the story of whose courtship and marriage runs through the whole of the *Furioso*, are treated as the 'ceppo vecchio' of the Estense family, to whom Ariosto's poem is a tribute, and their various adventures afford opportunities for reviews of the history and achievements of the Estense line. The link between past and present, and between fiction and reality is thus established, and it proves to be a fruitful one: for not only are the poet's immediate patrons introduced in this way into his poem, but a wide range of other contemporaries from Ferrara and elsewhere; and in the process the relations of Ferrara and its people with other states and foreign powers enter the poem as well as the preoccupations and interests of the Ferrarese. The *Furioso* is thus linked formally and closely with the environment out of which it arose.

That this has many advantages for the poem as a whole I shall try to show, although the so-called dynastic and political elements in the *Furioso* have frequently been condemned by critics, particularly in the nineteenth century when Ariosto's 'hypocrisy' was lamented, but also in more recent times by those who see a real lack of any poetic inspiration in these parts of the poem. The celebration of Ariosto's two main patrons, Ippolito and Alfonso d'Este, is perhaps particularly vulnerable to these charges. The poem was largely written (and first published) while the poet was still in the service of Cardinal Ippolito: his relationship with his patron, as was so often the case in Renaissance courts, was an uneasy one. For poets and

artists the balance between service and reward was seldom resolved
entirely to the satisfaction of both sides, and at Ferrara neither
Ippolito nor Alfonso was ready to accept Ariosto into their service
exclusively as a poet. His poetry alone did not earn him his rewards:
he was, as we have seen, kept busy with a great variety of tasks for
his patrons. But his poetry was one of his services, as his opening
stanzas to Ippolito make clear:

> Qual ch'io vi debbo, posso di parole
> pagare in parte, e d'opera d'inchiostro;
> né che poco io vi dia da imputar sono;
> che quanto io posso dar, tutto vi dono. (1,3)
> [What I owe you I can partly repay in words and the work of
> my pen, and I should not be reproved that this is a small gift
> for I am giving you all that it is in my power to give.]

From the beginning therefore Ippolito is established as the recipient
of Ariosto's poem which is addressed explicitly to him; the poet
imagines that he is speaking directly to his patron, addresses him as
'Signor', 'voi', refers to 'your brother' 'your mother' 'your ancestors'
'your recent victory' etc. Such references are not frequent, but they
are scattered throughout the poem together with occasional appeals
to 'invitto Alfonso'. Ippolito is praised for his justice, his military
skill (particularly his recent victory over the Venetian fleet at Polesella
to which there are several allusions (xv, 2; xl, 1 etc.)), his loyalty
(to Ludovico Sforza), his shrewdness (in administering justice).
Ruggiero is urged to prove himself worthy of his great descendants,

> Ippolito e il fratel; che pochi il mondo
> ha tali avuti ancor fin al dì d'oggi,
> per tutti i gradi onde a virtù is poggi. (vii, 62)
> [Ippolito and his brother, for the world has known few such to
> this day of any rank in which man scales the heights of virtue.]

Astolfo on the moon, among the skeins of life being woven, sees one
particularly remarkable as conferring 'tutte le grazie inclite e rade'
('all the rare and illustrious graces') (xxxv, 5). And Ippolito is among
those whom Ariosto sees as undertaking the onslaught on the monster
of Avarice, a characteristic court encomium which hopefully en-
courages as much as it acknowledges its recipient's generosity (xxvi,
51). Alfonso too is praised in this passage, as he is elsewhere for his
prudence, diplomacy, chivalry (his compassionate treatment of his
prisoner Fabrizio Colonna, xiv, 4–5), his skill as a general (as at
Ravenna, iii, 51).

These specific tributes to his two patrons are extended to more general encomia of the Estense family and line – to Ippolito's father, Ercole, the wise builder; to Alfonso's children, and their antecedents. Several lengthy passages are devoted to this: an account of a sort of Estense portrait gallery found by Bradamante in Merlin's cave (III); a description of the future famous deeds of the Estensi depicted on a tapestry bought for the wedding of Ruggiero and Bradamante (XLVI); and an account of the female descendants of Bradamante given her by Melissa (XIII). Much of the genealogical detail is fictitious, either invented by Ariosto or taken by him from unknown sources, but there is a substratum at least of historical truth and some support in legend and tradition, not least in the *Innamorato* which provided the precedent for the Estense link with Ruggiero and Bradamante. Ariosto modifies Boiardo's genealogy somewhat, improving the specifically Italian strain of the family.

In all of this Ariosto has borrowed from Boiardo but gone beyond him. Boiardo, for example, dedicates his poem not specifically to the Estensi but to the 'signori e cavalieri' whom he imagines gathered around him to hear his story:

Signori e cavallier che ve adunati
Per odir cose dilettose e nove ... (I, i, *1*)

Ariosto too is conscious of his local 'audience' and he addresses them directly from time to time; 'the ladies' in particular, addressed in the second person, receive the poet's sympathies, curses and apologies – ladies in general, of course, but above all the court ladies of Ferrara and nearby cities, Mantua and Urbino. Rinaldo is shown a magnificent fountain which has sculptures of eight fine ladies, supported by their admiring poets – Lucrezia Borgia, Isabella and Beatrice d'Este, Elizabetta Gonzaga etc. – for the last one, unnamed, who must be Alessandra Benucci, Ariosto imagines himself as the single unnamed admirer (XLII, *93*). Elsewhere he prefaces a canto with a long eulogy of famous women, the contemporary poetess Vittoria Colonna prominent among them (XXXVII) – and in the last canto the poet imagines himself at the end of his voyage, welcomed home by his many friends, who receive his tribute:

Oh di che belle e saggie donne veggio,
oh di che cavallieri il lito adorno!
Oh di ch'amici, a chi in eterno deggio
per la letizia c'han del mio ritorno!
Mamma e Ginevra e l'altre da Correggio
veggo del molo in su l'estremo corno. (XLVI, *3*)
[O what lovely, wise ladies, what gentlemen I see adorning the

shore! What friends whose joy at my return puts me in their
everlasting debt! Mamma, Ginevra and the other Correggio
sisters I can see at the very tip of the pier.]
The 'audience' is thus picked out by name and identified with the
poem – and the poet changes his allusions in the different editions as
times change; new friends appear and others disappear. Machiavelli
regretted that Ariosto had not found room for his name among the
writers welcoming the poet on the completion of his voyage!

   The eulogy of the poet's patrons thus extends to a note of more
general acknowledgement of his friends and acquaintances: the encomiastic note here is often restrained; a few lines, a few epithets,
perhaps only the name mentioned. The intention is rather to associate
the person named with the poem than to impress the reader with his
brilliance. The same effect is apparent in the fairly frequent allusions
to contemporary political events, where the eulogy of a prince or
general leads to a glimpse of current affairs of state. The court knows
that its very existence depends on the combination of diplomatic and
military skill of its leaders: Alfonso will need all his ability to keep
Ferrara independent:

   che si ritroverà, con poca gente,
   da un lato aver la veneziane squadre,
   colei da l'altro, che più giustamente
   non so se devrà dir matrigna o madre;
   ma se pur madre, a lui poco più pia,
   che Medea ai figli o Progne stata sia. (III, 52)
   [because he will find himself, with few troops, between the
   Venetian forces on the one side, and on the other someone who
   I don't know whether she should be called mother or step-
   mother; but if mother, then no kinder to him than Medea or
   Procne to their children.]
Here are the old enemies of Ferrara, the Venetians and the Pope –
and although in 1532 the whole face of Italian politics has changed,
many of the earlier allusions are retained in the final edition. The
reference to the Venetians' ingratitude to Ercole on whom they
waged war in 1492 despite his previous services to them, is kept
(slightly toned down – III,46); but a more friendly allusion to
Venetian 'giustizia' is introduced elsewhere (XXXVI,3). Julius II
(who had once threatened to throw Ariosto to the fishes) is pictured
reacting to the French and Ferrarese success at Ravenna:

   Si morde il papa per dolor le labbia,
   e fa da' monti, a guisa di tempesta,

scendere in fretta una tedesca rabbia. (xxxiii, *41*)
[The Pope bites his lips in pain, and hurriedly brings down over
the mountains, like a tempest, a German rabble.]
Julius's successor, Leo x, Ariosto's former friend, is treated more
generously: he is included among those fighting the monster Avarice,
and appealed to as a saviour appointed by God (xvii, *79*).

In the last years of the Italian wars Ferrara had changed allegiance
from the French to the Spaniards, and the final edition of the poem
acknowledges the new masters with allusions to 'il sagace Spagnol'
and to the achievements of the captains of Charles v (xv, *23*). So in
a long new passage (xxxiii) on the wars of Italy, added in the 1532
edition, the invaders of Italy are seen as the French. (Ariosto had
earlier prepared, in the unpublished 'Scudo d'Ullania' fragment, an
analogous passage in which the German invasions were described.)
But the old sympathy for the French is still apparent in various
passages of the 1532 edition : Francis i is praised alongside Charles v,
as 'il re gagliardo'; his invasion of Italy in 1515 is described as 'moved
by a just and noble anger' (xxvi, *44*); and his victory over 'quei
villan brutti', the Swiss, is praised (xxxiii, *43*).

These confusions, reflecting the changing sympathies of the poet
and of his Ferrarese readers, do not I think adversely affect his poetry.
They contribute indeed in some way to the vitality of the poem in
which the poet's own affairs seem to be moving no less than those of
his characters. The over-all effect is achieved of a country over-run by
war in which peace and independence are the great dream. So in spite
of the sympathy for Francis i, and the praise of Charles v, in spite of the
eulogies of the Estensi, long the allies of the French invaders, the lament
for the loss of freedom is perhaps the most constant note. Reliance on
the aid of foreigners is disastrous, as Agramante knows to his cost, and
  chiunque il regno suo si lascia tòrre,
  e per soccorso a' barbari ricorre. (xl, *40*)
[whoever loses his kingdom and resorts for help to foreigners.]
The invader is cruel and rapacious, even Francis's troops when out of
his control (xxxiii, *44*) – and Ludovico il Moro soon regrets his fatal
mistake:
  ... si pente Ludovico
  d'aver fatto in Italia venir Carlo;
  che sol per travagliar l'emulo antico
  chiamato ve l'avea, non per cacciarlo. (xxxiii, *31*)
[Ludovico repents of having invited Charles into Italy; he had
called him only to harass his old rival not to expel him.]

In another famous comment on the harpies which Astolfo hunts out of the Senapo's land, Ariosto curses the invaders of Italy and those who invited them in (Ludovico and Julius II are probably meant, though not named):

Oh famelice, inique e fiere arpie
ch'all'accecata Italia e d'error piena,
per punir forse antique colpe rie,
in ogni mensa alto giudico mena! ...
Troppo fallò che le spelonche aperse,
che già molt'anni erano state chiuse;
onde il fetore e l'ingordigia emerse,
ch'ad ammorbare Italia si diffuse. (XXXIV, 1-2)

[Oh ravenous, wicked, cruel harpies brought by divine judgement to every part of blind, errant Italy perhaps as a punishment for her past sins. It was a grave error to open the caves that had been closed for many years releasing the stench and greed to spread their taint over all Italy.]

It was a frequent cry among Ariosto's contemporaries that Italy's ills were due to her rapacious leaders, sent as a punishment by God:

... a noi, greggi inutili e mal nati,
ha dato per guardian lupi arrabbiati. (XVII, 3)

[he has given us, a wretched helpless flock, ravenous wolves as guardians ...]

The foreign rulers should seek elsewhere for lands to plunder: Italy is a Christian country, let them go and fight the Turk and liberate Jerusalem (XVII, 75). In the last resort, however, the Italians themselves are to blame, and in a literary lament traditional in Italy from the times of Petrarch to those of Leopardi he calls on the Italians to stir themselves:

O d'ogni vizio fetida sentina,
dormi, Italia imbriaca, e non ti pesa
ch'ora di questa gente, ora di quella
che già serva ti fu, sei fatta ancella? (XVII, 76)

[O foul sink of every vice, you're sleeping, drunken Italy, and do you not care that you've become the servant first of this people, then of that, who were once servants to you?]

It is not really an exhortation, but a lament – like Leopardi's. Ariosto's assessment is not so different from Machiavelli's (the fault lies in the leaders); but he has no faith in any practical solution and no possibility of implementing one, as Machiavelli, at certain stages at least, had; and this consciousness of present misfortunes cannot be kept out of a poem so intimately concerned with military valour, chivalry, honour, glory. So the parallel between the ancient and modern times is seldom long forgotten. The problem of leadership, for example, occurs on several occasions, as we have pointed out elsewhere, in the poet's comments on the military commanders, Agramante and Rodomonte (p. 90). So, too, in internal affairs, the tyrant who is hated, but obeyed is insecure (another Machiavellian thesis):

> Sia Marganorre essempio di chi regna;
> che chi mal opra, male al fine aspetta. (XXXVII, 106)
> [Let Marganorre be an example to all those who govern, that ill-doers can expect ills in the long run.]

And to pursue Machiavelli's preoccupations, what of the crowd, the people–is there anything more fickle? Ariosto shows us one shrewdly contrived scene where the inhabitants of an island off the Irish coast are freed by Orlando of the sea-monster to which they had had to sacrifice a maiden daily, and suddenly turn on their deliverer for fear that his action will bring some mysterious retribution on their heads (XI, 46).

What has disturbed Ariosto's admirers in these encomiastic and allusive passages is the lack of any original or individual style. The poet adopts the traditional rhetorical devices without it seems much real conviction and we, his readers, remain unconvinced of the brilliance of his patrons, the justice of the Venetians, shrewdness of the Spaniards, or valour of the French. We tend to 'shut off' to these conventional eulogies, as we do to exaggerated modern advertising. The hyperboles we have heard before, the mythological allusions are introduced almost mechanically, as of the baby Ippolito:

> sì bello infante n'apparia, che 'l mondo
> non ebbe un tal dal secol primo al quarto.
> Vedeasi Iove, e Mercurio facondo,
> Venere e Marte, che l'aveano sparto
> a man piene e spargean d'eterei fiori ... (XLVI, 85)
> [so fine a child appeared as the world had never known from the golden to the iron age. Jove came, eloquent Mercury, Venus and Mars scattering over him heavenly flowers.]

The poet seems often at a loss for alternative means of conveying his praise and resorts to lists of epithets:

> ... il liberal, magnanimo, sublime,
> gran cardinal de la Chiesa di Roma (III, 56)

– or to tediously repeated introductory phrases 'Ecco ... ecco ...', 'Si

vede ... si vede ...', 'Poi mostra ... poi mostra ...' (XXXIII, *37, 40, 54*).
Frequently he cuts short his eulogies or lists of famous men with the
lame explanation that he would never end if he really attempted to
do justice to his subject, or that he would offend others if he singled
out individuals for praise.

Yet one must remember that the conventional rhetorical devices
and the literary reminiscences sounded differently in early Cinquecento Italian ears – four centuries of repetition have dulled the rhetoric
which to the cultured Renaissance reader recalled the classical masters.
In many of these passages Ariosto is consciously raising his tone above
the pedestrian romance level, aiming towards the splendour of the
epic which increasingly attracted Italian poets, or deliberately recalling Dante's precedent and endowing his own verse with a hint of
Dante's solemnity: as in Bradamante's modest surprise at the invitation to see the gallery of her descendants:

> Di che merito sono io? (III, *13*)
> [Of what worth am I ...?] (cf. *Inferno*, II, *33*)

In these contexts he often adopts the cryptic, allusive style of the
Commedia; as of Ludovico Sforza after Beatrice's death:

> ... e fia stimata, senza
> costei, ventura la somma prudenza. (XIII, *63*)
> [And without her his great prudence will be judged good
> fortune.]

Similarly in reacting againts the so-called hypocrisy of the encomiastic verse the modern reader tends to forget the extent to which
these conventional flatteries form a part of any society, including our
own: the eulogies of Ariosto's patrons should perhaps be judged in
the same light as the modern author's grateful acknowledgement of
the generosity of the X Foundation, and of the unfailing courtesy of
his colleagues. Ariosto's attitude is to be judged by the standards of
his times: alongside many of his contemporaries he seems moderate
in the extent and nature of his encomia. There are perhaps a dozen
flattering allusions to Ippolito, half as many to Alfonso, and less to
Charles v or Francis i – in a poem of nearly 5000 octaves; and many of
his allusions are moderate in tone, and not at all sensitively attuned to
the changing political situation of his times. The political opportun-
ism is not marked.

The ultimate justification of the encomiastic and allusive material
however is in its function in the structure of the poem as a whole.
The dedication and address of the poem to the Cardinal serves to
establish the immediate circle for which it was written: Ippolito,

Alfonso, the Estense family, the Ferrarese court, the visitors from other cities, poets, painters, men of affairs. The poet thus keeps in constant touch with his own society: his fairy-story assumes a contemporary relevance. It reflects, for example, the current knowledge of geography and the interest in exploration. The previous fifty years had witnessed not only a series of fascinating voyages to the east and west of Europe but also the rediscovery or revival of interest in the classical treatises of Ptolemy, Strabo, Pomponio Mela and Pliny. Ferrara was a centre of cosmographical studies with a well-equipped library, and we know from the satires that Ariosto enjoyed armchair travel:

... il resto de la terra
senza mai pagar l'oste andrò cercando
con Ptolomeo ... (Satire III, 61)
[the rest of the earth I'll visit with Ptolemy without ever having to pay an inn-keeper.]

Seated comfortably in Ferrara therefore, studying his Ptolemy in a modern edition, he contrived a series of journeys which covered most of the known world. Ruggiero, equipped with a flying horse and a thirst for travel (x, 72), flies from Europe to India 'per la via occidentale', probably a reflection of Columbus' journey. From India he returned via Central China, Sarmazia, east of the Caspian sea, to the borders of Europe and Asia, to Poland, Hungary, Germany 'e il resto di quella boreale orrida terra', to England and the Thames (the Estense library had a *Narratione delle cose de l'Inghilterra*). Astolfo makes two epic journeys, the first from Alcina's island (probably Japan); he makes for England via the safer southern route (India, Persian Gulf, Red Sea, Cairo, Jerusalem, Tripoli, Syria, Armenia, Anatolia, Thrace, Hungary, the Rhine, the Ardennes, Aix-la-Chapelle and Flanders). In the final edition of the poem Ariosto added a passage in which Andronico, in answer to Astolfo's question about a sea-route from India to England, predicts the great geographical discoveries of the fifteenth and sixteenth centuries (xv, 18–36).

The wanderings of these medieval knights and their enchanted beasts are charted therefore with a precision not found in any of Ariosto's predecessors, and various topographical allusions show that Ariosto had acquired some knowledge of the regions to which he refers – he comments for example on the bad air of the port of Famagusta, in Cyprus (xviii, 136); he gives us in some detail the water-ways of the Po and its tributaries along which Rinaldo travels in Canto xliii; he likens a castle near Paris to one on the road from

Parma to Borgo San Donnino; he comments on the wooden houses
of Paris, and the swarming streets of Cairo (xv, 63).

However, in most cases we are given only the most cursory
references to the places through which his characters pass. Rinaldo
comes to Scotland, somewhere close to Berwick, but immediately
plunges into 'la selva Caledonia' (iv, 51) which like all other woods
provides trees and streams and glades, through which come the
sounds of clashing armour or weeping maidens. With this back-cloth
he is at home anywhere. Rarely do we pause to examine the local
peculiarities – a conventional, literary landscape meets us almost
everywhere, Ruggiero on the coast of Brittany for example:

> Sul lito un bosco era di querce ombrose,
> dove ognor par che Filomena piagna;
> ch'in mezzo avea un pratel con una fonte,
> e quinci e quindi un solitario monte. (x, 113)
> [On the shore was a wood of shady oak-trees, where Philomena
> seems to be always weeping, with a meadow and a stream, and
> here and there a solitary hill.]

This is of course a studied negligence. Ariosto is writing a poem not
a geographical treatise: if he permits himself some armchair travelling
it is for the pleasure of letting his imagination roam free, not in order
to convince us of the truth of his tale: when his inventions are set in
too precise a topographical framework we become uneasy (as in the
Mantuan allusions in Canto xliii). The balance between fantasy and
reality is a delicate one, and the poet knows it.

The *Furioso* is also closely related to its audience in its reflection of
some of the current debates of court society – the feminist controversy
for example which is discussed with such feeling in the *Cortegiano*.
It is particularly notable that apart from the explicit discussions of
feminist topics in the first edition, two of the episodes added for the
final edition (Marganorre, and the 'rocca di Tristano') are very largely
concerned with this issue. Classical and medieval sources were both
significant in influencing the feminist debate in Italy in the fifteenth
century, when a succession of humanist treatises discussed the rival
merits of the sexes, often declaring the equal worth of both or the
superiority of the female. A vast literature throughout Europe arose
during the fifteenth and sixteenth centuries in which these peren-
nial problems were debated with a new vigour. How far woman's
position in society was in practice improved by this debate it is not
easy to establish; certainly many of the attitudes expressed by Italian
writers in the high Renaissance were, like Ariosto's very liberal and

sympathetic towards women, and women of good birth generally enjoyed the benefits of a good education and a good status at court: a few exceptional women handled affairs of state in the absence of their husbands, and vied with men as poets – and to these privileged few Ariosto paid his tribute in his poem (XXXVII, XLII).

Yet the pages of the *Cortegiano* make it quite clear that opinion was much divided on this thorny subject, and Gaspare Pallavicino, with his violent anti-feminism, must have represented a broad section of opinion which buttressed the long-standing social conventions of female seclusion and suppression. Rodomonte's tirade against the female sex (Doralice has just jilted him), repeats several of the arguments common in Quattrocento feminist writing:

Credo che t'abbia la Natura e Dio
produtto, o scelerato sesso, al mondo
per una soma, per un grave fio
de l'uom ... (XXVII, *119*)
[I think that God and Nature, produced you, accursed sex, as a burden, a grave punishment for man in this world.]

That man can only be produced with the assistance of women is no credit to the female sex – roses grow from thorns, Rodomonte continues. The anti-feminists often declared in fact that women were a mistake of nature, which tries to produce males but isn't always successful!

Rodomonte here is being mocked by Ariosto who makes this lover suddenly turned misogynist into a lover again a few stanzas later when he meets the lovely Isabella. Another misogynist who is exposed by Ariosto is Marganorre, the tyrant who has established various harsh laws in his territory because women were the downfall of his two sons: the women are forced to live apart from their menfolk, and female newcomers have their skirts cut off at the waist, while male strangers are imprisoned or forced to hate women for the rest of their lives (XXXVII, *83–5*). The reason for this severe misogynism is that his two sons lost their lives because of their illicit passions for married women, both ladies being innocent (faithful to their husbands) while the two sons in pursuit of their lust resorted to violence against their guests (see p. 77 above). There could hardly be a more irrational anti-feminism than Marganorre's and he is maliciously punished in due course by an old woman with a sharp stick – while new laws are established in his land whereby the government is given into the hands of the women and husbands all have to swear to obey their wives. (An echo of another female community, the Amazonian women, described earlier in the poem, xx.)

A more explicitly pro-feminist note is struck elsewhere in various comments on the attitude of society towards illicit lovers. When Ginevra, Princess of Scotland, is accused of having a lover, the 'harsh law of Scotland' requires that she should be burnt unless a champion comes forward to prove her innocence. The episode not only shows the danger of a false accusation (Ginevra is in fact innocent), but affords an opportunity for Rinaldo, who intervenes in the incident, to inveigh against the injustice of the law:

> S'un medesimo ardor, s'un disir pare
> inchina e sforza l'uno e l'altro sesso
> a quel suave fin d'amor, che pare
> all'ignorante vulgo un grave eccesso;
> perché si de' punir donna o biasmare,
> che con uno o più d'uno abbia commesso
> quel che l'uom fa con quante n'ha appetito,
> e lodato ne va, non che impunito?
>
> Son fatti in questa legge disuguale
> veramente alle donne espressi torti ... (IV, 66–7)

[If the same passion, the same desire directs and drives both sexes to that sweet conclusion of love that seems to the ignorant crowd a grave intemperance: why should a woman be punished or blamed for doing with one or more men what a man does with as many women as he feels inclined to, and not only goes un-punished, but gets credit for? Women are manifestly wronged by this unequal law.]

Rinaldo's words may well be an echo of the debate that occurs in Ariosto's probable source, Juan de Flores' *Historia de Grisel y Mirabella* where the author discusses whether any one of two illicit lovers can be considered more guilty; and they recall the tone of various pass-ages in the *Decameron*, notably Madonna Filippa's reasoning in reply to the charge of adultery, 'the law should be the same for all, and made with the agreement of those it concerns' (Day VI, Novella 7). But they seem to reflect Ariosto's own feelings, repeating as they do the arguments he returns to elsewhere (and Rinaldo incidentally is the rare wise husband who later refrains from submitting his wife's fidelity to the test – XLIII, 6–8).

We are inclined also to see Ariosto in the elderly man who is not prepared to accept the Fiammetta story as valid evidence against the female sex. What of the men, he asks the innkeeper:

> Ditemi un poco : è di voi forse alcuno

ch'abbia servato alla sua moglie fede? (xxviii, 79)
[Tell me : has any of you here by any chance stayed faithful to
his wife?]
Women have often good reason to be dissatisfied with their husbands
and to look elsewhere. *He* would establish a new law:
Saria la legge ch'ogni donna colta
in adulterio fosse messa a morte,
se provare non potesse ch'una volta
avesse adulterato il suo consorte: (xxviii, 82)
[The law would be that every woman taken in adultery should
be put to death if she could not prove that her husband had on
some occasion committed adultery.]
The same arguments recur later when Rinaldo insists that if women
can be corrupted by money, men are even more susceptible, and the
story of Argeo (xliii) follows immediately as evidence of this.

The conflict between the sexes is a fruitful theme in a world where
women adopt the normally male role of fighters, and defeat men,
or are mistaken for men or, perhaps worse, are mistaken for gentle
ladies. These are a frequent romance motif, not frequently however
employed in a feminist or anti-feminist context. (Ariosto himself exploits one variant with the Ricciardetto-Fiordispina story – xxviii.)
On several occasions however he seems aware of its feminist potential:
the female warrior, who proves she is as good as a man, can hardly
be bound by the usual conventions: Bradamante refuses her parents'
choice of a husband and will only accept a man 'che più di me sia
valoroso in arme' (xliv, 70) [who is more valorous than I am in
arms.]. The aggressive Marfisa, who for once dons a dress at the
request of her companions, is taken by Mandricardo to be a fair
prey, but this lady is her own master:
Io sua non son, né d'altri son che mia :
dunque me tolga a me chi mi desia (xxvi, 79)
[I am not his, nor anybody's except my own; so if anybody
wants me, let him try to take me.]
The most thoughtful exploitation of this motif is in the 'rocca di
Tristano' episode added for the edition of 1532 (xxxii – see p. 80
above). The convention imposed by the jealous husband ejected by
Tristan was that entry to the castle should be competitive – the men
must joust for a place, the ladies be judged on their beauty. Bradamante jousts with the three knights who are accompanying Ullania,
defeats them and wins her place in the warm; but when she takes off
her helmet and reveals her hair, the guardian of the place is in a

quandary – Ullania is already inside and only one, and the most
beautiful, lady may remain. He judges Bradamante to be fairer than
Ullania and is for turning the latter out when Bradamante intervenes
with some clever and convincing arguments: 'Non venni una donna
qui' – she fought her way in as a man – and how do they know she
isn't a man?

> Ben son degli altri ancor, c'hanno le chiome
> lunghe, com'io, né donne son per questo. (XXXII, *103*)
> [There are plenty of others who have long hair, as I do, but still
> aren't women.]

Why treat her as a woman when in all ways she acts like a man? And
supposing she *were* a woman, and were judged less beautiful than
Ullania, would she still have to leave in spite of having defeated her
opponents with her lance? And finally, most convincing argument
of all, what are they going to do about it? It is a fine legalistic argument, much of it, a *reductio ad absurdum* of the futile distinctions made
between the sexes.

The feminist debate was one of a number of topics keenly discussed
at Renaissance courts; another, to which we have referred several
times previously, was the conflict between 'virtù' and 'fortuna'.
Ariosto's contemporaries were much concerned with what came
largely to be a discussion of man's ability to control his environment
and himself. The humanist thesis which set man in the centre of the
universe, a rational, dignified and noble being, a creature made in
God's image and, in the neo-Platonic view, participating in the divine
nature – such a thesis was the foundation for Renaissance man's
belief that he could by his own 'virtù', his inner worth, check the
power of forces outside him, the chance play of events which had
once seemed to be his master. Castiglione's courtier was a man who
could master the conflicts and stresses of an artificial court society, a
man who in the 'grace' of his conduct, his self-control, showed himself a superior being. Machiavelli's prince by a ruthless assertion of
rational principles was to master the tangle of forces which seemed to
dominate man's political life.

Fortune, usually personified as 'Fortuna', in the style of a deity
controlling men's lives, is a term frequently on Ariosto's lips. We
have seen how often it recurs in his treatment of his main themes, of
arms and love, both of which seem to proceed irrationally, even
perversely. Battles seldom turn out as expected, nor do love affairs.
Sudden caprices of Fortune make armies flee, horses bolt, men and
women kindle with passion; and in the process people's lives are

changed dramatically. It is 'Fortuna' which deprives Carlomagno of his best knights at a critical moment (xxvii, 7), and 'Fortuna' which at the same time 'smiles' on Agramante; it is the 'wheel of Fortune' which brings defeat and victory to the armies of Louis xii and Francis i (xxxiii, 42), and which kills off Francis's soldiers in an epidemic (xxxiii, 57). Chance brings Angelica across the wounded Medoro (xix, 17), or brings Zerbino into Isabella's world – and in so doing from happy, wealthy, princess she becomes a poor, miserable captive (xiii, 4). Love above all is irrational: valour, virtue, devotion may, or may not, win love as a reward.

Repeatedly therefore Ariosto presents us with situations in which men and women are not masters of their environment or of themselves, and it has been argued that this insistence on man's subjection to fortune runs as a leit-motif throughout the *Furioso* and is perhaps its most persistent thesis. It is not only in love and war that the point is made. All human affairs are affected, travel above all, which was indeed subject to untold hazards in Ariosto's day and could seriously thwart men's lives, hopes and intentions. His knights set off to sail to France, and are blown to Syria, or are captured by pirates, or drowned. Shipwrecks are frequent in the *Furioso*, a valuable narrative tool to throw into the machinery when it is running too smoothly – and Ariosto gives us some malicious accounts of sailors in storms when all their science and discipline are shown up as futile in the face of a puff of wind (xix, 44). In their bold adventures his knights may put forth all their skill and bravery and still really depend on luck – the heroic Norandino was guided by 'Fortuna' so that he arrived at the Orc's cave when Lucina was alone and the monster was fortunately out (xvii, 39)! Lucina is eventually rescued by Agricane and Gradasso, although it was 'aventura più che senno', ('good luck rather than judgement' – xvii, 63). The Saracen leaders are reduced to such a state of discord that they draw lots to decide who shall settle their disputes, thus readily acknowledging their own incapacity (xxx, 22).

There is therefore, in the *Furioso*, a frequently realistic, sceptical, anti-humanist note which seems almost a protest against the exaggerated claims of neo-Platonists and other idealists. Men and women are frequently shown as weak, fragile creatures, incapable of contriving their own happiness, subject to repeated misfortune through their own passions or the perversity of forces beyond their control. The *proemio* to the last canto but one, added in the final edition, seems to underline this, yet the tone ultimately is not pessimistic:

Si vede per gli essempii, di che piene

sono l'antiche e le moderne istorie,
che 'l ben va dietro al male, e 'l male al bene,
e fin son l'un de l'altro e biasmi e glorie;
e che fidarsi a l'uom non si conviene
in suo tesor, suo regno e sue vittorie,
né disperarsi per Fortuna avversa,
che sempre la sua ruota in giro versa. (XLV, 4).

[One sees from many examples in ancient and modern history
that good follows ill, and ill good, that glory ends in blame, and
blame in glory, and that man should not put his trust in his
wealth, his realms, his victories, nor should he despair if Fortune
is hostile for she always keeps her wheel turning round.]

Fortune's wheel therefore, bringing ills *and* blessings, is not an unmitigated evil; and man *has* the possibility of withstanding its force:
indeed the poem as a whole can be read as demonstrating the triumph
of 'virtù' over 'fortuna'. Ruggiero and Bradamante overcome progressively the obstacles put in their path (separate faith, separate
allegiance, jealousy, war), and come together at the last to establish
a long and powerful line: of one of their descendants, Azzo d'Este,
Ariosto wrote that he would be endowed above all with 'virtù,'
that determination and strength of character which can overcome
Fortune:

... di grandezza d'animo e di fede,
e di virtù, miglior che gemme et auro :
che dona e tolle ogn'altro ben Fortuna;
sol in virtù non ha possanza alcuna. (III, 37)

[with greatness of mind and spirit and of 'virtue', greater than
jewels or gold: for Fortune gives and takes away all else, but
against 'virtue' alone has no power.]

So the Christian cause triumphs: Orlando, Rinaldo, Astolfo and their
followers are successful in asserting their skill, their courage, and their
faith over the combined forces of a brave and powerful, but mis-
guided and often treacherous enemy – but only just! There were
moments when the outcome might well have been different, and
indeed in Ariosto's Italy the foreign invasions were in the process
of establishing a foreign domination for centuries to come. Small
wonder then that the balance is somewhat delicately poised in his
poem.

Formally of course the triumph of Carlomagno and his paladins is
owed to the direct intervention of their Christian God, who sends
rain to extinguish the fires in Paris, Silence to help the relieving armies

infiltrate the besiegers, Discord to ruin the Saracen forces, and St John
to advise Astolfo how to cure Orlando whose madness was directly
brought about by God as a punishment for his wicked love of a
pagan: the paladin has thus abused his divine authority:

Il vostro Orlando, a cui nascendo diede
somma possanza Dio con sommo ardire,
e fuor de l'uman uso gli concede
che ferro alcun non lo può mai ferire;
perché a difesa di sua santa fede
così voluto l'ha constituire. (xxxiv, 63)
[Your Orlando, to whom at birth God gave the utmost strength
and courage, and contrary to human custom made him invulnerable to all weapons because He decided to make him the
defender of His holy faith.]

Ultimately it is by the use of religious miracles that Astolfo creates the
forces and the ships which rout Agramante: St John's gifts and
instructions enable him to turn stones into horses, and branches into
ships. The main struggle is indeed of two faiths; and the ultimate
union of Bradamante and Ruggiero is dependent on the latter's conversion to Christianity.

Yet one would hardly claim that the *Furioso* is a monument of
religious devotion; indeed one could read the poem without forming
any clear picture of Ariosto's inner religious beliefs. The anti-
clericalism is of course traditional, and cannot be interpreted as anti-
religious. The angel Michael fails to find Silence in the cloisters; nor
any other of the prescribed Christian virtues:

Né Pietà, né Quiete, né Umiltade,
né quivi Amor, né quivi Pace mira. (xiv, 81)

Friars and priests come in for some conventional mockery – one
wicked hermit tries to rape the sleeping Angelica and proves too
senile to succeed (viii, 49); but the one who saves Isabella wisely
recognises the power of the senses and takes her off to where she will
be out of temptation, from him as well as everyone else (xxiv, 91).
There are slighting allusions to Julius ii and encouraging ones to
Leo x. The attitude to Church and Papacy is neither deferential nor
hostile, or perhaps it is a mixture of both.

Similarly the Christian devotion of the paladins seems hardly to
provide evidence of any deep religious conviction. Ariosto, compared with Pulci before him and Tasso later, seems relatively un-
interested in religious issues. He presents religion in the generally
naïve mode of the romances – where magic and enchantment and

religious miracles follow each other unceremoniously. Conversions occur rapidly and mechanically in deference to superior force. Praying is often a sort of bargaining: Ruggiero, swimming for his life, vows to become a Christian if he is saved (XLI, *48*); Carlo, praying for God's aid, seems eager to convince Him: Galileo commented, 'I'd prefer Carlo to be content with praying to God, and to leave off admonishing and advising him.' Counter-Reformation critics were particularly incensed that Astolfo should find stowed away with other useless things on the moon 'infiniti prieghi e voti ... che da noi peccatori a Dio si fanno' ('infinite prayers and vows that we sinners offer to God' – XXXIV, *74*). The Saracen forces are not presented as consistently black villains: they are often noble and warm-hearted. At one point Agramante resists the attempt of his former friend and fellow believer Brandimarte to convert him to the Christian faith, and his loyalty to his own creed is presented sympathetically, even heroically:

> Ch'io vinca o perda, o debba nel mio regno
> tornare antiquo, o sempre starne in bando,
> in mente sua n'ha Dio fatto disegno,
> il qual né io, né tu, né vede Orlando. (XLI, *44*)
> [Whether I win or lose, whether I return to my old kingdom or
> am for ever banished from it, God has decided that in his own
> judgement which neither I, nor you, nor Orlando know.]

The treatment of religion, as I have said, is close to that of the popular romances, formally deferential but far from pious. The attitude is one found frequently in early sixteenth century Italy, especially in Ferrara in the time of her struggle with the Papacy, and nothing that we know about Ariosto from his contemporaries or his other works suggests that it was uncharacteristic of him.

The reflection in the *Furioso* of contemporary currents of thought and feeling extends further than we have time here to pursue in any detail. The poet accompanies his narrative with a fairly frequent personal commentary aimed primarily at his Ferrarese patrons and friends, and related to their experience and culture. The feasting, carousing and pageantry of the court we have seen earlier, in the joust in Damascus, for example (XVII, *81*), and the accounts of buildings, gardens, paintings and tapestries implicitly and explicitly pay tribute to the poet's own Ferrara:

> ... la più adorna
> di tutte le città d'Italia. (XXXV, *6*)

The tone of his contemporary commentary is often critical, however, and we are reminded of the satires – indeed some of the favourite targets of the satires reappear here – women's cosmetics, for example, priests, lawyers and doctors. Astolfo's visit to the moon enables the poet to discourse at length on the things found there which had been lost on earth – time wasted in gambling, charitable gifts made on men's death-beds, the donation of Constantine, gifts made to princes in the hope of favours and other vain tributes.

The poet keeps contact therefore with the world he is living in – his dragons and hippogriffs and enchantresses have not entirely taken possession. The Italy and Ferrara of his day are frequently recalled and it is part of the poem's charm that this is so. We are conscious throughout of two contexts, the romance medieval world of Carlomagno and his paladins, and the Renaissance and humanist world of Alfonso d'Este and Francis I. The poet does not attempt to escape – he is in a sense committed. Yet we should not exaggerate the extent of this commitment. Ariosto does not polemicise: he has no sense of mission, no real political or social message for his trouble-laden times. He is not, like Machiavelli, championing a militia, or exhorting a leader to come forth and cure Italy's ills; nor is he, like a Savonarola, denouncing the sins of his countrymen and preaching a moral revival; nor was he like Guicciardini, a man of shrewd political insight and practical administrative ability. Like most of his fellows he is dismayed, bewildered by the military, political and social problems of his day and he has no real answer to them. His reaction is one of lament and protest, mingled with nostalgia for a past age which he knows is really in his imagination.

The contemporary commentary therefore is muted, discreet; it plays essentially a minor role in the poem. It is not the local, topical, contemporary relevance of his romance narrative which commands the scene, but the wider, human implications. Out of the loves and encounters of his knights and damsels come not so much answers for the ills of his society, but meditation and tentative counsel on the business of living with our fellows, friends, masters, enemies, daughters, wives.

7. The Arts of Narrative

We have said that Ariosto's first outstanding achievement was his creation of a structure for the heterogeneous romance material which he adopted. His is a long poem totalling nearly 5000 octaves, with numerous characters each going his different way, and a host of separate incidents, episodes and inset stories. Yet in spite of the episodic nature of much of its material it is not a collection of *novelle* in the style, say, of the *Decameron*, but a continuous narrative with a coherent story set in a given place and time which embrace all the characters and events however different they are. Any of these characters can meet any other, and the co-ordination of their movements alone must have taxed the writer's memory and ingenuity.

One might well wonder why Ariosto should have taken up this complex romance material and not limited himself to a simpler theme. His approach after all is more mature than Boiardo's : both the political and the cultural situation had changed and encouraged a more serious attitude. The wars of Italy made Boiardo's carefree pursuit of dragons and magicians seem escapist and irresponsible to many readers; and the further diffusion of classical literature over the past twenty years made the romance confusion seem naïve. Set beside the *Aeneid* the *Innamorato* looked strikingly deficient. In electing to follow in the romance tradition Ariosto was motivated in part of course by the continuing popularity of Boiardo's poem, particularly among the less cultured readers, and also by the degree of liberty which the loose romance structure offered the poet to include almost any material he chose. But he also saw that the variety and complexity of the romances could be exploited for a more serious purpose than they had served hitherto, that in relating the traditional themes of love and arms to a sixteenth-century context the 'confusion' of the romances could be made to reflect something of the confusion of life. So the complex material is kept, but is carefully organised. It is chosen and arranged with great care so as to reflect the poet's vision of the complexity of human experience; and under the influence of the classical epic a greater unity is achieved by emphasising certain main themes which run through the whole poem and which dominate the lesser incidents surrounding them.

These main themes, as we have seen earlier, are the courtship of Ruggiero and Bradamante, the madness of Orlando, and the war between Charlemagne and Agramante – and it is indicative of Ariosto's position in the history of the Italian narrative poem that he compromises between the heterogeneous nature of the earlier romances and the attempts at rigid unity of theme of later sixteenth-century theorists and poets – so he has three themes rather than one, but one is given preference, and all are related to each other. He decides to give priority to Ruggiero and Bradamante, thus emphasising the serious, encomiastic note in the poem: so this pair are kept in view most frequently – one or the other is present in 30 of the 46 cantos, and the final cantos are devoted exclusively to them. Their story is that of a thwarted marriage – so they are separated from each other for most of the poem and the narrative follows them separately, jumping from one to the other with only brief meetings in between.

This theme is linked to that of the war in that it is the hostility between the two lovers' countries and faiths which prevents their marrying – only as a result of his experience in battle and with the ending of the war can Ruggiero win the hand of Bradamante. The war provides a focussing point for the widespread hostilities of pagans and Christians, who ultimately are drawn back to a common battle-field, and its completion is delayed therefore as late as possible in the poem (XLII; and the last pagan resistance, of Rodomonte, is defeated only in the last lines of the poem). Yet the war is not of primary importance and is often forgotten – in 22 cantos it is entirely absent. The war is also related to the other main theme, the madness of Orlando, in that it is *his* absence which jeopardises the safety of the Christians, and his return which brings their final success. The madness itself is not a particularly fruitful theme (Ariosto did not have Cervantes' happy inspiration in his treatment of insanity) and Orlando is off stage for much of the poem (for 31 of the 46 cantos); and Angelica has no further interest for us once she is married, and so disappears effectively in Canto XIX. The chronological sequence is therefore rationally established as the madness of Orlando, his cure, the completion of the war and the marriage of Bradamante and Ruggiero – and so the key points in the structure become the Medoro-Angelica meeting (XIX), the madness (XXIII), the cure (XXXIX), the completion of the war (XLII), the marriage (XLVI). The outbreak of madness is thus placed in the very centre of the poem, overlapping the divisions between Cantos XXIII and XXIV. By his

conscious ordering of these main elements of his subject, his relation
of them to each other, and the prominence they acquire by comparison with the rest of the material, Ariosto assured his poem a degree
of unity and coherence which his predecessors had failed to achieve.

This was, however, only a partial answer to Ariosto's problem.
The subordination of the complex secondary material to the main
themes was a major consideration. The main events involving the
leading characters, and a host of minor ones take place at the same
time but in different places. The narrative cannot present them all at
once and the poet is obliged to make his choice. In describing Angelica
in the early cantos, for example, Ariosto follows her to the moment
when she finds the wounded Medoro (XII, 65) – but Medoro in fact
has not yet been wounded – and Ariosto now leaves Angelica and
initiates the sequence of events (the battle for Paris) in which Dardinello was killed and Medoro went out to fetch back his body (XVIII),
and is struck down (XIX). And so in XIX, 17 the poet has caught up
with his previous XII, 65. In the meantime he not only prepares for
the wounding of Medoro, but has to bring other characters forward
in time. Orlando has to be prepared to receive the news of Angelica's
'treachery', and so his meeting with Isabella is now introduced
(XII, 91), the contrast between Isabella's devotion and Angelica's
defection precipitating Orlando's madness. And meanwhile Ariosto
thinks forward to the completion of the Isabella story and initiates
the story of Doralice (XIV, 50), whose 'betrayal' of Rodomonte will
precipitate the latter's assault on Isabella. So the poet jumps frequently
from place to place keeping the scattered events in time with each
other:

> Ma tempo è omai di ritrovar Ruggiero (VI, 16)
> [But now it's time to find Ruggiero again]
> Tempo è ch'io torni ove Grifon lasciai (XVIII, 59)
> [It's time that I went back to where I left Grifone.]

Frequently Ariosto conveys the impression of a writer hovering
over the globe surveying a range of separate activities taking place at
different points. We are permitted to see what goes on in different
places at the same time, though the narrative has to present them in
sequence. So we leave Astolfo on his hippogriff:

> Resti con lo scrittor de l'evangelo
> Astolfo ormai, ch'io voglio far un salto, (XXXV, 31)
> [Let Astolfo stay with the writer of the gospel now, because I
> want to make a jump ...]

– or we leave Bradamante to see what Rinaldo is doing:

Or ch'abbiam vista Bradamante in pena ...
veggiamo ancor, se miglior vita mena
il fratel suo ... (xLII, 28)
[Now that we've seen Bradamante suffering, let's see if her
brother is faring better.]
Such references are frequently ironical: Ruggiero has been left cantos
back in a storm at sea while Ariosto describes the combat on Lipadusa.
Then at a critical moment in the duel:
Ma mi parria, Signor, far troppo fallo,
se, per voler di costor dir, lasciassi
tanto Ruggier nel mar, che v'affogassi. (xLI, 46)
[But it seems to me, sir, that I should be far too neglectful if,
through wanting to speak about these people, I left Ruggiero so
long in the sea that he drowned.]
– and so to prevent Ruggiero drowning we leave Lipadusa and move
out to sea. The action apparently stands still while the author makes
the next move. Ruggiero and Orlando are left making their way to
Marseilles while Ariosto goes to fetch Astolfo:
Ma quivi stiano tanto, ch'io conduca
insieme Astolfo, il glorioso duca. (xLIV, 18)
[But let them stay there until I fetch Astolfo, the famous Duke.]
The tone is often that of the story-teller confiding casually to his
audience:
Soviemmi che cantare io vi dovea
(già lo promisi, e poi m'uscì di mente) ...

Dovea cantarne, et altro incominciai,
perché Rinaldo in mezzo sopravenne;
e poi Guidon mi diè che fare assai ... (xxxII, 1–2)
[I remember now that I ought to have told you (I promised to,
but then it slipped my mind) about. ... I should have told you,
and then I started something else, because Rinaldo came in
between; and then Guidone gave me plenty to do.]
If he breaks off one story it is because he has forgotten something – or
because his imaginary source does so:
Turpin, che tutta questa istoria dice,
fa qui digresso ... (xxIII, 38)
[Turpin, who tells the whole of this story, makes a digression
here.]
These breaks in the narrative are quite frequent – they average
about two a canto, and the poet makes no effort to conceal them. On

the contrary he seems to draw our attention to them by his ironical comments; occasionally he glides quietly into another subject with an unobtrusive 'Parigi intanto ...' (VIII, 69), 'Ruggiero in questo mezzo' (XXVI, 88) – but more often he advertises the break explicitly. The effect in most cases is to distance the narrative from everyday experience: the characters are belittled, they seem like puppets dangled on the end of a thread, made to dance when their author decides to pick them up, but otherwise left suspended in an awkward immobility which reminds us that they are, after all, only puppets. When they move they are remarkably human, reacting sensitively to the spurs and checks which govern human activity – but, just when we begin to confuse them with our own selves they are suddenly interrupted in their eloquent movements and hung up to await their creator's pleasure. And we are left with a strong impression that human experience is similar – that *we* are dangled at the end of cords manipulated by some unseen power, and that all our eloquent gesturing is liable to be suspended at a moment's notice. So Ariosto's recurrent comment on the fallibility of human aspirations is reflected in the structure of his narrative.

For human experience is not a smooth continuous process in which our intentions are successfully realised, and Ariosto came to see the potential of romance for reflecting the complexity of our experience in which funerals and weddings jostle each other, in which men turn from fighting to making love, in which one man's amorous conquest is another man's pair of horns. The poet's vision could embrace the confused complexity of life and see not only its subtlety but its essential unity and so its harmony. Hence Ariosto's likening of his poem to a tapestry in which different threads are woven together into a whole:

> Ma perché varie fila a varie tele
> uopo mi son, che tutte ordire intendo ... (II, 30)
> [But since I need different threads for different tapestries, and I intend to weave them all.]
> Di molte fila esser bisogno parme
> a condur la gran tela ch'io lavoro. (XIII, 81)
> [I think I need many threads to weave the great tapestry on which I am working]

– or a piece of music with its various changes of note:

> Signor, far mi convien come fa il buono
> sonator sopra il suo instrumento arguto,
> che spesso muta corda, e varia suono,
> ricercando ora il grave, ora l'acuto. (VIII, 29)

[Sir, I must do as the skilled player on his keen instrument, who often changes key and varies the tone, using now the low, now the shrill.]

These breaks in the narrative therefore serve a multiple purpose – to keep the actions of the various participants in step with each other, to allow the poet to vary the colour or texture of his narrative, and also of course to maintain suspense, for the break occurs with only rare exceptions at an exciting point in the action where we are eager to hear more. In the early cantos the breaks are often motivated by the search for variety; as the poem progresses the motive is more often the need to explain how a character has arrived where he is.

These explicit breaks in the narrative show quite clearly that for most of the poem Ariosto is concerned to follow in turn specific characters: 'Di Rinaldo ho da dir ...' (xxxi, 7). And he 'follows' that one, as a film director's camera might follow a particular actor – 'Voglio Astolfo seguir ...' (xxxiii, 96). In so doing we see not only Rinaldo's or Astolfo's own deeds, but also the persons whom they meet on their way, with their activities and perhaps *their* accounts of their own past misfortunes – so that temporarily our attention is distracted from the knight to his acquaintances; but he remains present as interlocutor/audience, and we return to him when the interlude is over. So a certain continuity is given to a succession of separate incidents which are gathered together in what we might call a 'phase'. It is as though one character is on stage for a succession of scenes in which he may be the centre of interest, or he may only be a bystander – but this sequence of scenes acquires a coherence from the continued presence of that character – and by coherence I mean not only a formal continuity of action but a thematic or psychological consistency in the relation of the digressive or peripheral material to the attitudes or situation of the main characters who witness them.

So after the initial canto and a half devoted to Angelica and her pursuers, we follow Bradamante ('torno a dir di Bradamante', (ii, 30)) through Canto ii, iii, and most of iv, including a long account of her descendants, forecast in Merlin's cave. Then we leave Bradamante and turn to Rinaldo ('torniamo a Rinaldo paladino' (iv, 50)) in Scotland where he hears Dalinda's story and intervenes to help her and Ginevra (iv, v, vi). Then comes a phase devoted to Ruggiero (vi, 16–viii, 19) who comes to Alcina's island, hears Astolfo's story, and becomes Alcina's captive till released by Melissa. Then after a brief return to Rinaldo and Angelica, we follow Orlando in his search for Angelica and his involvement in the adventures of Olimpia and

Bireno (VIII, IX, X). From Canto X we follow successively Ruggiero (X–XI), Orlando (XI–XIII) and then make a brief return to Ruggiero and Bradamante before a phase concerned very largely with the war (XIII–XV). Thereafter we follow Astolfo and Grifone (XV–XVIII) with interludes for the war (XVI–XVII, and XVIII–XIX). Then we follow Astolfo and Marfisa (XIX–XX), Zerbino (XX–XXII) and Bradamante (XXII–XXIII). In the second half of the poem there are long phases devoted to Ruggiero (XXV–XXVI), Rodomonte (XXVII–XXIX), Bradamante (XXXII–XXXIII), Astolfo (XXXIII–XXXV), Bradamante (with Ruggiero and Marfisa) (XXV–XXXVIII), Rinaldo (XLII–XLIII) and Ruggiero (XLIII–XLVI).

The 'phase' it will be seen, often embraces several cantos which are thus given a degree of continuity they might otherwise lack. The transition from one phase to another is normally clearly signalled by the poet, as we have seen earlier, with explicit allusions about returning to a long-neglected character, and so on, but on occasions the change is unobtrusive. We are following Astolfo for example, in Canto XVIII, where he meets Marfisa who accompanies him on his exploits in the land of the Amazons (XIX–XX). We then follow Marfisa ('ma vo' seguir la bellicosa donna', XX, 106) who meets and takes into her care the old hag Gabrina until she is able to hand her over to Zerbino – and so Marfisa withdraws ('e subito s'imbosca', XX, 129) and the narrative moves on with Zerbino. So a chain of characters introduce each other, themselves withdrawing in turn in a technique reminiscent of the theatre.

While a sequence of incidents is most commonly linked together by means of a character there are occasions when these incidents centre on a number of different characters but occur in the same geographical context. Here the narrative takes its direction from the place, Paris, for example, during the siege, where a rapid change of actors against the backcloth of the city helps to convey the confusion and excitement of the action; or the magic castle in Canto XII, where the confusion of the inmates who are invisible is reflected in the quick movement from one character to another. In the latter half of the poem Ariosto concentrates in a long phase (XXXVIII–XLII) on the climax of the war with the action swinging to and fro between Africa where Astolfo and Orlando are assaulting the pagans, and France where Charlemagne is driving Agramante into the sea – and the breadth of the canvas, with its multiplicity of characters converging ultimately on the Mediterranean for the final combat, produces an effect of grandeur reminiscent of the epic.

A different component of Ariosto's structure is what has been called the 'episode'. The word was used by the Cinquecento commentators to signify the largely self-contained stories not directly relevant to the main theme of the poem. Tasso later argued lengthily with his critics as to whether some of his 'episodes' were or were not relevant to his action. It is clearly a difficult term to define accurately. Much of the main action of the *Furioso* is itself episodic in nature – each of the principal knights is successively engaged in a series of adventures most of which are self-contained and could occur in a different sequence (although, as we have suggested earlier, the sequence actually followed has invariably been carefully planned by Ariosto to achieve a specific effect). Where the main characters themselves are principally involved in such adventures there is little difficulty for the author in relating them to the main structure, which, as we have shown, is largely built around the activities of the main personalities. Thus the Alcina episode, which is certainly a fantastic digression from the war, is nonetheless a significant moment in the career of the young Ruggiero; so Astolfo is a prime actor in the story of the warrior female community and of Guidone Selvaggio; and the self-contained Rocca di Tristano episode is linked to the main structure by the active involvement of Bradamante.

At the other extreme are those episodes in which none of the actual participants in the action is involved except as a listener. So we have four stories, complete in themselves, which are told to Rodomonte (Fiammetta, xxvIII), Astolfo (Lidia, xxxIV) and Rinaldo (Melissa, and Adonio, xLIII). Each is related thematically to the action in that it exemplifies a sexual relationship such as the main characters are involved in – and each serves, at the point at which it occurs, to diversify the narrative. But none has any formal connection with the action of the poem and could be detached from it with little difficulty.

In between the two categories we have mentioned is a larger group of episodes which are perhaps more characteristically Ariostesque and which comprise some of the most successful parts of the poem – the stories of Dalinda (IV–VII), Olimpia (IX–XI), Isabella (XVI–XXIX) Gabrina (XX–XXIII), Ricciardetto (XXV) and Marganorre (XXXVII). In each of these the interest centres on one or more minor figures who appear only in the context of the episode and then disappear, but in whose stories the main characters of the poem are actively involved. In the case of Ricciardetto Ruggiero's involvement is minimal: he saves the condemned youth from execution and then

hears the story of his misdeeds – but Ariosto does not tell us the outcome of Ruggiero's action. Marganorre's story is also largely self-
contained but is linked to the main narrative in that it presents an
injustice which Ruggiero, Bradamante and Marfisa amend. Gabrina
is more subtly interwoven into the poem in that she is both an active
participant in the action, causing distress to both Marfisa and Zerbino,
but also a character in her own right with a particularly interesting
past, revealed by her murdered lover's brother, Ermonide.

The remaining three episodes (Dalinda, Olimpia and Isabella) are
all of them masterpieces of narrative skill and poetic invention and are
integrated into the action with great care. Each of them contains a
lengthy narrative put in the mouth of the main character, the suffering
female, who presents us with a picture of events very largely as seen
by herself. Against this we have the reaction of the knight, Rinaldo or
Orlando, his efforts to relieve the lady's misfortunes, and their influence on his own subsequent conduct. The Isabella-Zerbino story is
spread over Cantos XII–XXIX in five components: Isabella's own
account of her misfortunes to Orlando when he rescues her from the
robbers' cave (XIII), her lover Zerbino's activities on the battlefield
(XVI,XIX) and with Gabrina (XX–XXIII), the uniting of the lovers
through Orlando's intervention (XXIII–XXIV), the death of Zerbino
(XXIV) and Isabella's suicide (XXVIII–XXIX). It is thus interwoven
into a lengthy stretch of the narrative, and is in fact linked with at
least three other strands of the plot – first with the movements of
Orlando, who saves first one, and then the other of the lovers and
whose discovery of Angelica's 'infidelity' shortly after contrasts so
effectively with Zerbino's happy recovery of his faithful Isabella, so
that each influences the other, Orlando going mad, Zerbino being led,
out of gratitude, to defend Orlando's arms from Mandricardo and so
sacrifice his own life for his protector. The Isabella story thus fits
neatly around the madness of Orlando which occurs between the reuniting of the lovers and the death of Zerbino. Secondly it is linked
with the Gabrina-Ermonide story, not only in that both are tales of
the conflict of friendship and passion, but more directly in that Zerbino is forced to escort the old hag Gabrina whose betrayal of him
brings Orlando to the rescue. Finally it is linked to the Mandricardo-
Doralice-Rodomonte triangle, a contrasting tale of female disloyalty,
by Zerbino's duel with Mandricardo and Isabella's death at the hands
of Rodomonte.

The Olimpia-Bireno episode was inserted by Ariosto after the 1521
edition and was cleverly interwoven into the existing Orc of Ebuda

story, in which Ruggiero saved the bound Angelica from the sea-monster. We are given first the account of the Orc (VIII–IX), then Olimpia's story – her own description of Bireno's long courtship, their marriage and enforced separation followed by Orlando's intervention to bring the lovers together (IX) and Bireno's desertion, then a return to the Orc and the rescue of Angelica (X), followed by the bringing together of the two stories in the last section where Olimpia is the next victim of the monster (XI). The different strands of the narrative are thus woven together, as at a different level are contrasting pictures of the female victims, the fickle Angelica and the devoted Olimpia, and of the male rescuers, the libidinous Ruggiero and the chaste Orlando.

Ariosto's episodes are thus effectively integrated into the texture of his poem – they retain the advantages of the episode, allowing the author to depart from the main lines of his action and to diversify the picture he is painting, and allowing the audience to concentrate its attention on a limited subject-matter at a time. Yet the continuity of the narrative is maintained and the coherence of the ideas is reinforced.

A further narrative device for breaking up the long poem is the *canto*, analogous to the phase or episode, yet not coincident with these. It reflects clearly the oral tradition, each canto representing a single session or 'performance'. The length of a canto was then primarily determined by the patience of the audience and remained fairly consistent. Ariosto retains the canto structure of the romance tradition, but he is far from consistent in the length of his cantos, which vary from 72 to 199 octaves. Such cantos, if recited, would take anything from about half an hour to more than an hour, but it is clear that by the sixteenth century the romance was more often read silently than aloud. The canto division therefore provides a pause for the reader who is invited, so to speak, when he wishes to break off his reading, to do so at a canto break. So the poet signals the break by drawing his narrative to a close (*congedo*), and re-starting it (*proemio*) in a new canto.

The siting of this break in the poem was used by the *cantastorie* for narrative effect, most commonly of course to maintain suspense. The breaking off of an adventure at a critical moment would be accompanied by an invitation to the audience to hear the sequel on the next occasion, by a few words of thanks to the listeners for their attention, of God's blessing on their sleep or appeals to their generosity when the hat would be taken round. Ariosto's *congedi* are always very

brief – never more than four lines, and sometimes they come on us
abruptly in the very last line of the canto:

    Al fin le donne in campo, e in Arli è gito
    Ruggiero; et io il mio canto ho qui finito (xxxvii, *122*)
    [At last the women came to the camp and Ruggiero to Arles;
    and I have finished my canto.]

He observes the conventions of the oral tradition, keeping up a fiction
that he is addressing the listening Ippolito and the court, referring to
what he will *tell* them:

    All'altro canto vi farò sentire,
    s'all'altro canto mi verrete a udire. (ix, *94*)
    [In the next canto I will tell you if in the next canto you come to
    hear me.]

He is tired at the end of a long narration, or hoarse ('rauco' xiv, *134*);
he would not want to bore his audience by going on too long
(xxiii, *136*) but he hopes they will return to provide 'quella grata
udienza che solete' (xxxiv, *92*).

    He brings the canto to a close almost always at a critical moment in
the narrative when we are eager for him to go on; the middle of a duel
or battle, a danger about to overtake a maiden in distress, the beginning of a new character's account of his misfortunes. Frequently he
has half begun a new adventure when he stops short: a knight having
overcome one adversary or obstacle is going on his way when he sees
a stranger approaching, or he hears a loud noise, scream, weeping:

    Spinge il cavallo, e piglia il brando fido,
    e donde viene il suon, ratto s'invia:
    ma diferisco un'altra volta a dire
    quel che seguì, se mi vorrete udire. (xi, *83*)
    [He spurs on his horse, seizes his trusty sword, and makes
    straight for the place where the noise is coming from: but I will
    put off till next time to tell you what happened, if you want to
    hear.]

The mere suspension of the excitement would, however, have
little significance for the *reader*, who has only to turn the page, were
it not for a deliberate pause the poet enforces upon him in the opening
stanzas of the next canto. The *proemio*, like the *congedo*, was a natural
device of the oral poet for welcoming his audience and setting the
context of his narration. Ariosto's *proemi*, as we have said, force the
reader's attention away for the moment from the narrative: the poet
does not need to welcome his audience, or to recapitulate what the
reader can quickly recover for himself–(although he does occasionally

repeat the *cantastorie's* formulae: 'Di sopra vi narrai che ...' (XIII, 2)).
Nor does he waste time on religious invocations. Instead Ariosto uses
the *proemio* for his own particular narrative purposes: especially to re-
establish contact with his audience, to step out of the framework of
his poem and talk to them man to man, commenting on the moral
implication of his story or its relevance to his own situation:

> Gravi pene in amor si provan molte,
> di che patito io n'ho la maggior parte ... (XVI, 1)
> [Love makes men suffer many grave trials, most of which I have
> endured,]

or addressing his patron directly, or the 'cortesi donne' of his acquaintance. He is able to explain the general significance of the story in
which we are involved:

> La fede unqua non debbe esser corrotta ... (XXI, 2)
> [A promise never should be broken,]

or to set the tone of what is to follow: serious and pompous as before
the battle for Paris:

> E se alle antique le moderne cose,
> invitto Alfonso, denno assimigliarsi;
> la gran vittoria, onde alle virtuose
> opere vostre può la gloria darsi ... (XIV, 2)
> [And if, invincible Alfonso, modern matters can be compared to
> ancient; the great victory, the glory of which can be credited to
> your virtuous exploits ...]

– or bantering and ironical before the bawdy tale of Fiammetta:

> Donne, e voi che le donne avete in pregio,
> per Dio, non date a questa istoria orecchia. (XXVIII, 1)
> [Ladies, and those of you who prize the ladies, pay no heed to
> this story.]

The canto divisions therefore serve further to vary the rhythm and
tone of the narrative, and are thoughtfully related by the poet to his
other narrative devices, particularly the 'phase' and the episode. In
many cases the latter are themselves spread over several cantos, beginning and ending midway through the canto (the Bradamante phase,
II, 30–IV, 50; the Rinaldo phase, IV, 50–VI, 16; the Angelica-Medoro
episode, XVIII, 165–XIX, 42 etc.). The effect then is a counterpoint of
canto, episode and phase which brings out the colour and particular
character of each while blending them together in a harmonious
whole. And within the canto itself the narrative is varied not only by
the breaks between phases and episodes, but by a succession of lesser
incidents, different from each other in theme or tone. Canto VI, for

example, comprises the conclusion of the Dalinda story and the beginning of the Alcina episode, which divides into Ruggiero's arrival and meeting with the myrtle (Astolfo), Astolfo's story, and then Ruggiero's advance to meet Erifilla. Thus the canto embraces a frequently changing narrative with not only a quick succession of new characters and events but also a variation of method from commentary, to direct narrative, to dramatic monologue or dialogue.

It is notable how frequently Ariosto's narrative employs effects similar to those of his works for the stage. The canto divisions, and other breaks in the narrative, are often analogous to the scene or act-divisions of the comedies. There are some conventional 'agnizioni', as when Rinaldo discovers Guidon Selvaggio in Canto XXXI, and when Marfisa turns out to be Ruggiero's sister in Canto XXXVI – and we have the mistaken identity of Ricciardetto and Bradamante (XXV). Some of the tales work up to fine dramatic dénouements, the Dalinda story for example with Ariodante's surprise appearance (VI), and the Drusilla story with its final poisonings (XXXVII). And the poet makes frequent use of dramatic irony, as in the Leone episode, for example, where Bradamante fights Ruggiero believing her opponent to be Leone, or the Grifone-Orrigille story where we as audience are let into the secret of the fickle girl's treachery. In particular Ariosto's use of direct speech, monologue or dialogue, goes far beyond that of any of his predecessors – repeatedly he envisages a scene as a lively exchange of words between two characters. What happens when the false Odorico who has attempted to seduce his friend Zerbino's beloved Isabella is caught and handed over to Zerbino? The scene is vividly presented with the words of both men (XXIV, 20–41). So is the scene where Polinesso insists to Ariodante that his beloved Ginevra is false to him (V, 27–46); and the scene where Ferraù unwittingly insults Orlando (XII, 40–45), and where Astolfo and Iocondo discuss their memories of the night when Fiammetta cuckolded them both (XXVIII, 66–70). We also are given many eloquent or pathetic monologues; Bradamante's defence of her actions in the Rocca di Tristano (XXXII, 101–6) or Rinaldo's eloquent plea for the equality of the sexes (IV, 63–7), Fiordiligi's lament for the death of Brandimarte (XLIII, 160–3) or Olimpia's when she is abandoned by Bireno (X, 25–33). It is mostly at moments of particular tension when his characters are confronted with situations that stir their deepest emotions or beliefs that the poet turns to a dramatic form: it is an effective variant of the narrative, bringing the scene more vividly before us, and at the same time recalling the art of the theatre and thus distancing the fiction to some extent from the reality of our experience.

At the same time Ariosto achieves subtle effects by his juxtaposition of direct and indirect speech, setting up tension between the bluntness of the spoken words and the elegance and poise of the poet's narrative. Compare the crude challenge of the vindictive Ermonide with the courtesy of Zerbino's reply, set respectively in direct and indirect speech:

– O di combatter meco t'apparecchia, –
gridò con voce minacciosa e fiera
– o lascia la difesa de la vecchia,
che di mia man secondo il merto pèra.
Se combatti per lei, rimarrai morto:
che così avviene a chi s'appiglia al torto. –

Zerbin cortesemente a lui risponde
che gli è desir di bassa e mala sorte,
et a cavalleria non corrisponde
che cerchi dar ad una donna morte:
se pur combatter vuol, non si nasconde ... (xxi, 7–8)

['Either prepare to fight with me,' he shouted with fierce and threatening voice, 'or give up your defence of the old woman and let her perish by my hand as she deserves. If you fight for her you'll die; that's what happens to those who involve themselves in what is wrong.' Zerbino courteously answers him that it is a base and wicked desire not consonant with chivalry, to try to kill a woman; but if Ermonide insists on fighting, he will not refuse.]

This combination of narrative and dramatic techniques is one of the many devices that help to maintain the reader's interest through this long poem. It is particularly the variety of the form that holds our attention. Not only does the poet break his narrative as soon as he fears he is becoming tedious, but he is extremely careful within each story or incident to avoid unnecessary detail or elaboration. Characterisation is not detailed but it is more effective than we might expect in a long narrative poem of this period. The main features of the paladins and their opponents had been established long since and recently reinforced by Boiardo. Ariosto accepts the characters he had inherited from the *Innamorato*: he rarely stops to redefine them. But they act consistently within their characters and they come to life in vividly imagined scenes in a way that their predecessors generally

failed to do – Angelica, for example, helping the defeated Sacripante
to his feet and assuring him that his downfall was the fault of his
horse (I, 67); the warrior-maid Marfisa, who is persuaded to put on
female dress and then finds she has to fight off Mandricardo since her
male escort can't defend her from him (xxvI, 79); Orlando, restored
to his senses and staring in confusion at his own naked body and the
cords used to tie him up (xxxIx, 59). And there are some fine little
vignettes – the shepherd, for example, who thinks he can entertain
Orlando with his normally successful story of how Angelica brought
Medoro to his cottage (xxIII, 118).

In all of this Ariosto reveals a fine sense of proportion, an ability to
scale the detail to the whole. Character drawing, precedents, back-
grounds are not allowed to obtrude. The scene is often barely mentioned and is rarely particularised: this lively human action needed a
fairly generic back-cloth to avoid over-elaboration. It is the essential
art of the raconteur to know where to hurry on with his tale and
where to linger. The *cantastorie* had the yawns of their audience to
guide them, and Ariosto follows in their wake:

> Ma le parole mie parervi troppe
> potriano omai, se più se ne dicesse:
> sì che finirò il canto; e mi fia specchio
> quel che per troppo dire accade al vecchio. (xxvIII, 102)
> [But my words might seem excessive to you if I said any more;
> so I will finish the canto and let my warning be what happens to
> the loquacious old man.]

The structure of the poem serves therefore to sustain and unite a
complex mass of characters and incidents the variety of which is an
essential feature of its appeal. The selection of this character to follow
that, the breaking off of one story in order to pursue another is determined by the poet's vision of his subject. His aim as we have noted
before is to weave his many threads into a complete tapestry – but the
mere completion of the fabric with all threads tied away is not enough;
it is the pattern which emerges that justifies the whole operation. So
Ariosto brings in a villain here to offset a hero there, a trusty friend to
offset a false one, an innocent maid to balance a scheming old crone.
So he moves from a shady wood and murmuring stream to a rich
palace or a craggy mountain. Or he follows a realistic tale of the conflict of human passions, with a fantastic account of hippogriffs, orcs or
crocodiles. Or we indulge in the lighthearted banter of a bawdy story
followed by a tragic tale of love and devotion: we find ironical tilts at
the ladies of the court, and high-flown eulogies of the Estense rulers.

Ariosto himself smilingly comments on the art required to handle this narrative.

Or l'alta fantasia, ch'un sentier solo
non vuol ch'i' segua ognor, quindi mi guida,
e mi ritorna. ... (xiv, 65)
[My lofty fancy, which does not want me to follow a single path,
now guides me and sends me back.]

Ironical as this Dantesque reminiscence sounds (*Paradiso*, xxxiii, 142) it reflects nevertheless the essence of Ariosto's genius.

8. The Arts of Poetry

If Ariosto was a master of the arts of narrative, he was nevertheless essentially a poet – almost everything that he wrote was in verse, and it is difficult to imagine the *Furioso* in any other form than the *ottava rima*: the inspiration is essentially poetic. The subject-matter is of a literary, imaginative nature: we are presented with characters and settings that have existed only in the minds of writers and their public, and the poet is largely occupied in re-creating that imaginative vision of the past and relating it to his own; and his conception of the chivalrous world is coloured by his sixteenth-century culture and experience in subtle and confused ways which are not subject to rational or logical analysis. This delicate superimposition of Renaissance attitudes on medieval romance becomes a paradigm for a larger theme, the interaction of imagination and experience, of ideals and reality, truth and illusion.

That such a theme dealing broadly with an imaginative world and emotional reactions towards it is eminently suited to poetical expression is, I think, clear. A hundred years later Cervantes used prose when he undertook a similar theme in the *Quixote* – that is to relate the chivalrous tradition to his contemporary world – but Cervantes had a different literary tradition behind him, and his approach to his subject was also rather different. Don Quixote acts like a medieval knight in a world that is really seventeenth-century Spain, and with the sharp eye of a realistic novelist Cervantes recorded his exploits in prose. Ariosto's setting, characters and action are all those of the chivalrous tradition – Orlando is not thrust out into the harsh realities of, say, Machiavelli's Florence; he and his fellows while acting sporadically like sixteenth-century mortals, live nonetheless in the forests of medieval romance. Essentially these creatures of fancy had come down to Ariosto through a verse tradition, and he in his turn presents them to us with the resources of poetry, in the cadence of verse and the imagery of poetic language. His introduction of Orlando and Angelica in the opening stanzas of the poem illustrates this:

> Orlando, che gran tempo inamorato
> fu de la bella Angelica, e per lei

in India, in Media, in Tartaria lasciato
avea infiniti et immortal trofei. ... (1, 5)
[Orlando, who for a long time had been in love with the lovely
Angelica, and had left, in India, Medea and Tartary, infinite and
immortal trophies to her.]
Orlando, in a dominant position at the beginning of the octave, and
credited in resonant epithets with his immortal triumphs in the East,
as though with a glittering row of medals across his chest, already stirs
the imagination as a figure beyond the normal human proportions;
and the seductive Angelica insinuates herself into the picture, relegated into a quiet, subordinate role and contrasted with Orlando both
by her antithetical placing at the end of the clause and by the form of
her first presentation in which the priority of her beauty over her
identity is reinforced by the strong stress on 'bella' which echoes
through the quasi-rhyming 'Angelica'. The characters and relationship of the two are already suggested by the cadence of the lines
beyond the explicit meaning of the words.
    Rinaldo too is presented as a creature of the imagination, the knight
in shining armour:
    Indosso la corazza, l'elmo in testa,
    la spada al fianco, e in braccio avea lo scudo ... (1, 11)
    [His cuirass on his body, his helmet on his head, his sword by his
    side, and on his arm his shield,]
– the simplest and barest of descriptions which nevertheless conveys
a sense of his splendour and self-confidence in the careful symmetry
of the syntax (the arms enclosed by their qualifying positions in the
first line and enclosing them in the second) and of the rhythm
(the stress pattern of the first line is repeated, but in reverse, in the
second).
    So too the narrative action is underlined by poetic means. Carlo-
magno put Angelica in the safe keeping of Duke Namo before the
battle, planning to give her as a reward to the most valorous of his
knights. But the Christians were defeated and in place of an orderly
prize-giving there is a wild flight:
    Contrari ai voti poi furo i successi;
    ch'in fuga andò la gente battezzata,
    e con molti altri fu'l duca prigione ... (1, 9)
    [Contrary to their intentions was the outcome, because the
    baptised went off in flight, and the Duke was left a prisoner with
    many others ...]
The rout of the Christians is brought vividly before our eyes by the

stressing of 'fuga' at the beginning of the line (their instinct for self-preservation taking precedence over their religion ('battezzata')!); and in the next line, prominently sited and emphasised by the repetition of consonants, the crowd of unidentified prisoners seem to swamp the Duke who is in there somewhere among them. And introducing this unexpected turn of events is the poet's comment which not only tells us the result of the battle but suggests by the antithetical stressing of 'voti' and 'successi' a sort of proverbial truth revealed in this particular incident: so stark is the contrast in fact that we are led to smile at the naïveté of human illusions.

Such of course are the arts of poetry, of all poets. What distinguishes the poetry of Ariosto from that of Petrarch, say, or even Dante, is its essentially narrative character – that is to say, that Ariosto is largely concerned with people's actions, what they do next when something has happened to them, how the course of their conduct is affected by their encounters with other people. Orlando is jilted, goes mad, is cured and recovers his fighting strength and skill; Rodomonte is jilted, gets drunk, chases another woman, repents; Isabella's lover is killed and she commits suicide; Olimpia's lover deserts her and she marries someone else. A succession of actions and reactions is narrated and the poetry is adapted to this specific purpose. It is not generally lyrical; Ariosto does not delay long to convey states of feeling, although there *are* declarations of love and laments for the dead in which the verse takes on the richness of imagery and density of stylistic effects of the sonnet or *canzone*. But these are not frequent, nor are the epic outbursts, the rhetorical celebration of the Estense heroes. There are satirical passages in which the poet stops to criticise the failings of his society, very much in the style of his satires; and there is a dramatic component in his verse where situations are presented through the dialogue of the participants. But most characteristic of the *Furioso* is the narrative style in which the poet is pushing along the action, bringing characters from Africa to Paris, getting them in and out of ships (and shipwrecks), getting them courted, jilted, assaulted and rescued, and showing how they react to the stings and spurs of Fortune.

Essential to such poetry is movement, the movement of the narrative underlined and shaded by that of the verse. We haven't time, where the action is moving on, to stop to savour patient similes or to disentangle obscure word-order, we cannot look under every word for a symbolic meaning or ponder over bold images. We have a long way to go. So we find a poetry in which the normal features of the lyric are diluted, in which the intensity of epic is relaxed, a narrative style in a medium register, somewhere between, on the one hand, lyric and epic, and on the other a discursive prose – a poetry reflecting the actions and reactions of the characters and also the varying response to them of their creator.

In characterising Ariosto as a narrative poet we should remember that he was a poet before he was a narrator – that is, in the chronological sense. His early writing is all in verse, whether in Latin or Italian: sonnets, *canzoni*, *capitoli*, eclogues. In these forms, however, he is a rather undistinguished poet. Only when he turns to the octave does his genius emerge, and it is clear that (in spite of the skill he later displayed in the satires, which are in *terza rima*) the character of his poetry is closely affected by his choice of this particular form, his 'ottava d'oro' as it has been called.

The early history of the octave is obscure, but the first master, and probably the inventor of the form was Boccaccio, who employed it in his narrative poems, the *Filostrato*, *Teseida* and *Ninfale Fiesolano*. It seems likely that the authors of the *cantari*, or popular narrative poems of the latter fourteenth and the fifteenth centuries, in adopting the octave rhyme, were following Boccaccio's example. In these works the octave is a fairly simple metrical tool – essentially a sequence of four couplets of *endecasillabi*, the first three of which have alternating rhyme (ab ab ab), the last being a rhyming couplet with a new rhyme (cc). In the simplest examples the couplets are self-contained grammatical units, separate finite sentences or clauses, often with marked pauses at the end of each line. Rhyme may be replaced by assonance, but tends to be obvious and obtrusive, frequently a verbal inflection or cliché, dictating the word-order of the couplet. The rhyming couplets are barely distinguishable in function from the preceding ones in alternating rhyme.

The progress from this crude form to the sophisticated octave of the *Furioso* is too complex to describe here. Boccaccio made frequent use of enjambement to break up the formal pattern of the couplets, bringing the rhythm of the stanza closer to that of prose, and in the fifteenth century Pulci, Lorenzo de' Medici, Poliziano and Boiardo all used the octave with some degree of originality. Essential to any successful handling of the form was the relation of the metrical structure to the tone and mood of the material – which was severely hampered by a close adherence to the primitive practice described above. Poliziano, in his unfinished epic fragment, *Le Stanze per la*

Giostra, used the octave sensitively, moulding successive *endecasillabi* together by metrical and stylistic means to achieve subtle lyrical effects and to produce an octave that was a complete lyrical whole; and Boiardo showed his readiness to break up the octave, running couplets into each other and even thinking beyond the single octave, allowing his narrative the sweep of successive stanzas. But neither of these writers really mastered the octave as a narrative form. Poliziano's subtle use of enjambement only rarely extends to the octave as a whole; and Boiardo, in spite of his liberties with the octave structure, is mostly in too much of a hurry to achieve any subtlety of poetic effect from them. To combine Boiardo's narrative power with Poliziano's lyric sensitivity would be to create a genuinely narrative poetry, and that is what Ariosto did.

The stanza form, for example, is carefully moulded to the narrative action. The break between stanzas is used for a purpose, most commonly of course to enforce a pause where the reader is required to let what he has just read sink in, to take stock before continuing. It acts perhaps like a double full stop. When Angelica rushes off on Rinaldo's horse we follow her wild course through the first six lines of the stanza and are brought to a halt with her in the final couplet:

> La donna il palafreno a dietro volta,
> e per la selva a tutta briglia il caccia;
> né per la rara più che per la folta,
> la più sicura e miglior via procaccia:
> ma pallida, tremando, e di sé tolta,
> lascia cura al destrier che la via faccia.
> Di su, di giù, ne l'alta selva fiera
> tanto girò, che venne a una riviera.

> Su la riviera Ferraù trovosse
> di sudor pieno e tutto polveroso ... (I, *13–14*)

[The lady turns the palfrey round and drives it full speed through the wood, and does not take the best or safest course, through the clearings rather than the thickest parts, but pale, trembling and beside herself leaves her steed to make its way. Up, down, through the wild wood she careered, till she came to a river bank. On the bank was Ferraù, all covered in sweat and dust.]

We pause with Angelica at the end of the octave, sensing her frustration, and the unhurried repetition of 'riviera' in the first line of the next stanza contrasts vividly Angelica's speed with Ferraù's inertia –

while she has been careering through the forest he has retired from the battle to rest and have a drink. The two stanzas are thus related to each other not merely as successive moments in an action, but poetically as separate impressions, contrasting pictures of different characters. Elsewhere successive stanzas are linked by enjambement where the action carries us on: the speed of the abandoned Olimpia's rush after her lover allows of no pause:

... si getta
del letto e fuor del padiglione in fretta:

e corre al mar ... (x, *21–2*)

[leaping out of bed and the tent in haste: she runs to the sea.]

Interesting here is the near disappearance of the final couplet in a different structure. The rhyming couplet, by virtue of its rhyme and its position, has a special function in Ariosto's poem where it is used with much greater care and effect than in the poems of any of his predecessors. It frequently forms a genuine conclusion, completing the action of the first six lines (as in I, *13* quoted p. 146), or holding the point of interest as well as the rhythmical climax for which the reader is waiting (xxv, *64*; xlii, *38*). It may sum up a lengthy description (xxxvii, *115*) or provide a sort of finishing touch, a witty comment (viii, *80*; xii, *3*) or mythological adornment (I, *40*; xliv, *85*). Most commonly it concludes what has just been said, but it may look forward, setting off a new chain of action, stirring our interest in what is to follow (I, *25, 32*) like a canto ending; and where appropriate its independence may be merged in the following octave (as in x, *21–2*, quoted above), with a few words repeated to stress the continuity (xli, *19–20, 27–8*).

The quadripartite structure of the octave remains the basis of Ariosto's method, as in the stanza describing Angelica's flight quoted above (p. 146). This is, one might say, the standard pattern which conditions our ear to a certain cadence, any deviation from which we note consciously or subconsciously and which the poet can use for particular effects. In this stanza all lines except one are end-stopped, and there is a particularly strong pause at the end of each couplet (the repeated stopping and re-starting of the rhythmical flow reflecting perhaps Angelica's wild flight through the forest). In the introduction of Orlando (see p. 142 above), on the other hand, there is repeated enjambement between successive lines, couplets and stanzas, allowing the poet a more ample frame-work for the sweep of his long sentences, and at the same time speeding up the flow, not allowing us to

pause, except very briefly, for some fourteen lines – a practice frequently adopted where the poet does not want to place much emphasis on what he is saying, as, for example, in this recapitulation of
Orlando's previous history, which is hardly necessary when most of
his readers knew Boiardo's poem so well. So he hurries on until he
comes to the really significant lines (at the end of the sixth and beginning of the seventh stanzas) which are end-stopped.

Repeated enjambement thus can be used to set the narrative in the
tone of an aside, while the end-stopped lines or couplets restore
the emphasis – as, for example, where Drusilla, courted by Tanacro,
the murderer of her husband, resolves to use deceit, pretending to
welcome his proposal of marriage, but planning secretly to poison
him. Her hatred is intense:

Ma non però quest'odio così ammorza
la conoscenza in lei, che non comprenda
che se vuol far quanto disegna, è forza
che simuli ... (XXXVII, 59)

[But this hatred does not so blunt her understanding, that she
doesn't realise that, in order to do what she plans, she must
simulate.]

Compare this sottovoce soliloquy with the answer she makes
publicly:

Ella si mostra tutta lieta, e finge
di queste nozze aver sommo desio:
e ciò che può indugiarle a dietro spinge,
non ch'ella mostri averne il cor restio.
Più de l'altre s' adorna e si dipinge:
Olindo al tutto par messo in oblio. (XXXVII, 61)

[She makes a show of being very happy, and pretends that she is
very eager for this wedding; she rejects anything that might
delay it, let alone any sign that she is reluctant at heart: she
dresses and makes herself up more than the others. Olindo seems
to be entirely forgotten.]

A similar effect is apparent in Isabella's attempt to deceive Rodomonte
into testing her potion on herself, enjambement hurrying on her
words and forestalling his possible objections (XXXIX, 24).

So single words and images gain greater or lesser prominence by
their rhythmical context. In the Drusilla story the key image is given
prominence by rhythmical stress and contrast when the bride hands
the poisoned cup to the groom:

poi diè allo sposo con viso giocondo

il nappo: ... (XXXVII, 69)

[then with smiling face she gave the goblet to the bridegroom.]
Here the enjambement not only conveys the action more vividly (as
though stressing what is going on in the bride's mind – her eagerness
to be rid of the cup), but it also, in that stressed juxtaposition of
poisoned cup and smiling face, condenses in one striking image the
essence of the whole scene.

The cadence of the octave is thus used to distribute emphasis as the
poet wishes, in the style of the story-teller who knows that he must
ration his effects, speeding up where he may prove tedious in order
to win his listener's whole-hearted attention for matters of real
interest. In the scene where Agramante gives Doralice the task of
choosing between her two admirers and, to everyone's surprise, she
prefers Mandricardo to the mighty Rodomonte, her fateful judgement is hidden away in the fifth line of the octave, and the key name
in the middle of the line, as though sheltering behind a stress and tail-
ing away rhythmically :

... Et ella abbassò gli occhi vergognosi,
e disse che più il Tartaro avea caro ... (XXVII, 107)

[And she lowered her eyes shyly and said that she liked the
Tartar better.]

So Ariosto paints in sound the diffident girl's fear of angering her
choleric fiancé.

The poet's artistry in fusing sound and image is nowhere more
apparent than in the scene where Isabella, pining for her dead lover,
Zerbino, tricks the brutal Rodomonte into cutting off her head :

Quel uom bestial le prestò fede, e scorse
sì con la mano, e sì col ferro crudo,
che, del bel capo, già d'Amore albergo
fe' tronco rimanere il petto e il tergo.

Quel fe' tre balzi; e funne udita chiara
voce ch'uscendo nominò Zerbino ... (XXIX, 25-6)

[That bestial man believed her, and let fly with hand and cruel
sword so that he lopped the body bare of that lovely head, once
the abode of love. It bounced three times, and from it was heard
a clear voice calling Zerbino's name.]

The contrast between the crude violence of Rodomonte and the
gentle beauty of Isabella, underlined rhythmically in the first three
lines, is repeated in the last two between the clipped syllables of the
bouncing head and the drawn-out lament in which, with our last

ounce of breath, we reach the beloved Zerbino's name.

This scene of Isabella's suicide is one of the most admired passages in the poem. That it is a tragic, a pathetic moment we are at once aware – the noble sacrifice of the gentle girl whose chastity and devotion have been so warmly represented is given an epic setting with the Creator gazing down in approval, conferring beauty and virtue for ever on all those bearing the name of Isabella (Isabella d'Este no doubt prominent among them). Yet the harsh reality is pressed upon us with that 'perhaps' drunken executioner (XXIX, 25) and the bouncing head depicted only a moment previously in the most stylised Petrarchan language. This juxtaposition or overlapping of different stylistic levels and tones is frequent and characteristic in the *Furioso* arousing that complexity of reactions and interpretations which is the hall-mark of so much great literature.

It reflects of course the complexity of the subject-matter which embraces so many different levels of experience from the meanest and ugliest to the noblest and most beautiful. At its two extremes Ariosto's poetry derives from two different cultural traditions, the popular romance and the classical epic, and its stylistic diversity is essentially a reflection of the poet's cultural situation: characteristic of some of the greatest minds of his age was his ambition to embrace both traditions, the classical and the vernacular, and his combination of different stylistic levels in a coherent and individual poetry was one of his greatest achievements.

Ariosto was not then content to leave the romance in the key of the *cantastorie*: he has the classical epic frequently in mind. His opening lines are clearly reminiscent of the opening of the *Aeneid*, and his final stanzas, where in a last heroic duel Ruggiero kills Rodomonte, are closely modelled on Virgil's final duel between Turnus and Aeneas:

> Alle squalide ripe d'Acheronte,
> sciolta dal corpo più freddo che giaccio,
> bestemmiando fuggì l'alma sdegnosa,
> che fu sì altiera al mondo e sì orgogliosa. (XLVI, *140*)
> [To the grim banks of the Acheron, released from the body that was colder than ice, fled cursing the scornful soul that was so proud and arrogant on earth.]

The style is elevated and grave in a conscious recollection of the Virgilian precedent. In the new material added for the final edition the poet frequently repeats this note, and notably in the passages devoted to celebrating Ruggiero and Bradamante as the fountain-head of the illustrious line of the Estensi. Here the tone is, as we should

expect, high-flown and noble: in the long review of the Estensi in
Canto III for example:

Chi mi darà la voce e le parole
convenienti a sì nobil suggetto? (III, *1*)
[Who will grant me voice and words fitting for so noble a
subject?]

Such grandiose eulogies are scattered throughout the *Furioso* in
passages celebrating not only the Estensi, but other famous contemporaries, the heroes of the wars of Italy, the great explorers, the
famous ladies etc. Ippolito d'Este, whose patronage is so scathingly
treated in the satires, is here painted in epic colours:

Poi cardinale appar, ma giovinetto,
sedere in Vaticano a consistoro,
e con facondia aprir l'alto intelletto,
e far di sè stupir tutto quel coro. (XLVI, *90*)
[Then he appears as a cardinal, though still a young man, sitting
in council in the Vatican, eloquently displaying his profound
intellect and leaving the whole assembly amazed.]

Bradamante and Ruggiero are invested with the splendour of the
heroes of antiquity, and the battle between Christians and pagans
often assumes epic tones:

Grandine sembran le spesse saette
dal muro sopra gli nimici sparte.
Il grido insin al ciel paura mette ... (XVI, *19*)
[The dense arrows showered from the wall like hail upon the
enemy. The cry strikes fear into heaven itself.]

The tone here is serious: Ariosto's eulogies of his patrons and other
famous men are not ironical – and to assume that the poet was smiling
up his sleeve as he wrote them is quite unjustified – Ariosto could not
risk offending his protectors even if he wanted to. But we know that
he was a loyal subject, a Ferrarese and Italian patriot and one who
cared deeply about the fate of his country – and in a sense he writes
the epic of his time in which the splendid victory of the Christians
over the invaders reflects the hopes of the Italians struggling with
their invaders.

So the tone of the poem is often very far from ironical. It can be
epic and eloquent as we have seen – and it can be grave and elegiac, as
in some inspired death scenes, those of Brandimarte and Dardinello
for example:

Come purpureo fior languendo muore,
che 'l vomere al passar tagliato lassa;

o come carco di superchio umore
il papaver ne l'orto il capo abbassa:
così, giù de la faccia ogni colore
cadendo, Dardinel di vita passa;
passa di vita, e fa passar con lui
l'ardire e la virtù de tutti i sui. (XVIII, *153*)
[As a purple flower, cut by the plough as it passes, is left to
languish and die; or as a poppy laden with too much moisture
in the garden droops its head; so, all colour draining from his
face, Dardinel passes from this life; he passes away and with him
pass the courage and virtue of all his men.]

It is a close Virgilian reminiscence (with echoes from the *Iliad* and
Catullus: 'inque umeros cervix conlapsa recumbit:/Purpureus veluti
cum flos succisus aratro/Languescit moriens, lassove papavera collo/
Demisere caput pluvia cum forte gravantur./at Nisus ruit in medios!')
Ariosto takes up and extends the elegiac note of the *Aeneid* where the
similes give way abruptly to the stark narrative ('at Nisus ruit ...'; cf.
the pathetic 'passa di vita e fa passar con lui ...' . But essentially the
tones and the effect of Virgil are preserved. The tone may also be
elaborately didactic, as in the serious allegorical passages concerning
Alcina and Logistilla (VI, VII), or the personified forces controlling
the battle fortunes (XVIII, *28*), or committed and urgent – as in the
appeal to his invasion-ridden country (quoted above, p. 112) to
resist the foreign hordes now swarming over a lethargic Italy, or the
rebuke to the invaders:

Se Cristianissimi esser voi volete,
e voi altri Catolici nomati,
perché di Cristo gli uomini uccidete? (XVII, *75*)
[If you wish to be true Christians, to be reckoned Catholics,
why do you kill men who follow Christ?]

Often the note is consciously literary, not with any satirical or ironical
undertone but in serious emulation of some much admired poetic
precedent – as in the case of a delicately painted sky-forest-scene or
scape for example:

Era ne l'ora che traea i cavalli
Febo del mar con rugiadoso pelo,
e l'Aurora di fior vermigli e gialli
venìa spargendo d'ogn'intorno il cielo. (XII, *68*)
[It was the hour when Phoebus brought his horses out of the sea
with dewy coats, and Aurora came scattering the heavens all
around with vermilion and yellow flowers.]

Yet Ariosto knows that there is another side – the struggle often is not heroic. One dreams of the grandiose and lives with the trivial: and alongside the noble high-flown rhetorical eulogies of the epic are the realistic, down-to-earth, deflationary notes of the Italian romance tradition, not thrust crudely on us as in the *cantari*, but gently and gracefully insisted on nonetheless. The romances had tended more and more to bring the Carolingian legends closer to the experience of the popular Italian audiences. Andrea da Barberino is much concerned with the everyday background – explaining why people acted as they did, what they ate and drank, where they stayed (compare Don Quixote's insistence that he never read of any knight having money with him).

Ariosto inherits this tradition. We see the heroes in their unheroic as well as their heroic moments – in their squabbling arguments for example:

– Per Dio (dicea Ruggier), non te la lasso,
ch'esser convien questa battaglia mia.
– Va indietro tu! – Vavvi pur tu! – (xxvii, *66*)
[Good God (said Ruggier) I'm not leaving this to you. This is my fight – You just get back! – Get back yourself!]

Their language is often far from heroic or literary – almost that of everyday conversation:

Ruggier le disse : – Io v'ho veduto altrove;
et ho pensato e penso, e finalmente
non so né posso ricordarmi dove. (xxv, *21*)
[Ruggiero said – I have seen you somewhere else, and I've thought and I'm still thinking and I just can't remember where.]

The colloquialisms, the popular proverbial expressions, elegantly paraphrase the habitual mode of expression of the uncultured audiences of the romance tradition:

e presta pon l'impiastro ove il duol punge. (vii, *46*)
[and he puts the plaster where the pain hurts.]
e con tal modo sa tesser gl'inganni
che men verace par Luca e Giovanni (xvi, *13*)
[and he's so clever at telling lies that Luke and John seem less truthful than he does.]

The view-point is often that of the piazza where the *cantastorie* got their horse laughs from standard devices: crude force,

un pugno gli tirò di tanto peso,
che ne la gola gli cacciò duo denti. (xviii, *85*)

[he gave him such a punch that he knocked two of his teeth down his throat.]

(cf. Pulci, 'Dette a quell'altro un pugno tra gli orecchi/Col guante tal che non ne vuol parecchi' – *Morgante*, XIII, *64*) and stock witty paraphrases for slaughter and violence:

mandando or questo or quel giù ne l'inferno
a dar notizia del viver moderno. (XVI, *83*).
[sending first this and then that one down to hell to take them news about modern life.]
e 'l capo e 'l collo in modo gli divise,
che medico mai più non lo raggiunse. (XIX, *87*)
[and he split his head off from his neck so that no doctor ever joined it on again.]

(cf. Pulci, 'Chè se l'avessi giunto la percossa / Non bisognava il medico venisse' – *Morgante*, I, *38*).

So too we get some fairly broad laughs at love-making in generally transparent double-entendres:

Io senza scale in su la ròcca salto
e lo stendardo piantovi di botto,
e la nimica mia mi caccio sotto. (XXV, *68*)
[without a ladder I leap on to the castle, plant my standard on top, and thrust my enemy underneath.]

– the reverse perhaps of the Petrarchan coin.

These two notes, the popular and the high-flown, derive from different traditions familiar to the poet. What is new in the *Furioso* is the way in which the two traditions are combined. The poet often does not try to smooth out the transition between epic and romance: he simply juxtaposes them in a way that draws attention to their differences. So within a single stanza while the warriors are engaged in an epic struggle,

non che le piastre e la minuta maglia,
ma ai colpi lor non reggerian gl'incudi. (I, *17*)
[not just plate and chainmail but anvils could not withstand their blows]

– the fair Angelica is beating an unceremonious retreat:

che quanto può menar de le calcagna,
colei lo caccia al bosco e alla campagna.
[As fast as she can go she spurs that horse through the woods and open country.]

Knights in shining armour, ladies in sumptuous dresses, for all their fine airs and eloquent speeches, are frequently shown up as weak,

silly, impetuous children: even the dignified Bradamante and the
stern Marfisa squabble like naughty schoolgirls:

... che la battaglia fanno
a pugni e a calci, poi ch'altro non hanno. (xxxvi, 50)
[they carry on the battle with punches and kicks, since they
haven't anything else to fight with.]

Language and style here contribute towards a balancing of antithetical elements: the grandiose and the pedestrian exist side by side:
the paladin 'sees stars'. The same process is apparent in Ariosto's treatment of the fantastic and supernatural elements of literary tradition to
which he opposes the world of everyday reality. Ferraù in his pursuit
of Angelica loses track of her and finds himself back at the stream in
which he had earlier lost his helmet: he decides realistically that if he
cannot find Angelica he may as well try to recover his helmet and he
is fishing for it with a branch when out of the water rises the dead
Argalia to rebuke him for a broken promise – the two figures are
closely juxtaposed in a single octave :

Con un gran ramo d'albero rimondo
di ch'avea fatto una pertica lunga,
tenta il fiume e ricerca sino al fondo,
né loco lascia ove non batta e punga.
Mentre con la maggior stizza del mondo
tanto l'indugio suo quivi prolunga,
vede di mezzo il fiume un cavalliero
insino el petto uscir, d'aspetto fiero. (i, 25)
[With a great branch which he'd trimmed and made a long pole
of, he sounds and searches the river-bed, prodding and striking
about everywhere. While, extremely angrily, he stays on there,
he sees a knight with angry mien rise out of the water as far as his
chest.]

The juxtaposition of realistic and fantastic is a recurrent feature of
the poem as though in reflection of the constant interaction of our
imaginative and actual experience. The magician Atlante flying down
from his enchanted mountain castle on his hippogriff is attacked and
defeated by Bradamante who wields her sword to kill him when her
triumphant gesture is arrested by her glimpse of a sad, old man,

che mostra al viso crespo e al pelo bianco
età di settanta anni o poco manco. (iv, 27)
[who shows by his wrinkled face and white hair that he must be
70 years old, or very nearly.]

Ariosto delights in these sudden twists in his narrative tone – triumph suddenly dissolves in regret; or the tragic in the comic, as in Orlando's madness where the grief-crazed paladin goes berserk, uproots trees and throws his horse over his shoulders. Or the comic turns tragic or grim as in the death of Orrilo, where the farcical monster who chases after his severed head and claps it on again is intercepted by Astolfo who grabs the head and cuts the fatal hair:

> E tenendo quel capo per lo naso,
> dietro e dinanzi lo dischioma tutto.
> Trovò fra gli altri quel fatale a caso:
> si fece il viso pallido e brutto,
> travolse gli occhi, e dimostrò all'occaso
> per manifesti segni esser condutto. (xv, 87)
> [And holding that head by the nose he shaves it completely back
> and front. By chance he found that one fatal hair with all the
> others: then the face went pale and ugly, the eyes rolled, and
> it showed by clear signs that it had been brought to its final
> eclipse.]

This technique of blending the supernatural and the real in a continuous narrative must certainly owe something to Dante who convinces us of the reality of his other world often precisely by this close association of the two notes. In certain places the Dantesque reminiscence is clear as in the picture of Astolfo turned into a tree and giving his warning to Ruggiero of the wiles of Alcina – closely modelled on the *Aeneid* and on Dante's wood of suicides; and Ariosto derives frequent comic effect from this:

> Ruggier quel mitro ringraziò ... (vi, 56)
> [Ruggier thanked that myrtle ...]

Ruggiero in Alcina's enchanted palace is like a small boy in a sweet shop – his impatience for the arrival of the seductive witch is a very realistic detail in a highly fantastic picture. So too is his attempt to rape the naked Angelica when he is so excited that he fumbles with the knots in his armour – a miserable failure for one who has just arrived on a hippogriff: and he is justly punished by the magic disappearance of his fair prey.

This mobility of tone often comprises sudden changes of mood from serious or tragic to lighthearted and comic, or vice versa. The dedicated optimistic knights pursuing their unthinking sports are suddenly brought face to face with the reality of death and suffering – Bradamante seeing Atlante's wizened face, Astolfo with Orrilo's macabre skull, the drunken Rodomonte with Isabella's lopped-off head. Ariosto is not prepared to let his narrative settle for too long in any single key: we are not allowed prolonged or consistent emotional response. One cannot take any of these numerous episodes too seriously: this *is* a world of fiction, but doesn't it reflect the world we experience, in which *we* are tossed between hopes and fears, pity and impatience, dignity and pettiness? Olimpia's grand tragic moment when she is abandoned by Bireno is reduced to its petty essentials: half-asleep she stretches her hand across the bed for her husband:

Nessuno truova: a sé la man ritira;
di nuovo tenta, e pur nessuno truova.
Di qua l'un braccio, e di là l'altro gira,
or l'una or l'altra gamba; e nulla giova. (x, *21*)
[She finds no-one: she pulls back her hand; she tries again and still she finds no-one. She stretches round one arm here, the other there, now one, now the other leg; but it's no use.]

The intrusion of Olimpia's groping legs into this pathetic scene, otherwise so closely reminiscent of Catullus's Ariadne and Virgil's Dido, was much criticised by neo-Aristotelian critics – but if the genres seem to clash here, we can hardly say the same of the style which, apart from the one indecorous word, carries on in the same tone as before. Popular and realistic details are not flung crudely in the reader's face; when Orlando gets such a thump on the head that he sees stars we are not suddenly plunged into the crude jargon of the piazza: the measured pace and restrained language continues:

De la percossa Orlando stupefatto
vide, mirando in terra, alcuna stella: (xli, *96*)
[Orlando was stunned by the blow, and saw, although he was looking down on the ground, a few stars.]

His fall from his horse is a comic scene set in an elevated stylistic framework:

Con quel rumor ch'un sacco d'arme cade,
risuona il conte, come il campo tocca. (xxiii, *88*)
[With the same noise that a sack of arms makes when it falls, the count resounds when he hits the field.]

The separate traditions of romance and epic are to some extent reconciled by this adoption of a style which raises the tone of romance while depressing that of the epic. Linguistic and prosodic means contribute to this: Ariosto purges his language of its crudest dialect and popular terms, but also of many of its latinisms; and the framework of the octave helps to impose a certain uniformity of rhythmic effect. Certainly many critics have felt that the diversity of Ariosto's material only achieves unity through his style, and it was fashionable, a generation ago, to credit his much-vaunted irony with this function. This was a much exaggerated view, not only because it overlooked the importance of structure in contributing to the same effect, but also because it failed to recognise the important stratum of serious, epic, non-ironic material in the poem.

Far more significant in binding the poem together, in giving coherence to the diverse material and styles is the constant intrusion of the poet into his narrative. We noted earlier Ariosto's commentary on his story in the *proemi* to each canto, where he often points out the moral significance of what is to follow or relates it to some contemporary Ferrarese parallel, or to his own experience. The same practice is continued throughout the canto, where the poet maintains the illusion of oral poetry, as though speaking to a listening audience. Such intrusions are largely in a confidential, conversational, colloquial style, conveying a deceptive impression of spontaneous, almost careless informality. Much of this derives from the romance tradition where the rapport between audience and *cantastorie* was close, and where the narrative technique was often unsophisticated. Ariosto was a cultured poet and a skilful narrator, who wrote to be read, and his adoption of the ingenuous romance mode is a sort of stylistic archaism:

> Se mi domanda alcun chi costui sia,
> che versa sopra il rio lacrime tante,
> io dirò ch'egli è il Re di Circassia. (I, 45)
> [If anyone asks me who this is, shedding so many tears into the stream, I shall say that it is the King of Circassia.]

The rapport with the reader is regularly underlined, with appeals to members of the court, especially Ippolito or Alfonso 'Signori' or the ladies 'cortesi donne' – or to an indefinite 'voi' which would seem to comprise all of us, the bulk of unspecified and undistinguished readers who might have been thronging round the minstrel in an earlier day. With Alfonso or other Court dignitaries the tone is respectful, dignified and serious – but with *us*, the general audience, the poet is on terms of equality and he aims at a casual, informal note: 'come io dissi' (IV, 3), 'per dirvi quel ch'io non vi dissi inante' (VII, 66), 'mi si potrebbe dire' (XVIII, 46) etc. So the syntax is sometimes clumsy, the language repetitive in the romance tradition. The poet declares he has forgotten somebody, or only reveals his name when the tale is nearly finished; he admits he is repeating himself

> (Questo ho già detto inanzi) ... (XL, 65)

or interjects what seems a naïve afterthought:

> Si straccia i crini, e il petto si percuote,

e va guardando (che splendea la luna) ... (x, 22)
[She tears her hair, and strikes her breast, and stares to see (because there was a moon) ...]
  The effect thus is of a journey through the poem in the company of
the poet, who reminds us constantly of his presence and makes us see
his material through his eyes. It is this that gives unity to the poem,
enclosing the heterogeneous subject-matter within the focus of the
poet's vision. And it is his personality that colours the narrative and
conditions our response to it. The poet is in fact his own most interesting character, and it is the quality of his company that makes the
journey so agreeable. He is an interesting, well-informed companion,
knowledgeable about current political, social and cultural trends; and
he is a man of feeling, capable of indignation at abuses, compassion for
suffering, admiration for bravery, loyalty, and purity. But most characteristic is his sympathetic humour, his clear-sighted view of human
nature and his tolerant amusement at its deficiencies. He smiles as
he uncovers the hypocrisy, pretensions, self-deception of his creations.
  His irony is the vehicle of this balanced vision of his subject which
takes in the complexity of the world about us and of our reaction to
it. By ironical I mean an attitude that is not to be taken at its face value.
The words say one thing but the author means something different.
In its simplest form the poet writes the reverse of what he means, as
of the ugly old Alcina's use of cosmetics:
      Ma sì l'arti usa al nostro tempo ignote,
      che bella e giovanetta parer puote. (VII, 73)
      [But she makes such clever use of the arts unknown in our day,
      that she can appear beautiful and young.]
Cosmetics were only too well known in Ariosto's day, as his satires
show us. We think we understand the poet's intention here (although
this could be a non-ironic allusion to the arts of magic). Sometimes,
however, the note is subtler – as in his comments on the fickleness
of women: when Rodomonte is jilted by Doralice he curses the
female sex:

      e certo da ragion si dipartiva;
      che per una o per due che trovi ree,
      che cento buone sien creder si dee.

      Se ben di quante io n'abbia fin qui amate,
      non n'abbia mai trovata una fedele,
      perfide tutte io non vo' dir né ingrate
      ma darne colpa al mio destin crudele. (XXVII, 122–3)

[and certainly here he was acting most unreasonably; because for
every one or two you find who are wicked, you must realise that
there are a hundred good ones. Although of those whom I have
loved so far I haven't found one who was faithful, yet I won't say
that all women are treacherous and ungrateful, but I'll blame my
cruel fate.]

The ladies cannot really complain at this, but the men can guffaw over
the unspoken insinuation that Ariosto's experience is *not* uncommon.
Irony thus helps Ariosto to address a separate message to different
readers: the ambiguity is itself appealing. We are similarly left in
some doubt how to interpret the famous lines, quoted above 'Oh
gran bontà de' cavalieri antiqui!' (I, 22, p. 98) – When Rinaldo and
Ferraù patch up their quarrel in order to pursue the fleeing Angelica,
and the pagan even offers Rinaldo a lift on his horse, we are left to
smile our approval or snort our scorn according to our varying points
of view. It may be 'gran bontà' for enemies to treat each other chivalrously, but what of this unchivalrous pursuit of the lady? Irony here
exposes the ambiguity of our motivation, the naïveté of our moral
and social codes.

It is significant, however, that the ironical note is often broken by
a clear and forthright statement that dispels any ambiguity: Bireno's
attentions to the young girl he proposes as a bride for his brother are
judged to be kindly and paternal:

    che rilevare un che Fortuna ruote
    talora al fondo, e consolar l'afflitto,
    mai non fu biasmo, ma gloria sovente;
    tanto più una fanciulla, una innocente. (x, *14*)

    [to help up someone whom Fortune's wheel has brought
    down, and to console those in distress, has never brought blame,
    but often glory; all the more when it is a young, innocent
    girl]

– but Ariosto denounces them quite unambiguously in the following
lines:

    i modi di Bireno *empii e profani*
    pietosi e santi riputati furo. (x, *15*)

    [Bireno's conduct which was impious and profane was con-
    sidered pious and holy]

Similarly when Grifone pardons the faithless Orrigille and her lover
Martano who have cuckolded him, his motive is unambiguously
explained by Ariosto:

    (perché non osa dir sol d'Orrigille). (XVIII, *92*)

[because he daren't suggest that only Orrigille should be pardoned.]

Through his irony Ariosto embraces the varying interests and feelings of his mixed audience, and indeed the conflicting reactions of most of us caught between the worlds of our imagination and our practical experience. How does one react to a fiction? – with varying degrees of acceptance, involvement, amazement, amusement, scorn, according to one's culture and temperament. So Ariosto relates the beloved adventures, but with a wink to the more worldly ones; as when telling us of Orlando in the whale:

Si spinse Orlando inanzi, e se gl'immerse
con quella àncora in gola, e s'io non fallo
col battello anco; ... (XI, 37)
[Orlando pressed on and plunged into the orc's throat with that anchor and, if I'm not mistaken, with his boat as well.]

The ironical 's'io non fallo' is Ariosto's point of contact with his more sophisticated readers – hence the allusions to his 'source', his ironical admissions of his own surprise at the events in his tale:

(se la fama dal ver non si diparte);
[if the report is true]

– or his mock identity with the credulous romance audiences – as of Alcina's golden wall:

Alcun dal mio parer qui si dilunga,
e dice ch'ell'è alchimia; e forse ch'erra
et anco forse meglio di me intende:
a me par oro, poi che sì risplende. (VI, 59)
[Some people do not accept my opinion and say it's alchemy: and perhaps I'm wrong, and they know better than I do: I think it's gold because it shines so brightly.]

He teases the ladies frequently in a gentle courtly, flirtatious way. 'Don't listen to this story' he suggests to them at the beginning of one tale in which the fair sex show up badly – he only included it because it was in his source – they know he is really devoted to them, so let them skip this:

Passi, chi vuol, tre carte o quattro, senza
leggerne verso, e chi pur legger vuole,
gli dia quella medesima credenza
che si suol dare a finzioni e a fole. (XXVIII, 3)
[Anyone who wants to should skip these three or four pages and not read them, and those who do want to read them should put just as much faith in them as they would in fiction and fables.]

Similarly he addresses his courtly contemporaries with an ironical
explanation of the topography of Lipadusa where he has sited the
triple combat on which the war finally closes; Federigo Fulgoso, he
says, in chasing the Barbary pirates visited this island and found it so
rocky that there could not have been room for such a combat: however, he explains in the second edition, there *used* to be such an open
place as he described before a great rock fell in an earthquake and
covered it (XLII, *21*).

Elsewhere the smile is not at the credulity of the people but at
the remoteness of the cultured – at the strange conventions of literature, of classical mythology for example: Orlando in his search for
Angelica is likened to Ceres searching in dragon-drawn chariot for
her lost daughter:

> S'in poter fosse stato Orlando pare
> all'Eleusina dea, come in disio,
> non avria, per Angelica cercare,
> lasciato o selva o campo o stagno o rio
> o valle o monte o piano o terra o mare,
> il cielo e 'l fondo de l'eterno oblio;
> ma poi che 'l carro e i draghi non avea,
> la già cercando al meglio che potea. (XII, *3*)

[If Orlando had been equal to the Eleusine goddess in power as
he was in desire, he would have sought out Angelica through
field and forest, lakes and rivers, valleys, mountains, plains, land
and sea, heaven and the depths of everlasting oblivion; but since
he didn't have chariot and dragons, he went looking for her as
best he could.]

The final couplet reflects the realistic, uncultured reaction to the high-
falutin' world of the humanists. Another cultured obsession often
treated ironically are the artificial conventions of the Petrarchists.

> Parea ad Orlando, s'una verde riva
> d'odoriferi fior tutta dipinta,
> mirare il bello avorio, e la nativa
> purpura ch'avea Amor di sua man tinta,
> e le due chiare stelle onde nutriva
> ne le reti d'Amor l'anima avinta:
> io parlo de' begli occhi e del bel volto,
> che gli hanno il cor di mezzo il petto tolto. (VIII, *80*)

[On a green bank all painted with fragrant flowers, Orlando
seemed to see the lovely ivory and native purple coloured by
Love's hand and the two bright stars which fed with their light

Orlando's soul, captive in Love's nets: I mean the lovely eyes
and face which have stolen his heart from his breast.]
Here in the final couplet the poet mocks at the obscurity of his own
re-fashioning of the Petrarchan conceits. Or he may hint slyly at the
shortcomings of knights and ladies – at the romantic suicide who
plunges in the sea and then swims out to safety :

Ariodante, poi ch'in mar fu messo,
si pentì di morire: e come forte
e come destro e più d'ogn'altro ardito,
si messe a nuoto e ritornossi al lito. (VI, 5)

[Ariodante, when he was in the sea, changed his mind about
dying: and being strong and capable and extremely brave,
started swimming and returned to the shore.]

This is the author smiling at the romance-devotees, siding with the
realists, the unsophisticated, the incredulous; and in this way he
retains the ear and sympathy of all sides, idealists and realists, the
cultured and the ignorant, court and piazza.

Ariosto's irony also serves to sustain an atmosphere of fictive
remoteness in which the actions of his narrative are enveloped. Isabella, a captive in the brigands' cave, begins telling her sad tale to
Orlando :

Isabella sono io, che figlia fui
del re mal fortunato di Gallizia.
Ben dissi fui; ch'or non son più di lui,
ma di dolor, d'affanno e di mestizia.
Colpa d'Amor ... (XIII, 4)

[I am Isabella, and I was the daughter of the unfortunate king of
Gallicia; I was, indeed, for now I am no longer his, but the child
of grief, anguish and sorrow. The fault of Love.]

The conventional, highly stylised language which we have come to
accept in the lyric seems strangely out of place on the lips of Isabella;
we are alerted immediately to the idea that this is a fiction, a fairy
story: we do not need to feel too heart-broken and we can save our
tears: we may need them later: we still have a long way to go – and it
is characteristic of Ariosto's long romance that we are saved a succession of violent emotional reactions – joys and sorrows are muted. We
are removed from any close sense of identity with his characters who
speak the language of literature not of real life: so Isabella continues:

Già mi vivea di mia sorte felice,
gentil, giovane, ricca, onesta e bella :
vile e povera or sono, or infelice ... (XIII, 5)

[once I lived happy with my lot, noble, young, rich, virtuous, and beautiful: now I am mean, poor and unhappy.]

This 'distancing' technique is, we have suggested, a form of irony: the words do not quite mean what they say: their exaggeration settles the reader comfortably in the world of fiction, as, for example, the language of the inn-keeper whose jealousy lost him his wife – a pointed tale but the point is softened by this same stylised form:

Se Fortuna di me non ebbe cura
sì che mi desse al nascer mio ricchezza,
al difetto di lei supplì Natura,
che sopra ogni mio ugual mi diè bellezza. (XLIII, 12)

[If Fortune did not care for me and give me wealth when I was born, Nature supplied that lack and gave me beauty beyond all my companions.]

In all of this the range and depth of Ariosto's poetic inspiration is I think indisputable – but to write great poetry is not quite the same as to write a great poem. Whether or not Ariosto succeeded in reconciling his different stylistic levels in a unified poem is perhaps disputable. Over the long history of Ariosto criticism there has almost always been some partial dissent from readers who regret his so-called coarseness, or his adulation of his patrons, or his light-heartedness, his escapism or his didacticism. What at a stylistic level we have called mobility of tone reflects the juxtaposition at a structural level of conflicting situations. The grand epic battle of Chirstians and pagans is broken up by the adventures of the participants: a bawdy love story follows a fierce battle. The effect as we have said is to detach us from too close an involvement in any of the tales or episodes, and this perhaps was part of Ariosto's intention. But his intentions themselves were probably hybrid, not fully resolved. He did aim at a raising of the level of romance, at an emulation of the Virgilian epic, a celebration of his patrons, an involvement in the problems of his age, a realistic portrayal of human frailty – and these things mattered more to him than a consistent poetic style or a 'harmonious' presentation of his subject. But his technique of detachment, of distancing and disengagement have sometimes disengaged his readers not only from his romantic lovers and enchanted palaces, but also from his epic eulogies, his moral invectives, his disenchanted insights into human nature. This is in fact a serious poem perhaps too effectively disguised as an entertainment.

9. Problems of Language and Composition

The first edition of the *Furioso* was published in 1516, and consisted of 40 *canti*. This text was slightly revised for the second edition of 1521, which also consisted of 40 *canti*. The third and final edition, which is the one we read today, was a much corrected and amplified version of this in 46 *canti*, published in Ferrara in 1532 under the title *Orlando Furioso di Messer Ludovico Ariosto Nobile Ferrarese nuovamente da lui propio corretto e d'altri canti nuovi ampliato*. The corrections and modifications incorporated in the 1532 text are of a dual nature, consisting of extensive linguistic corrections of the earlier edition as well as some 700 new octaves added to the text of the poem as it had appeared in 1521, mostly in four new episodes. In this chapter we shall examine briefly the nature and purpose of the corrections and additions, and also consider the fragments associated with the poem and apparently rejected by the poet and left unpublished at his death.

The linguistic problem was one shared with all Ariosto's non-Tuscan contemporaries. In its simplest terms the question was to find a language which would be acceptable to a wide circle of readers in Italy; if he wrote for the immediate circle of the Estense court Ariosto could count on a fair measure of agreement as to what a word meant, in what contexts it could be used, how it should be spelled, pronounced and inflected. Outside Ferrara, however, he could count on no such consensus of opinion; and even in Ferrara itself the court circle comprised visitors from other cities whose ears were affronted by Ferrarese tongues or whose experience simply debarred them from understanding dialect.

Such had been the situation in the fifteenth century in the ferment of the humanistic revival when writers with serious subjects aiming at educated readers wrote in Latin, and the vernacular underwent a marked decline in prestige from the times of the 'tre corone'. The hundred years following the death of Boccaccio (1375) have been called 'il secolo senza poesia', the century without poetry, and in a national sense this is justified. The vernacular remained alive of course as a spoken language, as dialect or near-dialect, and there was a considerable increase in its practical use (in the chancelleries, for example), but with a few notable exceptions (such as Alberti) it was largely neglected by serious writers until the last quarter of the century.

By this time the dichotomy between the written and the spoken languages was sensed by many to be damaging to the national culture, and a number of writers emerged to dispute the supremacy of Latin for literary purposes. The popular literature of the romances, for example, was taken up by poets who succeeded in giving the crude jargon of their sources a form that could be appreciated beyond their regional and popular milieux: Pulci in Florence with his *Morgante* and Boiardo in Ferrara with the *Orlando Innamorato* each raised the tone and style of the romance and cast it in a language that could be read and enjoyed all over Italy. Similarly in the field of the lyric Lorenzo de' Medici and Poliziano used the very lively popular songs of Florentine dialect and gave them a literary shape and linguistic form which all educated Italians could appreciate. A further significant use of the vernacular was made in Naples by Sannazzaro, whose miscellany of pastoral prose and verse, the *Arcadia*, represented a conscious move in the direction of a vernacular that would be acceptable in other parts of the country, which essentially meant a move towards Tuscan. All of these writers see Tuscan principally in terms of the language of the *literary tradition* of the Trecento.

The revival of the vernacular in the late fifteenth century, however, raised as many problems as it solved, and essentially it provoked a controversy over what was thought to be widely acceptable. All of the writers referred to in the last paragraph used a vernacular that was consciously closer to a common norm than their sources and predecessors; the very increase in contacts between the Italian courts was pushing writers in this direction. But at the same time it made them aware of their very differences, and it soon became clear that a common norm was still remote. Pulci's language has a considerable measure of current Florentine slang and colloquialisms; Boiardo's Italian is markedly Emilian and Lombard; Poliziano and Lorenzo's language shows not only regional peculiarities but Latinate influences and numerous inconsistencies with itself; nor was Sannazzaro, who tried to bring his language closer to Florentine principles, able to achieve any reasonable measure of consistency. The revival of the vernacular had, in the view of some observers, resulted in anarchy.

A solution was proposed and indeed imposed by Pietro Bembo, who exerted a vital influence on Ariosto, and on the Italian language for the next generation: Bembo's answer was to return to the language of the great Florentine writers of the Trecento, to Petrarch for verse and to Boccaccio for prose: in these writers the vernacular had achieved its greatest perfection; the Quattrocento had witnessed a decline owing to regional and humanist influences, and a return to the source was essential.

Bembo's contribution to the linguistic debate dates from the very beginning of the century: he prepared an edition of Petrarch's *Canzoniere* in 1501, and published his *Asolani* with its Boccaccesque prose in 1505; the first book of his *Prose della Volgar Lingua* was ready in 1512, but the complete work was not published until 1525. Throughout this period he and Ariosto were in intermittent contact and there is no doubt that his influence on the *Furioso* was significant – particularly on the thorough-going linguistic revision to which the final edition was exposed. The *Prose* appeared therefore at a critical moment in the composition of the poem – as they did in that of another famous work, Castiglione's *Cortegiano*, which similarly underwent a linguistic revision under Bembo's influence between the penultimate and final editions (1519 and 1528).

Castiglione, like Ariosto, found himself in conflict with Bembo and others on two vital subjects – the influence of dialect and of Latin. The conflict was to a large extent between the Tuscans and the non-Tuscans, the former asserting the superiority of their ear and linguistic practice, the latter disputing the 'tyranny' of Tuscan and trying to establish a claim for a courtly language similar to the 'courtly, cardinal and curial tongue' which they thought Dante was championing in the *De Vulgari Eloquentia*; but there were further disputes among the supporters of Tuscan between those advocating a return to the archaic language of Petrarch and Boccaccio (Bembo) and those favouring contemporary Florentine usage (Machiavelli among them).

Ariosto wrote when this controversy was at its height and he could not fail to be influenced by it. However, he did not enter the lists as a theorist, unlike Castiglione or Machiavelli (and, later, Tasso). He offers only a few comments on linguistic questions, one of which we have quoted earlier – his apology in the Prologue to *Il Negromante*, that while the Cremona of his play has picked up words and expressions in Bologna, Florence, Siena, etc., he has not in the short period of his residence there learned enough to be able to hide totally its 'pronunzia Lombarda'. The non-Tuscans were often sensitive on this point: if current Tuscan usage were to be recognised as the main criterion, they would be at a great disadvantage. Indeed a Tuscan linguist who criticised Ariosto's comedies precisely on this score (see above, pp. 43–4): 'he did not like the Ferrarese expressions and did not know the Florentine ones, so did without'. He quoted as an example Ariosto's use of the word 'bigonzoni' for 'ears': 'a refined taste knows how offensive "bigonzoni" is, both to eye and ear'.

However, comedy was one thing, and romance was another; comedy dealt with lowly everyday characters and actions, and required a lively, racy dialogue. Romance concerned another world, essentially of the imagination, and here Ariosto's ignorance of Florentine colloquial usage would not disqualify him. In fact Ariosto had before him in Ferrara the precedent of Boiardo's successful *Orlando Innamorato* which was written, not in colloquial Florentine, nor in the current Ferrarese dialect, but in an essentially literary language deriving from the long romance tradition, with strong Tuscan influence, but a 'courtly' language nonetheless with strong Emilian and Lombard elements – and this 'emiliano illustre' was essentially the language which Ariosto's contemporary, Francesco Bello, used in Ferrara for his *Mambriano*, and which Ariosto also used in his first draft of the *Furioso* (1516).

The outstanding linguistic features of this text are its regional elements and its latinisms, and it is easy to set them against the two main cultural streams which met in the *Furioso* – the popular and the humanist. The influence of regional speech-habits (Lombard and Emilian) is strong: regional pronunciation is reflected frequently in words where single consonants occur in place of the Tuscan double: *mezo, azurro, aventura, adosso, letere* etc.; and where double consonants are used in place of Tuscan single: *fraccasso, diffetto, comminciare, commune*. Tuscan palatals give way to Northern sibilants in forms such as *azzaio* (*acciaio*), *zurma* (*ciurma*), *scaramuzza* (*scaramuccia*). There is also, as in Castiglione, considerable confusion over atonic 'i' and 'e': Ariosto writes *gettar* (*gittar*), *pregione* (*prigione*), *meglior* (*miglior*), but *liggiadro* (*leggiadro*), *mischin* (*meschin*), *impire* (*empire*). There are significant northern influences in the morphology too: for the article, for example, Ariosto used *lo* and *li* before a vowel, *il*, *el*, *li* or *e* before a consonant: for the dative pronouns he uses *gli* (*le*), and *gli* (*loro*). In verbal forms we find the characteristic Northern *tremarò, schivarei* (*tremerò, schiverei*). Latin influence is apparent in the vocabulary: *nece* (*morte*), *tuta* (*sicura*), *crebri* (*spessi*), *inulto* (*senza vendetta*); but also contributes to confusion, for example, in the region of atonic vowels: between *u* and *o; suave* (*soave*), *argumento* (*argomento*), *populo* (*popolo*); and between *e* and *i; intrar* (*entrar*), *artifice* (*artefice*) etc. There are frequent apparent inconsistencies:

giovane appears also as *giovene* and *giovine*; we find *due, dui, duo* and *dua* all with the same meaning.

This text was clearly far from the taste of the Florentines and was bound to occasion adverse criticism. There is a report (by Baruffaldi) that Ariosto consulted a considerable number of people about his poem: Bembo, Molza, Navagero, Sadoleto, Marcantonio Magno, and various others. Giraldi says that Ariosto put a copy of the *Furioso* out in his house for two years, for anyone to see and comment upon. Certainly his familiarity with spoken Tuscan must have increased in the period between the first and the subsequent editions: he was in Tuscany for six months in 1520, and he spent three years in the (Tuscan) Garfagnana from 1522–5. However, it was not the current spoken language of Tuscany which influenced his revision so much as the literary Tuscan advocated by Bembo. This was already apparent in the second edition (1521) which marks a modest advance towards Tuscanization, with the reduction of many dialect and Latinate forms.

However, the most thorough-going linguistic revision does not occur until the 1532 text, by which time Bembo's *Prose* had been published, and it is clear that Bembo's influence at this stage was all-important. The corrections made between 1521 and 1532 are very largely in conformity with the principles set out in the *Prose*, the goal of which was a consistent literary language on the model of the great Trecentisti, but notably of Petrarch. Some of the more significant changes we give below, but it is necessary at the same time to point out that for almost every category of correction there are exceptions; there are examples in the 1532 text where Ariosto fails to correct a form he corrects regularly elsewhere; and there are frequent examples of corrections in the opposite direction; so there are good literary Tuscan forms occurring in the 1516 edition which are changed to Northern or Latinate forms in the final text. We cannot always be confident that these were not due to oversights on Ariosto's part, or mistakes on the part of his printers, but the numbers are such as to lead us to believe that Ariosto was firmly claiming his poet's licence. He was a poet, and not a grammarian, and in the last resort his poetic judgement prevailed. But his acute interest in the language of his poem is apparent not only in the numerous corrections he made for the last edition (which leave barely a stanza unmarked), but also in the variants between different copies of the 1532 edition which show that the poet intervened to correct his text after the printing had actually begun.

The phonology is manifestly revised to bring it closer to Tuscan: *mezo* > *mezzo*, *sofrendo* > *soffrendo*, *vorete* > *vorrete*, *connoscere* > *conoscere*, *dibbattere* > *dibattere*. Dialect sibilants give way to Tuscan palatal forms, *azzaio* > *acciaio*, *zurme* > *ciurme*; or dialect palatals give way to Tuscan gutturals, *giaccio* > *ghiaccio*, *giotto* > *ghiotto*. Large numbers of dialect forms are corrected among the atonic vowels: *deciotto* > *diciotto*, *diece* > *dieci*, *occidere* > *uccidere*, etc. The morphology is brought very largely into line with Bembo's *Prose*: the article assumes its present-day form: in particular the poet puts himself to a great deal of inconvenience in correcting to *lo* and *gli* before *s* impure, which leads to whole lines and even octaves being rewritten. The pronouns similarly assume the form we use today *el* > *il*, *li* (dative) > *gli*, *gli lo* > *glielo* etc. Verbal forms similarly bow to Bembo, the future notably: *tremarò* > *tremerò*, *andaren* > *andremo* etc. And the apocopation characteristic of the Lombard dialect is substantially reduced. Latinisms, already reduced in the 1521 version, are now pruned more drastically: *marmori* > *marmi*, *suade* > *persuade*, *servasse* > *salvasse*.

Yet, as we have said earlier, the linguistic revision is far from mechanical. Thus while he generally corrects the Latinate forms *patre*, *matre*, *latroni* to the Tuscan *padre*, *madre*, *ladroni*, he changes one *padron* to *patron* (the dialect form used by Boiardo and Castiglione, see the *Cortegiano*, Book I (XXXV)). He changes *fabula* > *favola*, but keeps a *fabulosa*; he changes *triunfale* > *trionfale*, but also *trionfante* > *triunfante*. The Latinisms may be retained as a conscious classical or learned association, or perhaps because they are phonetically preferable in their context ('così murmura e stride e si coruccia', VI, 27); indeed a large number of Latinisms remain in the 1532 edition, single words: *vepri* (VII, 32), *passe* (VII, 50) *animanti* (VIII, 79); as well as phrases *geniali letti* (introduced in XVII, 13), *edera seguace* (XIV, 93) and Latinate constructions: *Sola di tutte Alcina era più bella* (VII, 10). Other unexpected corrections occur in diphthongisation: there are changes from *prova* to *pruova*, and vice versa (*prova* ↔ *pruova*); *nova* ↔ *nuova*, *mover* ↔ *muover*, *leve* ↔ *lieve*. The Tuscan diphthongised forms were in conflict with courtly and dialect non-diphthongised forms; and literary associations, particularly Petrarchan, must often have influenced Ariosto's choice of the non-Tuscan form. On occasion he rejects a Tuscan verb form advocated by Bembo for a dialect form (as in *abbiam* > *abbin* (XXX, 30) *avanzerà* > *avanzarà* (XXVI, 108), *partisse* > *partissi* (XXX, 93), probably because it fitted the tone of the context, or the rhythm of the line: his choice of *giovene* – *giovine* – *giovane*, *due-dui-duo-dua* seems to be governed by such considerations, and no effort is made at consistency. He corrects, for example, *dui* to *duo* in the line *duo chiari rivi mormorando intorno* (1, 35), with a very happy effect – as though throwing into relief the *chiari rivi* and isolating the phrase in a framework of different vowels and sounds (*duo, intorno*) in reflection of the natural scene he is depicting.

The language of the 1532 edition is therefore a good literary Tuscan, despite its inconsistencies, its Latinisms and its scattered regionalisms – the Crusca later pointed to the *Furioso* as an example of correct Tuscan and used Ariosto as a rod to beat Tasso whose *Liberata* was adjudged to be far too Latinate and eccentric for Tuscan ears. On wider issues of style the Crusca also championed Ariosto whom the Tassisti criticised for his excessively popular and hybrid form. It was no mean achievement for a Ferrarese poet to win the support of the fastidious Florentines.

In addition to the linguistic revision for the third edition Ariosto incorporated in this text substantial extensions to his poem, auto-graph manuscripts of which are extant. These extensions are not, however, the only evidence we have of the poet's intention of en-larging his poem. In 1545 the publisher Manuzio printed a text of five additional *canti* which had not been included in the 1532 edition. This text of the *Cinque Canti* was based on the copy of a manuscript provided by the poet's son, Virginio. A fuller text was published by Giolito in 1548. This text consists of four complete cantos and a fifth left unfinished. Their authenticity is not in doubt and we are led to wonder what is their relation to the 1532 poem. Although never published by the poet, the *Cinque Canti* nevertheless provide valuable evidence of the way in which Ariosto's ideas about his poem were evolving in the latter part of his life, and they help us to understand better the changes actually effected in the 1532 edition.

The manuscript extant in the Biblioteca Comunale of Ferrara begins with a stanza of the *Furioso* (XLV, 40 of the 1521 edition; XLV, 68 of the 1532) showing clearly that it is intended to follow that point in the action. The war against Agramante is finished, and Ruggiero has been accepted by Bradamante's parents as their son-in-law. Nevertheless the memory of earlier conflicts between the rival houses of Maganza and Chiaramonte has left smouldering resent-ment and Gano is awaiting a chance of revenge. This hint of further trouble was not followed up in the 1532 edition, but in the *Cinque Canti* it provides the impetus for an extensive range of new hostilities engineered against Carlomagno by Alcina and Gano. Alcina, to avenge her abandonment at the hands of Ruggiero, now contrives a

great conspiracy of spirits against Carlomagno, allegedly to avenge
the wrongs done to her sister Morgana by Orlando (in the *Innamorato*). Her instruments in this are Gano, stirred by Invidia, and
Desiderio, King of the Lombards, motivated by Sospetto, who start
a new war against Carlomagno, in which the Emperor Constantine
and other Eastern powers are involved. The most prominent episode
is a long account in Canto IV of Ruggiero being swallowed by a
whale, inside which he finds Astolfo and a graveyard of other former
lovers of Alcina. This story is left unfinished in Canto IV and Canto V
ends abruptly with the retreat of Carlo's forces in the face of extensive
attacks in Germany. This development of the action, in which
Ruggiero, as ally of Carlo, is fighting against the Emperor Constantine, certainly conflicts with the 1532 text in which Ruggiero is King
of the Bulgars and friend of Constantine. It seems likely therefore
that the *Cinque Canti* were superseded by the 1532 additions.

The date of composition of the *Cinque Canti* is disputed, and the
evidence is certainly inconclusive. The most likely explanation would
seem to be that Ariosto began drafting these additional cantos as an
extension to his poem as early as 1519, but that he left them aside
when preparing the 1521 text and only returned to them later, at
some time bteween 1525 and 1532, when revising the poem for the
third edition. During this period they were probably re-written or
at least revised in the form in which we now have them. However,
the poet still was not satisfied and put them aside once more, composing in their place a different ending for his poem, the Leone
episode, which *precedes* Ruggiero's marriage – and it was this ending
that he finally adopted in the 1532 edition, together with the other
new material inserted elsewhere in the poem.

This explanation is conjectural, based entirely on internal evidence:
Ariosto himself tells us virtually nothing about his plans and intentions: he refers in a letter of 15 October 1519 to 'un poco di giunta'
to his poem, and in a letter of January 1532 to 'approximately 400
new stanzas' that he has recently added and his hope of adding 'molte
più'. Whether the first reference is to the changes in the 1521 edition
or to the *Cinque Canti* is not certain; and what the second reference
means is also obscure. Unlike Tasso, who commented so freely in
letters to his friends on the process of composition of the *Liberata*,
Ariosto tells us nothing.

What then was Ariosto's motive in writing the *Cinque Canti* and
why did he abandon them in favour of the 1532 additions? They
show, as we shall see, considerable differences in spirit and style from

the *Furioso* text of 1521. The poet is narrating here not the duels and chivalrous adventures of the early *Furioso*, but great wars between nations, an epic struggle between Franks and Lombards. There is from the start a notable attempt at grandeur – an elaborate apparatus is established to explain the new hostilities, a large-scale quinquennial council of supernatural spirits headed by Demogorgon 'principe saggio del gran Consiglio'; they meet in a remote Oriental temple, a vast, imposing building. The language is grandiose – the council is un 'alto Concistoro': their principal weapon is 'la maiestade', and an elaborate allegorical structure is devised merely in order to persuade Gano to betray Carlo. Alcina consults Invidia ('o delli imperatori imperatrice,' I, *44*), then shipwrecks Gano on Gloricia's territory where he is lured into her superb palace, 'splendida e gran corte', with its habits of 'gran splendor'. Symptomatic of the new approach is the abandonment of the old ironical jumps from one phase in the story to another. Here the transitions are smooth and dignified : 'Or, sopra gli altri, quei di Chiaramonte …' (I, *66*); 'In questo mezo che l'Invidia ascosa …' (I, *107*).

Except for a few passages in Canto IV the old light-heartedness and irony are missing. Throughout there is a greater seriousness and in many senses a greater realism. The tone is often sad and disillusioned :

O vita nostra di travaglio piena,
come ogni tua allegrezza poco dura!
Il tuo gioir è come aria serena,
ch'alla fredda stagion troppo non dura : … (II, *34*)
[O our travail-laden life, how brief your every joy. Your happiness is like the clear air which does not last long in the cold season.]

Times have changed since the happy, peaceful days of Boiardo:

Chi si ricorda il dì di san Giovanni,
che sotto Ercole o Borso era sì allegro?
che poi veduto non abbian molt'anni,
come né ancora altro piacere integro,
di poi che cominciar gli assidui affanni
dei quali è in tutta Italia ogni core egro : (II, *120*)
[Who remembers the day of Saint John which used to be so happy in the times of Ercole or Borso? which we haven't seen for many years nor any other unmixed pleasure since the constant trials began which have caused sickening hearts all over Italy.]

Not only the rules of chivalry but the spirit itself is abandoned. At the end Carlo is left struggling in the water with no-one helping him:

quivi la cortesia, la caritade,
amor, rispetto, beneficio avuto,
o s'altro si può dire, è tutto messo
da parte, e sol ciascun pensa a se stesso. (v, 92)
[Courtesy, charity, love, respect, gratitude and all else are put
aside, and each one thinks only of himself.]

The poet cannot forget the contemporary political situation of Italy,
the cruelty of commanders (II, 5), the suspicions of tyrants (II, 10),
the grimness of war:

Per le cittadi uomini e donne errando,
con visi bassi e d'allegrezza spenti,
andavan taciturni sospirando ... (II, 36)
[Men and women wandering through the towns with faces
lowered and reft of all joy, went about in silence, sighing.]

So too Ariosto seems more conscious of the darker side of human
nature, of the cunning, deceit and trickery which tend to submerge
the old chivalrous virtues: in place of the bland schematic portraits
so frequent in the first edition we find considerable psychological
penetration in the characters of Gano, Gloricia and Orlando, for
example. Compared with the 1521 edition the *Cinque Canti* show a
greater moral complexity: the few loves illustrated here emphasise
the potential violence and wickedness of sexual drives – the betrayal
of friends (II, 68) and disregard of honour:

... La qual tosto ch'io vidi, ogni ragione,
ogni onestà da me fece partita ... (IV, 56)
[... as soon as I saw her all reason, all sense of honour left me.]

In this greater emphasis on the sinfulness of human nature the poet
raises the religious tone of his poem: Ruggiero is now the Christian
hero: Alcina fears that she cannot recapture him, not because he is
now married, but because he is converted:

che se fosse, qual dianzi era, pagano,
miglior speranza avria di ricovrarlo ... (I, 22)
[if he had been a pagan, as he was before, I should have had a
better chance of getting him back.]

Ruggiero himself is conscious of his greater moral responsibility:
although captured again by Alcina, he compares his present situation
in the whale with his previous shameful capitulation to lust:

S'allora io fui – dicea – degno d'aita,
or ne son più, che son miglior di vita. (IV, 77)
[If I was then worthy of aid – he said – now I am all the more,
as I lead a better life.]

In all of this the poet seems to anticipate attitudes to the romance characteristic of the later Cinquecento. A striving for moral and religious seriousness and for epic grandeur marks many of the subsequent attempts to adapt the chivalrous romance to the climate of the later Renaissance from Giraldi and Trissino to Tasso. Ariosto's rejected *Canti* seem to show his dissatisfaction with the traditional romance and with his own first draft, and clearly denote his attempt to improve the structure and the tone of his poem. But the outcome did not satisfy him, nor does it appeal to us. If the poem needed a 'complicazione finale', some new, stirring events to provide a climax, the new hostilities conceived in the *Cinque Canti* are far too ambitious: they seem more appropriate to a new poem. The new allegorical and epic material is heavy and mechanical, often repetitive and lacking in invention. It draws heavily on other writers, already well-known in Ariosto's day, Pulci for example. The poet was caught, it would seem, in a crisis of self-confidence, no longer believing in his earlier detached and deft treatment of the chivalrous myths, yet lacking the moral and religious conviction necessary to sustain the different treatment he has attempted.

It is at this point, in all probability, about 1529, that he wrote a different set of extensions to his poem, those ultimately included in the 1532 edition. The bulk of this material is concentrated in the four new episodes concerning Olimpia, Marganorre, the Rocca di Tristano and Leone – each of which warrants a brief examination. I have discussed each of these briefly elsewhere but I should like now to consider them in the context of the poet's revision of his text, and particularly to assess their purpose and function in the enlarged poem. The one that has generally been judged most successful is the Olimpia episode, interpolated in Cantos IX–XI (see above, p. 68). Some 180 octaves are added in two lengthy passages (IX, *8*–X, *34* and XI, *21–80*). In the latter half of Canto VIII of the 1521 text we heard that Angelica had been seized by the people of Ebuda and tied to a rock as a sacrifice to the sea-monster. The poet then turned to Orlando who went off in search of his missing lady, but failed to find her and was lured into an enchanted inn. Meanwhile Ruggiero, mounted on his hippogriff, had left Alcina and Logistilla, and it was he who happened to see Angelica and rescued her from the monster: he was about to ravish her when she escaped him, and he was then lured to the same enchanted inn where Orlando was a captive. In the first of the 1532 insertions Orlando in search of Angelica hears of the Ebuda orc and sets off to intervene, but is distracted by Olimpia who tells him the story of her love for Bireno, now captured by the King of Frisa whose son she had killed rather than accept him as her husband. Orlando defeats the King and re-unites Olimpia with Bireno who marries but then deserts her. We then return to the 1521 text to follow Ruggiero on the hippogriff and his liberation of Angelica. Now comes the second insertion, in which Orlando arrives at Ebuda to find Olimpia the next victim of the orc: he kills the monster, frees Olimpia and leaves her with the Irish king, Oberto, who marries her. Then we return again to the old text at the point where Orlando is lured into an enchanted inn.

The effect is really to add *two* new stories – that of Olimpia and Bireno, and of Orlando and the orc. The latter essentially repeats the situation already described in the 1521 edition where Ruggiero saved Angelica: here Orlando saves Olimpia. The contrast between the two rescues is marked: Ruggiero comes upon the scene by chance, he uses a magic shield to stun the orc and fails to kill it, and he attempts to take advantage of the victim – whereas Orlando arrives by design, discards all weapons but his sword and relies on his own strength and astuteness, kills the orc and safeguards the lady's chastity. There are certainly traces of moral allegory in the Ruggiero scene: Ruggiero has been taught by Logistilla how to control the hippogriff (reason restraining passion?), but reason is not enough because

> raro è ... che di ragione il morso
> libidinosa furia a dietro volga (XI, 1)

[rarely does the bridle of reason turn back the passion of lust] – and Ruggiero fails to control the hippogriff and his lust, both of which 'take flight'. Orlando, however, is chaste, and the naked Olimpia is safe with him. Ariosto does not insist on the superiority of Orlando's conduct to Ruggiero's but the moral contrast is clear enough and gives us some insight into Ariosto's motives. The poet may also have decided to return to the orc of Ebuda because he felt that the full potential of the motif had not been realised in the Ruggiero-Angelica scene. It is indeed justified by its poetic effective-ness, and it fits logically into the sequence of tales of passionate love leading to disaster: Dalinda's obsession with Polinesso, and Ruggiero's with Alcina. The attribution of these two adventures to Orlando may well have been due to Ariosto's feeling that he had previously neglected his titular hero: in the 1521 edition Orlando takes virtually no part in the action until Canto x. Here the balance is somewhat restored. Here too the succession of faithless or wicked women of the early cantos (Angelica, Dalinda, Alcina) is halted with a fine tribute to female constancy and chastity.

The second of the 1532 additions, concerning the 'rocca di Tristano', was inserted between stanzas 47 and 48 of Canto XXX of the 1521 edition, comprising in the final edition Canto XXXII, 50 to Canto XXXIII, 76. A few other octaves are displaced but essentially this is a simple addition of one continuous passage of about 130 octaves with virtually no disturbance to the rest of the poem. In the earlier text Bradamante, in a fit of jealousy after hearing of Ruggiero's activities in the company of Marfisa, leaves her home in Montalbano and goes after her errant lover; Ariosto then describes several other incidents (notably Astolfo's activities in pursuit of Orlando's senses) before re-introducing Bradamante who rescues Brandimarte from Rodomonte's attack before going on to Arles to challenge Ruggiero.

The new episode relates an adventure that Bradamante is involved in soon after she leaves Montalbano in search of Ruggiero. It comprises effectively three separate incidents. The first concerns Bradamante's meeting with the Queen of Iceland's messenger, Ullania, who has been sent with a shield by her Queen to Charlemagne to offer it as a token of marriage to the knight whom the Emperor judges the best in all Christendom. Three Scandinavian kings accompany Ullania, each hoping to win the shield. Bradamante reflects on the dissensions this will cause and passes on. The remainder of the canto is devoted to her adventure at the castle, which we have mentioned earlier (see pp. 80, 119 above). Bradamante expels the Scandinavian escorts but protects Ullania.

In the following canto we find a long account of a series of paintings in the castle which depict the wars of Italy, past and future, up to the sack of Rome, with a special eulogy of the patron of Ariosto's last years, Alfonso d'Avalos, Marquis of Vasto. This is a self-contained section which has no special relevance to the Clodione story or Bradamante's adventure which follow. Its function is to celebrate the poet's patron and to relate his poem more closely to contemporary events. The tone is serious and high-flown, closer to epic than to romance.

The next morning the three Scandinavian kings, who have spent the night out in the rain, again challenge Bradamante, are again defeated, and are further discomforted by hearing that their victor is a woman. Ullania reappears briefly at the beginning of the next of the 1532 additions, some four cantos later, having had her skirt cut

off by Marganorre. She is rescued by Bradamante but her quest on
behalf of the Queen of Iceland is not mentioned again – a ragged end
that Ariosto must have intended to tie off later. The Ullania incident
is closely related to an autograph fragment, 'Lo scudo della regina
Elisabetta', which came to light only in this century, and which
may well have been a draft made after the poet had given up the
idea of using the *Cinque Canti*. The shield was the last survivor of
the twelve created by the Cumaean Sibyl to dissuade Constantine
from his intention of transferring the Imperial Headquarters to
the East – it could well have been the starting-point of new adventures.

There is something of a makeshift quality about this insertion as a
whole. The three components (Ullania, Clodione and the wars of
Italy) are juxtaposed clumsily, and the central episode is only barely
relevant. The poet seems concerned to exemplify further a favourite
theme, the love-sickness that influences conduct for the worst, possessiveness destroying the knightly obligation of courtesy and hospitality. As an example of unwarranted jealousy it is perhaps intended
as a warning to Bradamante at this point in the story. Perhaps more
important was the basis it provided for further debate on the subject
of women's rights. Yet in spite of its mechanical structure and somewhat didactic tone it is strangely appealing and has not lacked admirers – including Spenser who produced his own version in *The
Faerie Queen* (III, iv). The exaggerated conventions and fantasies of
romance acquire colour here from the realistic flashes introduced
by Ariosto, the cold wet night with Bradamante at the door and
Ullania's party inside by the fire, waiting for their supper but obliged
to conform to the chivalrous law:

Si levan pure e pigliòn l'arme adagio: (XXXII, 71)

[They get up nevertheless and pick up their arms, slowly.]

Ariosto inserted the Marganorre episode with a minimum of
structural disturbance to the poem: it is a self-contained story comprising a whole new canto (XXXVII) with only a single octave at the
end of Canto XXXVI to link it to the preceding narrative. There is a
further distant link with the 'rocca di Tristano' episode in that the
Queen of Iceland's messenger Ullania reappears here. We have a long
proemio in praise of women and of the men who have championed
them in their writings. The Marganorre story proper then begins
with the encounter of Ruggiero, Bradamante and Marfisa with
Ullania and her female companions who are squatting in embarrass-
ment on the ground because their clothes have been cut off at the

waist. They are victims of Marganorre's misogyny, the origins of which are explained in the stories of his two sons, which follow (see p. 77 above). This episode would appear to centre on misogyny and to stress its irrationality. The *proemio* is a eulogy of women and an attack on the prejudices of male writers who have not only failed to give women their due but

... anco studian di far che si discuopra
ciò che le donne hanno fra lor d'immondo (xxxvii, 3)

[are even eager to reveal what is foul and unclean about women] – which is precisely what Marganorre does in cutting off women's skirts. So Marganorre becomes a symbol of misogyny, a tyrannical, powerful giant with always a thousand men to back him up (xxxvii, 84). The total effect is certainly not harmonious : the poet seems more concerned to press home some bitter truths about his fellows than to preserve a smooth façade. There are some touches of fine psychological penetration, particularly in the portraits of Marganorre who is both villainous and pathetic, and of Tanacro, who can love and yet harm his lady, who regrets and yet persists in his folly and crime.

The main purpose of this late addition would seem to be Ariosto's wish to pursue the male-female debate (as in the 'rocca di Tristano') and to pay further tribute to his female audience, explicitly in the *proemio* to the episode and implicitly in his portraits of the loyal wives (as in the episode of Olimpia who is also forced to marry against her will and kills the bridegroom). Its insertion here is apposite if somewhat mechanical. The liberation of the offended woman is appropriately attributed to the two female warriors Bradamante and Marfisa who are particularly horrified at this affront to their sex; and the story carries further the study of the effects of sexual passion on men of honour : in the preceding episode (xxxiv) love drives Alceste twice to forsake his allegiance to his king, and in the episodes that follow (xliii) it drives the two husbands in their jealousy to lay deceitful traps for their devoted wives. Ariosto may also have felt that he needed some variation at this point in the long section between Cantos xxxiv and xliii which is devoted almost entirely to arms at the expense of love.

The last of the four major additions, the Leone episode, comprises some 250 new octaves which form the larger part of Canto xliv, all of Canto xlv and the first half of Canto xlvi, the last canto of the poem. In the 1521 edition the marriage of Ruggiero and Bradamante is celebrated as soon as the war is completed and the lovers are reunited at Charlemagne's court: the sequence of the final Cantos was then that in Canto xxxvii the triple combat between Christians and Saracens was begun, and Ruggiero, swimming for his life, vowed to become a Christian: in Canto xxxviii the combat was completed, and Rinaldo was cured of his jealousy, in Canto xxxix we have the two tales of the fidelity-cup and Adonio, followed, in the final canto, by the triumphal entry into Marseilles, the marriage of Ruggiero and Bradamante, and finally Ruggiero's duel with Rodomonte. In the 1532 edition, following the triumphal entry into Marseilles and gathering together of the scattered Christians forces, Ariosto introduces a final complication in the form of a further obstacle to the marriage: the introduction of Leone as a rival suitor for Bradamante's hand. Ruggiero departs to fight on the side of the Bulgars against Leone and the Greeks, is captured, but chivalrously released by Leone. He then finds himself under an obligation to fight for Leone against Bradamante and to allow Leone to claim Bradamante's hand. But in a final complication of this 'gara di Cortesia' Leone in turn renounces his claim on Bradamante so that she can marry Ruggiero. The marriage, and the Ruggiero-Rodomonte duel, then end the poem as in the earlier version.

The effect of the insertion, critics have aptly pointed out, is to provide a dramatic climax to the poem, in the earlier version of which the smooth passage of events seemed something of an anticlimax. Now the happy outcome of the long courtship is only brought about in the final canto. The episode also serves to bring extra prestige to Ruggiero and to throw greater emphasis on the wedding. The epic, encomiastic note is thus accentuated. However, the choice of this particular story in this final prominent section of the poem is also significant. The *proemio* to the new Canto xlv insists on the power of Fortune:

> Quanto più su l'instabil ruota vedi
> di Fortuna ire in alto il miser uomo ...
> [The higher you see unhappy man rise on the inconstant wheel
> of Fortune ...]

Ruggiero, from being the triumphant hero of the victory over the Greeks, plunges into the misery of imprisonment, torture and the threat of execution. Man's weakness before the capriciousness of Fortune's wheel, is stressed here once more; but Ruggiero triumphs, together with those qualities which he displays in this last test. Amid the cruelty, selfishness and bad faith that surround them the young lovers are true to their ideals: in the most bitter dilemma he could face Ruggiero keeps his plighted oath fighting for his rival at the cost of his lady:

> e ben che or questo or quel pensier l'assaglia,
> tutti li scaccia, e solo a questo cede,
> il qual l'esorta a non mancar di fede. (XLV, 60)

[and although assailed by conflicting thoughts, he rejects them all, yielding only to the voices exhorting him not to break faith.]
As in the classic 'gare di cortesia' (Boccaccio, Chaucer) one act of generosity sparks off another, so Leone's respect for his opponent's valour provokes Ruggiero's supreme self-sacrifice, which in its turn induces Leone's renunciation of his rights. So virtue triumphs over fortune: the chivalrous ideal, which has striven so shakily against the hard realities of self-interest so often in the poem, comes out on top. So too does Bradamante's faithful love for her spouse, as once again her 'vera fede' is stressed:

> O siami Amor benigno o m'usi orgoglio,
> o me Fortuna in alto o in basso ruote,
> immobil son di vera fede scoglio
> che d'ogn'intorno il vento e il mar percuote: (XLIV, 61)

[Whether Love is kind or harsh with me, whether Fortune's wheel turns me high or low, I am a steadfast rock of true faith, beaten all around by wind and sea.]
It is, I believe, Ariosto's conscious assertion of the validity of that ideal, notwithstanding all the doubts he has seemed to cast on it before. The poem was to end on a positive note.

Yet even here the note is muted: Ruggiero is a most reluctant chivalrous hero and in the end he cannot resist declaring his legal claim to Bradamante's hand, and his lady is sorely tempted to break her oath. The poet in fact seems in some difficulty in handling this grand climax, and his invention falters at times: the existence of a binding contract between the lovers is divulged first by Marfisa and then by Ruggiero at a strangely late stage in the proceedings: Bradamante's shilly-shallying between filial obedience and aggressive self-assertion is difficult to follow; Ruggiero's treatment at the hands of Teodora, and Leone's secretive release of his enemy, are also clumsily contrived, and the introduction of Melissa to help Leone find Ruggiero is singularly inept. The poet I think is over-concerned with the effect of this episode on the poem as a whole: in the search for a dramatic climax he ends up with a comedy of intrigue – rich suitor, poor suitor, nagging mother; gesturing lovers making their parallel laments, and the final identity hoax, with Leone as a master of ceremonies revealing the lost Ruggiero to his wife and sister. And alongside these relics of the comedy we find passages of lyric (Bradamante's declaration of constancy echoes closely one of Ariosto's *capitoli*). Yet many readers, particularly in the sixteenth century, have found this last episode moving and in keeping with the spirit of the poem. For the admirers of the Bradamante-Ruggiero relationship, who were numerous in the poet's day, this seemed a superb climax in which a noble and chaste passion is in conflict with the claims of honour and duty, and where in the end passion and virtue are both triumphant.

Here as elsewhere in the 1532 additions, and in the *Cinque Canti*, Ariosto seems to anticipate trends characteristic of the later Cinquecento, certainly of Tasso who carries further many of Ariosto's precedents: the staging of a poetic conceit, for example: Ruggiero's lament,

    Io m'ho dunque di me contra a me stesso
    da vendicar, c'ho tutto il mal commesso, (XLV, *87*)
    [I must then take my own revenge myself, for all the guilt is mine,]

might well have strayed from the lips of Olindo or Tancredi. The tone of most of the later Ariosto is serious, solemn, didactic, as his successors were so often to be; and the romance fantasy is linked more closely to historical or contemporary allusions (here the battle between Bulgars and Greeks recalled the capture of Belgrade by the Turks in 1529). So too the later Cinquecento was to emphasise the Christian, moral note we see in the *Cinque Canti*; and in the process the handling of the supernatural becomes increasingly uncomfortable. Ariosto's concern for the balance of his material is also reminiscent of the late neo-Aristotelian debates on the structure of the narrative poem. These strains in the fabric of his poem caused essentially by the pressures of neo-classical and moralising forces on the traditional popular romance are not new in the *Cinque Canti* or in 1532 insertions: they are already evident in the earlier versions, but they are certainly more serious in the later Ariosto and they explain I think some of the deficiencies of the later material.

Within a year of the publication of the 1532 edition Ariosto died and with him died any plans he may have had to extend his poem further. The letter written in January 1532, quoted earlier (p. 172) announcing that he had written 400 new stanzas and hoped to add 'many more' may well have meant that he was intending to carry his narrative on beyond the wedding of Bradamante and Ruggiero to Ruggiero's death, as forecast by Boiardo. It is difficult to imagine Ariosto writing full stop to the *Furioso*, and it would have been in keeping for him to carry on and complete Boiardo's plan. Had he lived another ten years we might well have had a fourth edition that would have pleased his contemporaries, but it is very doubtful whether it would have pleased us.

10. Fortune; Conclusion

The first (1516) edition of the *Furioso* did not at once take Italy by storm – some few hundred copies only seem to have been sold; and there was no reprint of the 1521 edition before 1524. But by 1532 there had been 21 editions, and there were 16 of the 1532 text by 1540, and another 29 by 1550. We have very little evidence about the early readership and critical reaction to the *Furioso* but there is reason to believe that it soon attracted popular interest, and certainly by the middle of the century it had achieved a very wide appeal. A mid-sixteenth-century writer asserted that people sang songs in the streets to the words of the *Furioso*, and indeed one of the jibes of Ariosto's opponents was that he was read by the crowd – 'il Furioso che piace al vulgo' was Trissino's criticism. For Ariosto's supporters, however, the breadth of his appeal was evidence of his genius: 'If you frequent the Courts, or you go about the streets or the market place, if you go into a place of learning or any social gathering, all you find are people reading or reciting Ariosto. Did I say courts and places of learning? If you go into private houses, villas, even hovels and shacks you still find the *Furioso* and people chanting it. Of course there's not a school, University or Academy where they don't prize this remarkable poem, and even among uneducated country-girls and rough shepherdesses, you won't find one of them, however ignorant she is, who doesn't know some stanzas of the *Furioso*' (G. Malatesta).

It has been reckoned that about 25,000 copies of popular editions of the *Furioso* appeared in Italy in the sixteenth century, establishing it as the favourite reading of the general literate public. There was a decline in the number of editions at the very end of the sixteenth century and the early seventeenth, but even then the numbers do not fall substantially below those of the recently printed *Gerusalemme Liberata*. Further evidence of the appeal of the poem is seen in the large number of continuations published in the sixteenth century: *Rinaldo Furioso, Astolfo Borioso, Bradamante Gelosa, Marfisa Innamorata, La Morte di Ruggiero, La Cortesia di Leone e di Ruggiero* etc.

Nor is there any shortage of critical commentary – on the contrary the poem soon became the centre of an extensive critical debate in which passions were quickly aroused. Machiavelli at once recognised its merit: 'The whole poem is fine, and in many places wonderful'. However, the initial reaction, particularly among Tuscan fans of Pulci, was not always favourable. A late sixteenth-century critic remembered that his father's generation 'because they were used to reading Pulci's *Morgante*, found it very difficult to acclimatise to the *Furioso*'; and they obstinately preferred the *Morgante* or the *Innamorato* to what most people soon recognised as their superior. The main current of hostile comment came in the second half of the century with the spread of neo-Aristotelian literary theory, but there were criticisms before this of the lack of unity, the digressiveness, the mingling of noble and lowly characters, the title, the lack of decorum shown by the knights, by Orlando, for example, in his madness. Yet the objections to the lack of decorum and to the popular appeal of the *Furioso*, which would seem obvious targets for opponents of Ariosto, are not so notable in the first half of the century as the contrary insistence on the seriousness and dignity of the poem as compared with its predecessors. The genealogical action is taken seriously by most commentators as being in the true spirit of the epic, and Ariosto is praised precisely for his achievement in raising the tone of romance – by G. Giolito in 1548, for example: 'With the wings of his rare and happy genius he raised the lowly Romance to a higher peak than the great Virgil raised the arms of Aeneas.' Rarely do we find any comments on Ariosto's comic vein, or his 'irony': on the contrary L. Dolce in 1536 finds his style 'lofty and grave and most appropriate for heroism and majesty'; he has brought 'authority and splendour' to the octave rhyme.

The most severe critical attacks coincide with the revival of interest in neo-Aristotelian theory which is generally held to develop after Robortello's commentary on the *Poetics* in 1548. Much of the criticism concerns Ariosto's alleged failure to observe the laws of the epic – his lack of unity, coherence, decorum and of invention. Castelvetro, for example, condemned especially Ariosto's anachronisms and 'inverosimiglianze'. Against this Ariosto's admirers insisted that he *was* in accord with the rules (S. Fornari) or that he didn't try to observe the rules (A. Minturno), or that what he wrote was not an epic, bound by classical precepts, but a romance with its own language and criteria (G. Malatesta).

Another current of criticism was based on moral and religious principles and gathered force as the Catholic reaction against the spread of heretical beliefs brought increasing pressure on literature and the arts. This is a comparatively late development in Ariosto criticism, rare in fact until the 1580s and the Tasso controversy. Before this the *Furioso* was widely accepted as a serious and indeed morally uplifting poem. T. Folengo in 1533 declared that Ariosto influenced the young to acts of courtesy and essentially Christian conduct; and from 1542 many editions contained moral commentaries which explained how Ariosto's action exemplified basic moral principles: 'Here one sees the prudence and justice of a perfect Prince, here the temerity and negligence of a foolish monarch and his tyranny; here courage and timidity, here valour and cowardice ...'. The so-called 'allegories' prefixed to each canto are in many cases little more than morals to be drawn from the tales: Medoro going out to recover his king's body shows 'the strength of true friendship' (G. Giolito); Angelica's falling in love with Medoro shows 'that love arises rather according to inclination than birth' (Ruscelli). The first serious attempt to equip the poem with a consistent allegory is Simone Fornari's *Spositione sopra l'Orlando Furioso* (1549) and this was followed by a spate of allegorising commentaries which bear witness to the vividness of imagination of their authors. Fornari provided a series of 'allusions' to contemporary or historical events: Doralice seized by Mandricardo was said to be an allusion to Cesare Borgia's capture of the bride of a Venetian captain; Ginevra and Ariodante were allusions to Ferrarese court characters; Martano's cowardice at the tourney reflected a similar episode in a recent tourney where a Florentine knight actually vomited through fear. Similarly the actions of knights and beasts were seen as allegorical representations of moral situations: 'The hippogriph rises up and Ruggiero cannot stop it. By which we understand that Ruggiero is an incontinent but not intemperate youth. First he resists vice; then he develops a taste for pleasure. The poet calls the hippogriph a large and strange bird, because the effect of lust is violent and varied.'

In the course of the next thirty years allegorical interpretations were provided for every remote nook and cranny of the poem. These allegorisations of the *Furioso* should be viewed alongside the widespread allegorisation of classical poetry in the latter half of the sixteenth century. The classical epics were then widely interpreted according to contemporary allegorical schemes: Homer's Italian translator, Baccalli, depicts the *Iliad*, for example, as showing 'how much the passions and errors of Princes cause suffering to their unhappy peoples'. Ariosto was allegorised partly to prove that he measured up to the standards of classical literature – also of course to meet the moralising criticism of the Counter-Reformation which objected to the licentious love stories (Ricciardetto and Fiammetta, for example) and the anti-clerical or 'blasphemous' passages (the libidinous friar, the 'wasted' prayers found on the moon).

The fortune of the poem in the sixteenth century is closely affected therefore by neo-Aristotelian literary theory and Counter-Reformation moralising, both influences being marked in the dispute between the supporters of Ariosto and of Tasso which broke out on the publication of the *Gerusalemme Liberata* in 1581. The debate went on for several years and virtually dominated literary thinking for the remainder of the century. Tasso shared the misgivings of critics of the *Furioso* that Ariosto had failed to produce a poem worthy to rival the classical epics, that he had written a romance rather than an epic, and Tasso's aim was to write an epic that would 'overgo' the *Aeneid*. He could not, however, get Ariosto out of his mind: the attempts of Ariosto's followers, Trissino, Giraldi and others, to improve on the *Furioso*, had been conspicuously unsuccessful. Who read *L'Italia Liberata da' Goti*? Who failed to read Ariosto? 'He is read, and re-read', Tasso noted, 'by people of all ages, by both sexes; he is known in all countries, everyone likes him.' So Tasso in effect compromised by producing an epic-romance, a poem that avoided Ariosto's main deficiencies of unity, decorum and morality, that was based on a Christian historical subject and maintained a consistently epic grandeur; but at the same time he retained Ariosto's popular use of episodes, especially love stories, and he re-wrote some of Ariosto's most successful material (Alcina's palace, for example, which re-appears in Armida's garden).

The Ariosto-Tasso dispute also brought to a head the linguistic debate that had been conducted about the *Furioso*. As we have seen, Ariosto revised the language of the earlier editions of his poem in order to conform to Bembo's *Prose della Volgar Lingua*, but he was open to the criticism that he had not consistently followed Bembo's advice. L. Dolce defended him in 1539 against the criticism that he 'offends in many of his words, in the majority in fact, some of which are Lombard and not a few are contrary to the laws observed by the ancient Tuscans'. However, the 1532 text was recognised by most moderate critics as employing an acceptable Tuscan, and in the controversy between Ariostisti and Tassisti, Leonardo Salviati and the Crusca Academy came down firmly in support of Ariosto's language, and in opposition to Tasso's.

The critical reception and influence of the *Furioso* in Italy largely determined the attitudes of readers all over Europe, where the poem soon established a widespread reputation. The first complete translation into French, an anonymous prose version edited by Jehan de Gouttes, appeared in 1543; in spite of its poor quality, it was reprinted frequently in the sixteenth century. The first Spanish version, published in 1549 by Jerónimo de Urrea (condemned by the Curate in *Don Quixote*), enjoyed 18 editions in the next 40 years, and there were two other complete Spanish translations in 1550 and 1585. The first English version, by John Harington, did not appear till 1591, but the poem was well known in England long before this: Roger Ascham reported that by 1570 it was on sale at every street corner in London. Up to the middle of the seventeenth century there can have been few persons of culture who did not have some acquaintance with the *Furioso*. Many of Ariosto's characters became legendary: an 'Alcina', a 'Lydia', a 'Gabrina' became stock names for seductive, cruel or treacherous women. Among the Précieux in the salon of Arthénice Mlle de Beauvais was known as 'Bradamante', Georges de Scudéry as 'Astolfe'. One lady is reported to have been rebuked: 'Vous ne citez ny le Tasse, ny l'Arioste. Pensez-vous qu'avec cette indifférence on puisse faire admirer son esprit?'

It was in the lyric that the impact of the *Furioso* was most marked. The very length of Ariosto's poem led his admirers to chop it up, to extract passages that were of a manageable size for translation or imitation; the sections most admired and imitated were the love lyrics: the portraits of Alcina and Olimpia, the idyll of Angelica and Medoro, the jealous frenzy of Orlando and of Rodomonte, the plaints of Bradamante and Isabella. In France it was the Pléiade which established Ariosto's fame as a model of sincere love poetry, frankly sensual but not lacking in delicacy and idealism. In this and in his simpler, less abstract style he seemed less affected than Petrarch, and was imitated by Ronsard, Du Bellay, and particularly by Desportes and his followers. The Spanish lyric poets show a similar reaction: Garcilaso in particular admired and reproduced the lamentations of Bradamante, as did Gascoigne and Daniel in England. This is an interest in Ariosto as a serious poet: the Bradamante-Ruggiero relationship was highly praised by readers all over Europe as a portrait of a profound and moving love; and such lyrics as 'La verginella è simile alla rosa' (1. 42–4) were taken up and remodelled repeatedly: one of the earliest English madrigals is a setting of two of these stanzas in 1581, by William Byrd.

Another interesting area of influence is the theatre. The dramatic possibilities of Ariosto's material were soon appreciated in England, for example, where a performance of a *Historie of Ariodante and Ginevra* was given before the Queen in 1582. The French court had witnessed a tragi-comedy on the same subject, *Genèvre*, as early as 1564. The texts of both these works are lost but it is significant that among the earliest tragi-comedies in France there should have been a number of themes taken from the *Furioso*. It would seem that Ariosto's blend of a potentially tragic story with a happy ending, a reflection of that intermingling of the serious and light-hearted fundamental to his poetry, gave a stimulus to what was essentially a new genre. Robert Garnier's *Bradamante* (1582), which follows closely the Ariosto text, preserves some of the main features of the new tragi-comedy: an amorous subject, less noble than that of tragedy, neglect of the unities, a mixture of the tragic and the comic with a happy ending. There were other French tragi-comedies, on Angelica and Medoro, for example, and even Zerbino and Isabella (cut short at the happy reunion of the lovers *before* Zerbino's death). In England the Isabella story reappears in Marlowe's *Tamburlaine* (1592), and Orlando's madness in Robert Greene's *The Historie of Orlando Furioso* (1594), but most interesting, I think, is the continued appeal of that essentially tragi-comic Ginevra story which helped to shape *Much Ado About Nothing*. The comedy ending is pushed even further in one Spanish poem (Jerónimo de Huerta's *Florando de Castilla* (1588)) where the Spanish version of Polinesso repents and marries his Dalinda. Lope de Vega returned frequently to Ariostesque subjects, particularly to those of jealousy and jealous frenzy (*Los Celos de Rodomonte* (1588), *Angélica en el Catay* (c. 1600)) which were later taken up by Moreto, Calderón and others. The Spanish dramatists from Lope to Calderón seem particularly to have been attracted to the possibility of transferring to the stage Ariosto's magic and enchantments. In Lope's *Angélica en el Catay* the jealous Orlando discovers Angelica and Medoro together but fails to take his revenge as they float off into the air together thanks to Angelica's magic ring.

In the narrative poem and prose romance the influence of the *Furioso* is very considerable although few writers can be said to have followed directly in Ariosto's footsteps. In Italy as we have seen the trend towards a regular epic was modified by the vast success of the *Furioso*, but the temper of the later sixteenth century led to a serious, moral and allegorical reading of the poem. A similar pattern is to be found outside Italy. In Spain in particular the *Furioso* left its mark

on the content and structure of numerous narrative works whose
authors valued the serious, heroic elements in Ariosto, the battles
and duels in particular which were widely imitated by Ercilla in the
Araucana (1569–90), for example. Ariosto's duels were also imitated
by Ronsard in the *Françiade* and by Du Bartas in *Judith*. But in France
in particular there was severe criticism of the romance features of the
Furioso: the lack of unity or of orderly structure, the lack of decorum,
the offence to morality and religion. Ronsard likened it to a 'deformed
and monstrous body'. Later French classical critics were also severe:
Rapin, criticising Ariosto's failure as an epic poet, likened the *Furioso*
to 'those fertile lands that produce flowers and thistles together', and
Boileau could not approve

    ... en un sujet chrétien
    un auteur follement idolâtre et païen. (*Art poétique*, I, 217–18)

  So in each of the European countries Ariosto loses favour by the
close of the sixteenth century, and poets who look to Italy are more
likely to be impressed by Tasso's *Gerusalemme Liberata* than by the
Furioso. The poets who continued to admire Ariosto, and who continue his poem or repeat his material, as they still do in Italy and Spain
until late in the century, are more serious, decorous, concerned with
moral and allegorical meanings. Spenser's example is particularly
illuminating. He was a warm admirer of the *Furioso* and set out in
The Faerie Queene 'to overgo' Ariosto; but in the temper of late
sixteenth-century Europe Spenser read the *Furioso* with the allegorising commentaries of his contemporaries; so he fitted Orlando into
the scheme of 'a good governour and a vertuous man', following the
'Allegory' appended to Tasso's *Gerusalemme Liberata*, which was in
many ways closer to his own taste. Indeed throughout Europe poets
were abandoning the old romance characters in favour of their own
national heroes: Spenser in *The Faerie Queene*, Ronsard in *La Françiade*,
Ercilla in *La Araucana* – all of them admirers of Ariosto, but of special
aspects of the poet, heroic and moral, which suited their own aims.

  Ariosto's fortune declined substantially in Italy in the seventeenth
century; the number of editions of the *Furioso* falls off (only 31 in the
Seicento, as compared with 154 in the Cinquecento), and the decline
is marked as the century progresses (only seven editions between
1635 and 1679, and none at all between 1679 and 1713). Ariosto still
has many admirers (Galileo among them), but their admiration is
more restrained. Serious moral and religious objections were voiced
by Paolo Beni in his *Comparatione* (1612) and by U. Nisiely in his
Proginnasmi poetici (1620–39) which attacks the poem for a wide

range of defects, especially for its lack of true epic decorum: Ariosto is found guilty of anachronisms, tedious repetitions, coarseness, impiety, immorality, harshness of rhythm and barbarism of language. Nisiely like many other critics who saw literature as the nourishment of a cultured elite regretted Ariosto's popular appeal: 'he was perhaps more concerned to entertain the crowd than to please the learned'. Yet seventeenth-century critics could still find in the *Furioso* a truth of human emotions and a pathos, particularly in the madness of Orlando, which Nisiely (like Casanova later) had read a hundred times: 'And each time I read it I fall in love with this episode, I weep with pity and I am overcome with amazement.' Outside Italy Ariosto's fortune undergoes a similar decline: the *Furioso* has more critics than supporters, although the latter include some great names: Cervantes, for example, who is perhaps the closest of any of Ariosto's admirers to his subtle irony – and La Fontaine who composed three verse tales based on episodes in the *Furioso*, and who has often been spoken of as being akin to the Italian poet in spirit. Boileau thought La Fontaine's imitations of Ariosto superior to the original.

With the eighteenth century a new interest in Ariosto is evident, an appreciation particularly of his fluency, 'naturalezza' and freedom of invention; the impression of 'spontaneity' appealed to an age that nurtured improvisation, and which reacted against the pedantry of classical literary theorists. In praising Ariosto, Bettinelli insists : I am speaking now of feeling and spirit, not of trifling and pedantic laws'. To the voices of the Italian critics must be added those of several great foreign writers. Voltaire's admiration for Ariosto grew throughout his life; while initially expressing his pleasure in the *Furioso* but his inability to class it with the great epics, he later wrote enthusiastically of Ariosto's range and variety, the natural ease of his style, his narrative fluency and his moral wisdom: 'Once upon a time I did not dare put Ariosto among the epic poets; I considered him only the first of the grotesques: but on re-reading him I have found him as sublime as he is agreeable'. Goethe in his *T. Tasso* (1790) refers to Ariosto as the poet of serene human vision expressed in harmonious verse. Neither Voltaire nor Goethe, nor indeed most of the eighteenth-century critics, for all their enthusiasm, seem really to have understood the essential seriousness of the *Furioso*. They were too preoccupied with his naturalness, his independence of the rule books, and his humour. A symptom of the eighteenth-century's limitations in this respect is the great popularity enjoyed by the very deficient French translation by the Comte de Tressan (1780), reprinted 23 times in spite of its abundant mistakes, largely on the strength of its deft and colourful presentation of the gallant stories and voluptuous descriptions of the original.

It was Hegel in the *Aesthetics* who recognised the source of Ariosto's irony: his reaction to an outdated medieval world from the new viewpoint of the Renaissance and under the influence of classical culture: but alongside Ariosto's comic vein Hegel underlined his ability to bring out the serious side of medieval chivalry, his depiction of generosity, love, honour and bravery. Foscolo, writing in the *Quarterly Review* in 1820, took a similar view, praising Ariosto's experience of the 'passions and propensities of human nature' and his knowledge of man as he appears in every class of society: 'He speaks of crimes, he laughs at follies, not like a stern censor who is out of humour with mankind, but as a playful and charitable observer of human nature'. De Sanctis emphasised the 'decadence' of Ariosto's society, dedicated to the cult of beauty, incapable of concern for the serious political and moral problems of its day. De Sanctis's earlier views (in the 1840s) had been clearly influenced by Hegel and did injustice to the seriousness of Ariosto's depiction of human emotions but his later criticism forces Ariosto into the pattern of his historical view of Italian literature, in which the Renaissance is condemned as abdicating moral responsibility with its cult of pure form, and the *Furioso* is seen as the masterpiece of art for art's sake: 'This world in which there is no seriousness of inner life, no religion, no fatherland, no family, no feeling for nature, no honour and no love'. Connected with this school of thought is a criticism much repeated in the nineteenth-century, of Ariosto's insincerity, his 'fawning' adulation of the Estense court. Many nineteenth-century Italian critics narrowed the angle of vision, judging the *Furioso* critically in its historical context as escapist and immoral, seeing it as part of a decline in Italian literature from the time of Dante. But out of the nineteenth-century historical approach came a number of writers who worked seriously to illuminate the cultural background of the poem, G. Bertoni with his studies of the Ferrarese court, and P. Rajna with his researches into Ariosto's sources.

Croce with his rigorous theory of 'poesia' and 'non poesia' derided those 'illogical' enquiries in his *Ariosto, Shakespeare e Corneille* (1920) where he pursued De Sanctis' interpretation of the *Furioso* as a temple of pure art: 'As soon as one affirms of Ariosto or of any other artist that their content is pure Art and pure Form, one really means that their content is the feeling for the pure rhythm of the Universe, for the unity of dialectic, the Harmony of evolution.' So 'Harmony' becomes Croce's definition of Ariosto's art, the resolution of the multiple facets of human experience in a serene and harmonious blend under the controlling and disciplining influence of the poet's style. This style is defined as predominantly ironic, remote and un-committed, 'like the eye of God that sees the movement of His creation, of all creation, loving it all equally, good and ill, seizing only the movement of it, the eternal dialectic, rhythm and harmony.' Croce's interpretation seemed to absorb and supersede all previous ones and it was extremely influential – but it encouraged a one-sided view of the poem, against which scholars and critics were slow to react for a whole generation.

A reaction came in the direction of closer attention to Ariosto's historical context on the one hand and an attempt on the other to define more closely the nature of his style. Both are apparent to some extent in W. Binni's *Metodo e poesia di Ludovico Ariosto* (1946) which emphasises the conscious method in Ariosto's poem: the *Furioso* is seen as the masterpiece of an age to which it is closely linked, and from which at the same time it is dissociated by a conscious process of 'deformation'. R. Spongano, R. Battaglia and others, in opposition to De Sanctis and Croce, insisted on the essential seriousness of the poem and the poet's sincere concern for human values which are *not* 'dissolved in his all-pervasive irony'. Closer attention has more recently been paid to Ariosto's language, particularly to the process of linguistic revision of successive editions, and closer stylistic studies have related the poet's diction to his predecessors in the Quattrocento. These and other recent trends have been discussed in the course of this book. There has been no lack of scholarly and critical comment but I think it is true to say that no new critical approach comparable with Croce's has emerged.

The present study perhaps reflects the modern hesitation to pin any of the traditional labels on Ariosto. Indeed it would seem rash, in the light of the history of the poet's reputation which we have just made, to attempt any precise definition of the nature of Ariosto's genius; so rarely in the past has the *Furioso* been appreciated in its complexity. It has been seen as heroic and didactic on the one hand, and as immoral and irreligious on the other; it has been judged both committed to its age and escapist; it has seemed serious to some, frivolous to others. It has been squeezed into narrow critical or moral frameworks, neo-Aristotelian, Counter-Reformist, Classicist, Romantic, Crocean

Marxist – from which it has emerged still essentially undefined and uncategorised.

It is of course the essence of great poetry that it does escape definition, that it is more than the sum of its parts, however cleverly the latter have been isolated. But the *Furioso*, is I think, particularly resistant to the attempts of critics to classify it, or to define its 'dominant' theme or mode. Like other great Renaissance narrative poems its very size and scope contribute to its complexity. Unlike a tragedy or a lyric poem, the conception and composition of which may represent only a fraction of its author's output, the long Renaissance epic-romances take years to write, often a lifetime. Ariosto is occupied for nearly 25 years on the *Furioso* and the rest of his writing is slight by comparison. Within this poem the poet tends to encompass the experience, the culture, the inspiration of a lifetime: over these years he himself changes; his friends, his court, his country changes. Even within the span of the single draft of his work the direction and tone of his poem is likely to change, whether in response to conscious or subconscious factors.

The forces for change in Ariosto's poem are particularly strong. As we have tried to show, the years of the composition of the *Furioso* are among the most critical in Italian cultural and political history, spanning the last twenty years of the Italian wars. And, if we look back to the beginning of the story which Ariosto completed, to the years when Boiardo began the *Innamorato*, in 'the good old days of Duke Ercole', we can see Ariosto's poem embracing two generations in time during which the divisions of the old and the new world seem very real. The *Furioso* reflects these changes – to some extent almost directly in the revised drafts of 1516, 1521 and 1532, but more significantly indirectly through their presence in the poet's inner self; and this is a source of strength for the poem which acquires not merely a relevance but a vitality from its identification with the mood of its changing society. Ariosto is himself caught up in this changing society which leaves him bewildered: what has happened to the world of his youth, not just the members of the happy circle of Ercole's court, but their values and their culture? He is too shrewd to retreat into a general denunciation of 'modern times' which he knows is useless, but also which he suspects is ill-founded. *Were* they such good old times? *Have* men ever lived up to those happy ideals which coloured the imagination of the poet in his youth? So the poet lives in both worlds, committed really to both, which means that he is only half-committed to either.

So Ariosto finds his primary inspiration in the reading of his youth, in books of chivalry. These were what first stirred his imagination, not the real world of the Estense Court but the books in the Estense library – like Don Quixote he falls a victim to chivalrous romances. And his first achievement is to have recaptured that fascination, to recall the spell of an imaginary world so effectively that his readers down to the present day can experience it with him – from Cervantes in an African gaol to Walter Scott reading the *Furioso* aloud on Salisbury Crags overlooking Edinburgh, or Milton:

Towred Cities please us then
And the busie humm of men
Where throngs of Knights and Barons bold
In weeds of Peace high triumphs hold ...

The generations of readers who have warmed to Ariosto's chivalrous world were not just laughing at an outdated convention. They have relived it, and we must insist that theirs was a legitimate reading of the poem – that the appeal of an imaginary chivalrous society is an essential feature of Ariosto's poem. In this respect it is indeed escapist.

Yet there is barely a page of poem, as we have seen, that is not stamped with the date of its composition. The poet's own experience is constantly recalled in those fluent allusions to his misfortunes or joys in love, and his audience is constantly reminded of its own experience, from the Duke and Cardinal, to the court ladies, and the fighting soldiers of Ferrara. The military action in particular, remote as it may seem, continually elicits parallels with the harsh realities of the war-ridden Italy of Ariosto's day. So the two actions are seen together, the action of imagination and that of experience – and the poet makes no effort to escape the cold realities of modern warfare even while he delights in the glamour of the 'arms' of romance.

However, Ariosto goes further. It is not merely the contrast between chivalrous romance and Renaissance Italy that he underlines but that between romance and human experience generally – and here too he is able to combine the two spheres in the same poem, on the same page. Lovers leap to their deaths, but swim out to safety; they vow eternal fidelity and then abandon each other. Ariosto knows that on the modern, Machiavelli-analysed battlefield the captains may still dream of chivalrous distinction while they set their cannons against their outnumbered opponents, and he suspects that this is not just the dilemma of his own generation but that of all generations, caught between self-interest and principle, or between reality and imagination; and in one area of human experience in particular he explores and illustrates that sad ambiguity, that is in the relations between a man and a woman.

All of this is comprised between the covers of his book, presented not as a social or historical thesis, but as a poem which in the subtlety of its expression can convey the feelings of human beings confronted with this ambiguous world. So the poem is grave or gay, heroic or facetious, sceptical or didactic as the mood and the material changes. It *does* aim to divert at times with a blithe disregard for moral or religious implications; and elsewhere it pushes home a moral lesson with insistence. It *is* prepared simply to follow a good story at times, apparently regardless of the course of the poem as a whole; although generally there is a careful control of the heterogeneous material in the interest of a balanced whole. There are times when the poet's wink is so broad that it cannot be missed, and other times when he is plainly moved about something, stirred to pity or admiration or indignation. This complexity of tone reflecting the diversity of his material and his view of the intricacy of human experience is perhaps the most characteristic feature of his poetry.

He was not, we have suggested, always wholly successful in reconciling this complexity of tone and material with the demands of artistic unity and cohesion, but this judgement is a personal one; and it would be remarkable if, at this distance in time, we could respond fully to every section of this lengthy poem. Where he fails, where the spell fades or the interest slackens it is most often an ambitious failure, a symptom of his seriousness rather than of his boredom or his dilettantism. In a sense his subject matters more to him than his poetry – we could reply to Croce that Harmony plays second fiddle to Truth. But his failures seem to me rare, and they have seemed rare to generations of readers over the last four hundred years. To so many readers in the past Ariosto has grown in stature as they came to know him better, and a long list of Europe's greatest minds have paid their tribute and acknowledged their debt to him. His appeal today, to the few who have learned to know him, is as strong as ever. It is hoped that this study may have helped to enlarge that limited circle of his admirers.

General Note
The bibliographical notes below are intended as a select guide to the more useful works relating to the various chapters. For a fuller bibliography readers are advised to consult the 'Nota bibliografica' appended to L. Ariosto, *Opere Minori*, ed. C. Segre (Milan 1954) and to the literary history of Cecchi and Sapegno, *Il Quattrocento e l'Ariosto* (Milan 1965) – supplemented by the annual lists of current work published in *La Rassegna della Letteratura Italiana*, *The Year's Work in Modern Languages*, and the *Publications of the Modern Languages Association of America*.
Ariosto's works are cited in the two volumes of the Ricciardi series *Letteratura Italiana, Storia e Testi: Orlando Furioso*, ed. L. Caretti, *Opere Minori*, ed. C. Segre (Milan 1954). These need to be supplemented by L. Ariosto, *Le Commedie*, ed. M. Catalano, 2 vols. (Bologna 1940) and *Le Opere Minori*, ed. G. Fatini, 2nd ed. (Florence 1961). For a critical edition of the *Furioso* see the edition by S. Debenedetti and C. Segre, *Orlando Furioso secondo l'edizione del 1532 con le varianti delle edizioni del 1516 e del 1521* (Bologna 1960). Among the numerous editions with commentaries note the following: Papini (Florence 1903); Zingarelli (Milan 1934); Sapegno (Milan 1940); Binni (Florence 1942); Ramat (Milan 1955); Ceserani (Turin 1969).
Of the English translations note those by J. Harington (1591), W. S. Rose (1823–31) and Barbara Reynolds (forthcoming in Penguin Books).

CHAPTER ONE: Life
The standard biography is that by Michele Catalano, *Vita di L. Ariosto*, 2 vols. (Geneva 1930). See also E. G. Gardner, *The King of Court Poets*, *L. Ariosto* (London 1906), and L. Ariosto, *Lettere*, ed. A. Stella (Milan 1965).
For Ferrara at this time see:
G. BERTONI, *La Biblioteca Estense e la cultura ferrarese ai tempi del duca Ercole I* (Turin 1903)
E. G. GARDNER, *Dukes and Poets in Ferrara* (London 1904)
G. BERTONI, *L'O.F. e la Rinascenza a Ferrara* (Modena 1919)
H. HAUVETTE, *L'A. et la poésie chevaleresque à Ferrare* (Paris 1927)
A. PIROMALLI, *La cultura a Ferrara al tempo di L.A.* (Florence 1953)
R. BACCHELLI, *La Congiura di Don Giulio d'Este* (Verona 1958)
R. LONGHI, *Officina ferrarese* (Florence 1956)
S. PASQUAZI, *Rinascimento ferrarese* (Rome 1957)
W. GUNDERSHEIMER, *Towards a Re-interpretation of the Renaissance in Ferrara* (Florence 1963)
— *Ferrara: The Style of a Renaissance Despotism* (Princeton 1972)
PAOLO NEGRI, 'Milano, Ferrara e Impero durante l'impresa di Carlo VIII in Italia' in *Archivio Storico Lombardo* 44 (1917) 423–571
R. BATTAGLIA, 'L'A. e la critica idealistica' in *Rinascita* 7 (1950) 141–50
G. GETTO, 'La corte estense di Ferrara ...' in *Letteratura e critica nel tempo* (Milan 1954)
E. GARIN, 'Motivi della cultura filosofica ferrarese nel Rinascimento' in *Belfagor* 6 (1956) 612–34

Among the contemporary accounts note:
GASPARO SARDI, *Historie ferraresi* (Ferrara 1556)
UGO CALEFFINI, *Diario*, ed. G. Pardi (Ferrara 1938–40)
BERNARDO ZAMBOTTI, *Diario ferrarese*, ed. G. Pardi (Ferrara 1934)

CHAPTER TWO : Minor Works
For Ariosto's lyric poetry see:
A. SALZA, *Studi su L.Ā.* (Città di Castello 1914)
C. GRABHER, *La poesia minore dell'A.* (Rome 1947)
G. CARDUCCI, 'La gioventù di L.A. e la poesia latina in Ferrara' in Carducci's
    Opere, vol. xiii (Bologna 1936)
G. FATINI, 'Su la fortuna e l'autenticità delle liriche di L.A.' in *Giornale
    Storico della Letteratura Italiana* Supp. 22–3 (1924) 1–164
E. BIGI, 'Vita e letteratura nelle poesie giovanili dell'A.' in *Giornale Storico
    della Letteratura Italiana* 145 (1968) 1–37
ANNA CARLINI, 'Progetto di edizione critica delle liriche di L.A.' in
    Giornale Storico della Letteratura Italiana 135 (1958) 1–40
For the satires see:
J ÜRGEN GRIMM, *Die Einheit der Ariost'schen Satire* (Frankfurt 1969)
G. FATINI, 'Umanità e poesia dell'A. nelle Satire' in *Archivium Romanicum*
    17 (1933) 497–564
C. BERTANI, 'Identificazione di personaggi delle Satire di L.A.' in *Giornale
    Storico della Letteratura Italiana* 102 (1933) 1–47
S. DEBENEDETTI, 'Intorno alle Satire dell'A.' in *Giornale Storico della
    Letteratura Italiana* 122 (1946) 109–30
For the comedies see:
C. GRABHER, *Sul teatro dell'A.* (Rome 1946)
D. RADCLIFF-UMSTEAD, *The Birth of Modern Comedy in Renaissance Italy*
    (London 1969)
K. F. THOMPSON, 'A note on A.'s *I Suppositi*' in *Comparative Literature* 12
    (1960)

CHAPTER THREE : The Literary Tradition
On the romance tradition in Italy before Pulci there is no comprehen-
sive study. Apart from the entries in the literary histories of Flora,
Cecchi and Sapegno, etc., I have found the following helpful:

JESSIE CROSLAND, *The Old French Epic* (Oxford 1951)
J. D. BRUCE, *The Evolution of Arthurian Romance* 2 vols. (Göttingen 1923)
R. S. LOOMIS, *The Development of Arthurian Romance* (London 1963)
E. G. GARDNER, *The Arthurian Legend in Italian Literature* (London 1930)
E. CARRARA, *Da Rolando a Morgante* (Turin 1932)
PAOLO TOSCHI, *Fenomenologia del canto popolare* (Rome 1947)
A. LIMENTANI, *Dal 'Roman de Palamedes' ai cantari di Febus-el-Forte*
    (Bologna 1962)
G. B. BRONZINI, *Tradizione di stile aedico dai cantari al 'Furioso'*
    (Florence 1966)
LINA CESATI, 'Contatti e interferenze tra il ciclo brettone e carolingio
    prima del Boiardo' in *Archivium Romanicum* 11 (1927) 108–17
Among the large bibliography on Fulci and Boiardo note especially:
L. PULCI, *Il Morgante* ed. F. Ageno (Milan 1955)

D. DE ROBERTIS, *Storia del 'Morgante'* (Florence 1958)
G. GETTO, *Studio sul 'Morgante'* (Florence 1967)
G. MARIANI, *Il 'Morgante' e i cantari trecenteschi* (Florence 1953)
R. SCRIVANO, 'L. Pulci nella storia della critica' in *La Rassegna della Letteratura Italiana* 59 (1955) 232–58
M. M. BOIARDO, *Orlando Innamorato* ed. A. Scaglione, 2 vols (Turin 1966)
G. REICHENBACH, *M. M. Boiardo* (Bologna 1929)
E. BIGI, *La poesia del Boiardo* (Florence 1941)
Il Boiardo e la critica contemporanea (Atti del Convegno di aprile 1969) (Florence 1970)
R. A. PETTINELLI, 'L'*Orlando Innamorato* e la tradizione cavalleresca in ottave' in *La Rassegna della Letteratura Italiana* 71 (1967) 383–418
C. P. BRAND, 'Ariosto's continuation of the *Orlando Innamorato*' in the forthcoming volume of studies presented to P. O. Kristeller, edited by C. H. Clough (Liverpool 1974)

CHAPTER FOUR: The Theme of Love
The critical literature on the *Furioso* is very extensive and I give here only a brief selection. General works are given below, more specialised studies under the relevant chapters.

The best studies in English are the short chapter in G. G. Hough's, *A Preface to the 'Faerie Queene'* (London 1962) and the longer and more detailed chapters in R. M. Durling's *The Figure of the Poet in Renaissance Epic* (Cambridge, Mass. 1965), which is particularly valuable. See also:

B. CROCE, *Ariosto, Shakespeare, Corneille* (Bari 1920)
A. MOMIGLIANO, *Saggio sull'O.F.* (Bari 1928)
L'Ottava d'oro: Letture (Milan 1933)
R. SPONGANO, 'La poesia delle *Stanze*; L'ironia nell'*O.F.*' in *La Prosa di Galileo e altri scritti* (Florence 1949)
R. BATTAGLIA, 'L'A. e la critica idealistica' in *Rinascita* 7 (1950) 141–50
R. RAMAT, *Per la storia dello stile rinascimentale* (Florence 1953)
A. PIROMALLI, *Motivi e forme delle poesia di L.A.* (Florence 1954)
W. BINNI, *Metodo e poesia di L.A.* 2nd ed. (Florence 1961)
L. CARETTI, *Ariosto e Tasso* 2nd ed. (Turin 1967)
M. TURCHI, *Ariosto o della liberazione fantastica* (Ravenna 1969)
R. NEGRI, *Interpretazione dell'O.F.* (Milan 1971)
P. RAJNA, *Le Fonti dell'*O.F.'* 2nd ed. (Florence 1900)

CHAPTER FIVE: The Theme of Arms
RICCARDO TRUFFI, *Giostre e cantori di giostre* (Rocca San Casciano 1911)
R. M. RUGGIERI, *Umanesimo classico e unmanesimo cavalleresco italiano* (Catania 1955)
A. B. FERGUSON, *The Indian Summer of English Chivalry* (Durham, N. Carolina, 1960)
S. PAINTER, *French Chivalry* (Ithaca 1967)
RICHARD BARBER, *The Knight and Chivalry* (London 1970)
P. PIERI, *Il Rinascimento e la crisi militare italiana* (Turin 1952)
J. R. HALE, 'Gunpowder and the Renaissance' in *From the Renaissance to the Counter-Reformation* ed. C. H. Carter (New York 1965) 113–44

J. R. HALE, 'International Relations in the West, Diplomacy and War' in *New Cambridge Modern History*, vol. I, ed. G. R. Potter (Cambridge 1957) 259–91.

E. SACCONE, 'Cloridano e Medoro' in *Modern Language Notes* (1968) 67–99

W. MORETTI, 'La storia di Cloridano e Medoro' in *Convivium* 37 (1969) 543–51

CHAPTER SIX : Dynastic and Political Themes

MICHELE VERNERO, *Studi critici sopra la geografia nell' 'O.F.'* (Turin 1913)

A. SALZA, *Studi su L. A.* (Città di Castello 1914)

G. DE BLASI, 'L'A. e le passioni' in *Giornale Storico della Letteratura Italiana* 129–30 (1952–3) 318–62, 178–203

A. GILBERT, '*O.F.* as a 16th century text' in *Italica* 37 (1960) 239–56

J. A. MOLINARO, 'Ariosto and the seven deadly sins' in *Forum Italicum* (1969) 252–69

CHAPTER SEVEN : The Arts of Narrative
Relatively little has been written on the structure and narrative technique of the *Furioso*, although most studies comment briefly on these (see the general works listed under chapter IV). Much of this chapter is original although I have drawn on R. M. Durling (see chapter IV) and C. Segre (see chapter VIII) and also:

N. CAPPELLANI, *La sintassi narrativa dell'A.* (Florence 1952)

E. LI GOTTI, 'L'A. narratore' in *Saggi* (Florence 1941)

A. JENNI, 'Raziocinio dell'A.' in *Rivista di Cultura Classica e Medioevale* 7 (1965) 577–85

CHAPTER EIGHT : The Arts of Poetry
A great deal has been published in recent years on aspects of Ariosto's poetic technique, but no comprehensive study of his style has appeared (cf. Chiappelli's *Studi sul linguaggo del Tasso epico* (Florence 1957)). This chapter is a personal assessment taking into account particularly the works listed below:

G. CONTINI, *Esercizi di lettura* (Florence 1947)

L. PARRINO, *Come sorride l'Ariosto* (Ancona 1953)

C. SEGRE, *Esperienze ariostesche* (Pisa 1961)

D. BIANCHI, 'Della musicalità considerata nella struttura del verso' in *La Rassegna della Letteratura Italiana* 33 (1925) 81–113

G. DE ROBERTIS, 'Le Stanze o dell'ottava concertante' in *Studi* (Florence 1944)

— 'Lettura sintomatica del primo dell'*Orlando*' in *Paragone* 4 (1950) 12–17

G. G. FERRERO, 'Sermone e poesia nell'*O.F.*' in *Scritti vari dell'Università di Torino* (Turin 1951) 185–202

E. BIGI, 'Petrarchismo ariostesco' in *Giornale Storico della Letteratura Italiana* 130 (1953) 31–62

M. MARTI, 'Il tono medio dell'*O.F.*' in *Convivium* 23 (1955) 29–42

E. TUROLLA, 'Dittologia e enjambement nell'elaborazione dell' '*O.F.*'' in *Lettere Italiane* 10 (1958) 1–20

E. SACCONE, 'Note ariostesche' in *Annali della Scuola Normale di Pisa* 27 (1959) 193–242

A.LIMENTANI, 'Struttura e storia dell'ottava rima' in *Lettere Italiane* 13 (1961) 20–77 – but cf. C.Dionisotti, 'Appunti su antichi testi' (*Italia Medioevale e Umanistica* (1964) 99 ff.)

E.BIGI, 'Appunti sulla lingua e sulla metrica dell'*O.F.*' in *Giornale Storico della Letteratura Italiana* 138 (1961) 239–53

L.BLASUCCI, 'Osservazioni sulla struttura metrica dell'*O.F.*' in *Giornale Storico della Letteratura Italiana* 139 (1962) 169–218

L.BLASUCCI, 'Ancora sulla *Commedia* come fonte linguistica e stilistica del *Furioso*' in *Giornale Storico della Letteratura Italiana* 144 (1968) 188–231

CHAPTER NINE: Problems of Language and Composition
There is no up-to-date study of Ariosto's language, although most of the general works comment on this and there are some useful brief studies. Note especially:

B.MIGLIORINI, 'Sulla lingua dell'Ariosto' in *Italica* 3 (1946)

M.DIAZ, *Le correzioni dell'O.F.* (Naples 1900)

S.DEBENEDETTI, 'Le tre edizioni dell'*O.F.*'; appendix to his edition of the *Furioso* (Bari 1928)

B.TERRACINI, 'Lingua libera e libertà linguistica' in *Archivio Glottologico Italiano* 35 (1950)

N.CAPPELLANI, *La sintassi narrativa dell'Ariosto* (Florence 1952)

C.SEGRE, *Esperienze ariostesche* (Pisa 1961)

On the *Cinque Canti* and the 1532 additions note, in addition to Segre's volume, the following:

S.DEBENEDETTI, *I Frammenti autografi dell'O.F.* (Turin 1937)

E.CARRARA, 'Marganorre' in *Annali della Scuola Normale di Pisa* 18 (1940) 1–20

F.CATALANO, *L'Episodio di Olimpia nell'*'O.F.*' (Lucca 1951)

PIO FONTANA, *I 'Cinque Canti' e la storia della poetica del 'Furioso'* (Milan 1962)

C.DIONISOTTI, 'Per la data dei *Cinque Canti*' in *Giornale Storico della Letteratura Italiana* 137 (1960) 1–39

C.DIONISOTTI, 'Appunti sui *Cinque Canti* e sugli studi ariosteschi' in *Studi e problemi di critica testuale* (Bologna 1961)

E.SACCONE, 'Appunti per una definizione dei *Cinque Canti*' in *Belfagor* 20 (1965) 381–410

E.PIERMARINI, 'Un episodio inedito dell' *O.F.*' in *Pegaso* 2 (1929) 169–181

S.DEBENEDETTI, 'Le nuove ottave dell'Ariosto' in *La Cultura* 7 (1929) 171–6

CHAPTER TEN: Fortune; Conclusion

W.BINNI, *Storia della critica ariostesca* (Lucca 1951)

R.RAMAT, *La critica ariostesca dal secolo xvi ad oggi* (Florence 1954)

G.FUMAGALLI, *La fortuna dell' 'O.F.'* in *Italia nel secolo xvi* (Ferrara 1910)

A.SAMMUT, *La fortuna dell'A. nell' Inghilterra elisabettiana* (Milan 1971)

A.BENEDETTI, *L'O.F. nella vita intellettuale del popolo inglese* (Florence 1914)

A.CIORANESCO, *L'Arioste en France* (Paris 1939)

M.CHEVALLIER, *L'Arioste en Espagne* (1530–1650) (Bordeaux 1966)

J.A.SCOTT, 'De Sanctis, Ariosto e *La Poesia Cavalleresca*' in *Italica* 45 (1968) 428–61

(a) PERSONS
Alamanni, Luigi, 43
Alberti, Leon Battista, 166
Alexander VI, Pope (1492–1503), 27
Aragona (d'), Eleonora, 18
Aragona (d'), Ferdinando, 15
Avalos (d'), Alfonso, 12, 177
Aretino, Pietro, 43
Ariosto, Ludovico,
   I Cinque Canti, 171-5, 182
   Le Commedie: Il Negromante, 9, 11,
   32, 40-4, 167; I Studenti, 42;
   I Suppositi, 9, 32-4, 42-3; La
   Cassaria, 9, 12, 32-3, 35, 39-40, 43,
   45; La Lena, 12, 32, 36-9, 43
   Italian lyrics, 17-22
   Latin lyrics, 15-17
   Letters, 13-14
   Orlando Furioso, 9, 11-12, 14-15,
   21-2, 28, 30-2, 35-6, 46-196
   Satire, 10-11, 22-31, 159
Ariosto, Nicolò, 3-4, 6
Ariosto, Giambattista, 6
Ariosto, Virginio, 6, 12, 15, 23, 171
Ascham, Roger, 188

Baccelli, Gerolamo, 186
Bandello, Matteo, 65
Barbaro, Francesco, 73
Barberino, Andrea da, 46, 48, 49, 50,
   84, 153
Baruffaldi, Girolamo, 169
Bartas, Guillaume du, 190
Bellay, Joachim du, 188
Bellini, Giovanni, 8
Bello, Francesco (il Cieco), 8, 54, 168
Bembo, Pietro, 5, 8, 16-19, 30, 44, 59,
   166-7, 169, 170, 187
Beni, Paolo, 190
Benucci, Alessandra, 7, 10-14, 18,
   20-1, 29, 30, 57, 58, 109
Bettinelli, 191
Bibbiena (il – Bernardo Dovizi), 43
Boccaccio, Giovanni, 36, 54, 58, 59,
   93, 118, 126, 145, 165, 167, 181
Boiardo, Matteo Maria, 1, 5, 8, 46,
   50-5, 57, 74, 84, 85, 88, 94, 95, 102,
   106, 109, 126, 139, 145-6, 148, 166,
   168, 170, 173, 183, 194

Boileau, Nicolas, 190-1
Borgia, Cesare, 5, 186
Borgia, Lucrezia, 15, 109
Botticelli, Sandro, 59
Burchiello (il – Domenico di
   Giovanni), 22
Byrd, William, 188
Byron, George Gordon, 54

Calderón de la Barca, Pedro, 189
Cammelli, Antonio, 8, 22
Cantelmo, Ercole, 91
Cariteo (il – Benedetto Gareth), 22
Casanova, Giovanni, 191
Castelvetro, Ludovico, 185
Castiglione, Baldassare, 28, 59, 102,
   116, 120, 167, 168, 170
Catullus, 5, 15, 20, 54, 152, 157
Caxton, William, 93, 94
Cecchi, Giovanni Maria, 43
Cervantes, Miguel de, 56, 100, 127,
   142, 153, 188, 191, 195
Charles V, Emperor, 12, 93, 111, 114
Charles VIII, of France, 5, 16, 111
Chaucer, Geoffrey, 181
Cicero, 15
Clement VII, Pope (1523–34), 11, 12
Colonna, Fabrizio, 108
Colonna, Vittoria, 109
Columbus, Christopher, 115
Correggio, Niccolò da, 8, 31
Cosmico, Niccolò Lelio, 18
Cossa, Francesco, 8
Costa, Lorenzo, 8
Croce, Benedetto, 192-3, 196
Crusca, Accademia della, 171

D'Ambra, Francesco, 43
Daniel, Samuel, 188
Dante Alighieri, 27, 47, 54, 58, 77, 79,
   114, 141, 144, 156, 167, 192
De Sanctis, Francesco, 192-3
Desportes, Philippe, 188
Dolce, L., 44, 185, 187
Dossi, Dosso, 8

Ercilla, Alonso de, 190
Este (d'), family, 1-3, 9, 52-3, 56, 68,
   76, 88, 90, 95, 107, 109, 111, 115,
   150-1

Este (d')—*contd.*
Alfonso, 6, 8-12, 14-15, 18, 23-4, 27,
  32, 89-90, 92, 107-10, 114-15, 125,
  158
Azzo, 122
Beatrice, 5, 109, 114
Borso, 2-4, 7
Ercole (I), 3-8, 16, 18, 31, 109-10,
  194
Ercole (II), 32
Ferrante, 5, 18
Giulio, 6, 9, 18
Ippolito, 6-11, 23-6, 107-8, 113-14,
  136, 151, 158
Isabella, 74, 109, 150
Obizzo, 2, 18

Ficino, Marsilio, 59
Flores, Juan de, 118
Folengo, Teofilo, 186
Fornari, S., 185
Foscolo, Ugo, 192
Francis I, of France, 10, 11, 12, 93,
  105, 111, 121, 125
Frere, J. H., 55
Frescobaldi, Girolamo, 8
Fulgoso, Federico, 162
Fusari, Giovanni, 26

Galilei, Galileo, 124, 190
Garcilaso de la Vega, 188
Garnier, Robert, 189
Garofalo (il – Benvenuto Tisi), 8
Gascoigne, George, 34, 188
Giolito, G., 171, 185, 186
Giraldi, Giambattista Cintio, 39, 88,
  169, 175, 187
Goethe, J. W. von, 191
Gonzaga, Elisabetta, 109
Gonzaga, Isabella, 8
Gouttes, Jehan de, 188
Greene, Robert, 189
Guicciardini, Francesco, 12, 125

Harington, John, 188
Hawes, Stephen, 94
Hegel, Friedrich, 192
Homer, 74, 88, 152, 186

Horace, 15, 16, 22-5, 30, 54
Huerta, Jerónimo de, 189

Julius II, Pope (1503–13), 9, 10, 25,
  90, 110-11, 123
Juvenal, 22, 24

La Fontaine, Jean de, 191
Leo X, Pope (1513–21), 10, 11, 27,
  32, 111, 123
Leopardi, Giacomo, 112
Lope de Vega, Felix, 189
Louis XII, of France, 5, 9, 32, 121
Lucan, 54

Machiavelli, Niccolò, 14, 27, 28, 37,
  42, 43, 56, 94, 101, 110, 112, 113,
  120, 125, 142, 167, 185, 195
Magnanino, Antonio, 89
Magno, Marcantonio, 169
Malaguzzi, Daria, 4
Malatesta, G., 185
Malegucci, Annibale, 29-30
Malory, Thomas, 93
Manuzio, Aldo, 171
Marlowe, Christopher, 189
Medici, Giuliano de', 18
Medici, Lorenzo de', 34, 49, 59, 145,
  166
Mela, Pomponio, 115
Milton, John, 195
Minturno, A., 185
Molza, Francesco Maria, 169
Monteverdi, Claudio, 8
Moreto, Agustín, 189

Navagero, Andrea, 169
Nisiely, U., 190-1

Ovid, 5, 15, 17, 54, 70

Palestrina, Giovanni Perluigi da, 8
Petrarca, Francesco (and Petrarch-
  ism), 18, 19, 22, 29, 45, 52, 54, 57,
  58, 59, 70, 73, 112, 144, 150, 154,
  162-3, 166, 167, 169, 170, 188
Pio, Alberto, 5
Pio, Marco, 17
Plautus, 7, 31, 33, 37, 42

Pliny, 115
Poliziano, Angelo, 45, 49, 59, 145-6, 166
Prés, Josquin des, 8
Propertius, 15
Ptolemy, 115
Pulci, Luigi, 49, 50, 54, 123, 145, 154, 166, 175, 185

Raphael Sanzio, 15
Rapin, Nicolas, 190
Renée, de Valois, 12, 32
Robortello, Francesco, 185
Ronsard, Pierre de, 188, 190
Rossetti, Biagio, 7
Rovere, Guidobaldo della, 17
Ruscelli, Girolamo, 186

Sacchetti, Franco, 92
Sadoleto, Jacopo, 169
Salviati, Leonardo, 187
Sannazzaro, Iacopo, 45, 166
Sardi, Gasparo, 18
Savonarola, Girolamo, 125
Scott, Walter, 195
Scudéry, Georges de, 188
Seneca, 15, 54
Sforza, Francesco, 5
Sforza, Ludovico, 5, 16, 108, 111, 112, 114
Shakespeare, 65, 189
Silvestri, Guido, 11
Sixtus IV, Pope (1471-84), 3, 4

Spenser, Edmund, 61, 65, 80, 178, 190
Spoleto, Gregorio da, 5, 10
Statius, 15, 54, 87
Strabo, 115
Strozzi, Ercole, 5, 9, 18, 31
Strozzi, Tito, 10

Tasso, Torquato, 1, 123, 133, 167, 171, 172, 175, 182, 184, 186, 187, 188, 190
Tebaldeo, Antonio, 8, 18
Terence, 7, 15, 31, 33, 37, 42
Tibullus, 15
Titian (Tiziano Vecellio), 8
Tossici, Niccolò, 18
Tressan, Comte de (Louis-Elizabeth de La Vergne), 191
Trissino, Gian Giorgio, 88, 175, 184, 187
Tura, Cosme, 8

Urrea, Jerónimo de, 188

Valerio, Gian Francesco, 79
Villani, Filippo, 93
Vinciguerra, Antonio, 22
Viola, Alfonso della, 8
Viola, Francesco della, 8
Virgil, 5, 15, 51, 54, 70, 74, 84, 86, 87, 88, 126, 150, 152, 156, 157, 164, 185
Voltaire (F. M. Arouet), 191

Willaert, Adriano, 8

(b) CHARACTERS IN *Orlando Furioso*

Adonio, 76, 81, 133
Agramante (African king), 51, 53, 63, 75, 84-6, 89-90, 105, 111, 113, 121, 123-4, 126, 132, 149
Agricane (Tartar king), 51, 103-4, 121
Alceste, 59, 179
Alcina, 65-8, 70, 98, 105, 115, 131, 133, 138, 152, 156, 159, 161, 175, 176-7, 187-8
Andronico, 115
Angelica, 51, 53, 59, 61-4, 66, 69, 71, 74, 77, 80, 82-3, 87-8, 98-9, 101, 103-4, 121, 123, 127-8, 131, 134-5, 137, 140, 142-3, 146-7, 154-6, 160, 162, 175, 176-7, 186, 188-9
Argeo, 72-3, 119
Ariodante, 59, 65-6, 83, 104, 138, 186, 189
Astolfo, 53, 62, 65-7, 71, 76-7, 86, 89, 95, 105, 108, 112, 115, 122-5, 128-9, 131-3, 138, 156, 177, 188
Astolfo (King of Longobards), 79-80
Atlante (Ruggiero's guardian-spirit), 67, 155-6

Bireno, 65, 68-70, 80, 104, 132, 134-5, 157, 160, 176
Bradamante, 21-2, 51-3, 59, 61-4, 67, 71, 76, 80, 82-5, 87-8, 101, 103-4, 107, 109, 114, 119-20, 122-3, 126, 128-9, 131-4, 137-8, 150-1, 155-6, 177-81, 182, 188-9
Brandimarte, 85, 104-5, 124, 151, 177

Caligorante, 95
Carlomagno (Carlo), 47, 48, 50, 51, 53, 56, 59, 61, 84, 86, 89, 90, 105, 120, 122, 124-6, 132, 143, 177
Cilandro, 77
Cimosco, 91, 92
Clodione, 80, 177-8
Cloridano, 86, 87

Dalinda, 65-6, 131, 133-4, 138, 176-7, 189
Dardinello (African king), 86, 128, 151

Doralice, 59, 74-5, 79, 80, 99, 117, 128, 134, 149, 159, 186
Drusilla, 59, 77-8, 138, 148

Erifilla, 138
Ermonide, 72, 101, 134, 139

Ferraù, 97-8, 102, 146, 155, 160
Fiammetta, 76, 78-80, 118, 133, 137, 187
Filandro, 71-3, 77
Fiordiligi, 99
Fiordispina, 54, 59, 76, 83, 119

Gabrina, 59, 71-3, 85, 100-1, 132-4, 188
Gano, 49
Ginevra, 59, 65-6, 83, 104, 118, 131, 186, 189
Gradasso, 51, 74, 85, 104, 121
Grifone, 59, 74-5, 98-9, 128, 132, 138, 160
Guidon Selvaggio, 105, 129, 133, 138

Iocondo, 79, 80
Isabella, 59, 71-5, 99, 100, 103-4, 117, 121, 123, 128, 133-4, 144, 148-50, 156, 163, 188-9

Leone, 63, 138, 175, 179-81
Lidia, 59, 77, 133, 188
Logistilla, 67-8, 152, 175-6
Lucina, 74, 83, 121

Mandricardo, 51, 60, 74-5, 99, 103, 119, 134, 140, 149, 186
Marfisa, 80, 100-1, 119, 132, 134, 138, 140, 155, 177-9, 181
Marganorre, 77-9, 104, 113, 116-17, 133-4, 175, 178-9
Martano, 74-5, 96, 98-9, 104, 160, 186
Medoro, 53, 60, 63-4, 66, 71, 74-5, 83, 86-7, 99, 121, 127-8, 137, 140, 186, 188-9
Melissa (Bradamante's guardian-spirit), 67-8, 109, 131, 181
Melissa (another *maga*), 78, 81-2, 133
Michael (Archangel), 123
Morgana, 52, 67

Namo (Duke), 143, 144
Norandino, 21, 74-5, 83, 121

Oberto, 71, 83, 176
Odorico, 71-3, 77, 101
Olimpia, 60, 65, 68-70, 78, 80, 83,
   91-2, 104, 131, 133-5, 144, 147,
   157, 175-6, 179, 188
Oliviero, 85
Orlando, 47-53, 57, 59, 61-5, 69-71,
   73-7, 80, 84, 87-9, 91, 95-101,
   103-5, 122-4, 126, 128-9, 131-2,
   134-5, 140, 142-4, 147-8, 156-7,
   161-3, 175-6, 185, 188-9
Orrigille, 74-5, 98-9, 138, 160-1
Orrilo, 156

Polinesso, 65-6, 104, 176, 189

Ricciardetto, 21, 54, 60, 76, 83, 103,
   105, 119, 133, 138, 187
Rinaldo, 47, 50-1, 61, 65, 80-1, 84,
   86-8, 90, 98-9, 101, 104, 109,

115-16, 118-19, 122, 129, 131-4,
   137-8, 143, 146, 160, 180
Rodomonte, 72-3, 75, 79, 80, 85-8, 90,
   95, 99, 101, 113, 117, 127, 132-4,
   144, 148-50, 156, 159, 177, 180, 188
Ruggiero, 21, 51-4, 59, 61-71, 77, 80,
   82-4, 86-8, 95, 98, 101, 103-5,
   107-9, 115-16, 122-4, 127-35, 138,
   150-1, 156, 175-83, 186, 188

Sacripante (Circassian king), 101-2,
   140
Sansonetto, 98
Sobrino, 85

Tanacro, 77-8, 148, 179
Teodora, 181

Ullania, 111, 119-20, 177-8

Zerbino, 59, 60, 71-5, 85, 87, 99, 100,
   103, 121, 132, 134, 139, 149-50,
   189